DEVOURING CULTURES

FOOD AND FOODWAYS

SERIES EDITOR:
JENNIFER JENSEN WALLACH

OTHER TITLES IN THIS SERIES

American Appetites: A Documentary Reader

Edited by Jennifer Jensen Wallach
and Lindsey R. Swindall

*Dethroning the Deceitful Pork Chop:
Rethinking African American Foodways
from Slavery to Obama*

Edited by Jennifer Jensen Wallach

Devouring Cultures

PERSPECTIVES ON FOOD, POWER, AND IDENTITY FROM THE ZOMBIE APOCALYPSE TO *DOWNTON ABBEY*

EDITED BY CAMMIE M. SUBLETTE
AND JENNIFER MARTIN

The University of Arkansas Press
Fayetteville
2016

20   19   18   17   16   5   4   3   2   1

Designed by Liz Lester

⊛ The paper used in this publication meets the minimum requirements
of the American National Standard for Permanence of Paper for Printed
Library Materials Z39.48-1984.

Library of Congress Control Number: 2015948065

SUBSIDY CREDITS

We gratefully acknowledge the following support and permissions:

The University of Arkansas–Fort Smith for providing sabbatical support
to Cammie M. Sublette during the completion of this project;

The University of Minnesota Press for allowing the republication of Kelly
Erby's "'Between Bolted Beef and Bolted Pudding': Boston's Eating Houses
and Nineteenth-Century Social and Cultural Change," a version of which
appears in her book *Restaurant Republic: The Rise of Public Dining in Boston*
(University of Minnesota Press).

Cover image: Erin Kirk New

Cammie M. Sublette

To my wonderful family, Len, Drew, Brody, Gavin, and Clara. You all inspire me. And to my parents, who have always nourished my spirit with their unflagging love and support.

Jennifer Martin

To my mom, who allowed me to "help" in the kitchen when I was so young I had to stand on a chair to reach the counter, tolerated my messes when I was learning to cook, instilled in me the knowledge that I could achieve my dreams, and, then, lovingly supported me in my quests.

CONTENTS

SERIES EDITOR'S PREFACE

The University of Arkansas Press series Food and Foodways explores historical and contemporary issues in global food studies. We are committed to telling lesser-known food stories and to representing a diverse set of voices. Our strength is works in the humanities and social sciences that use food as a lens to examine broader social, cultural, environmental, ethical, and economic issues. However, we recognize that food—perhaps the most central of all human concerns—is not only a barometer by which to gauge social, cultural, and environmental conditions, it can also be a source of pleasure. In addition to scholarly books, we publish creative nonfiction that explores the sensory dimensions of consumption and celebrates food as evidence of human creativity and innovation.

The ten essays that comprise *Devouring Cultures: Perspectives on Food, Power, and Identity from the Zombie Apocalypse to Downton Abbey,* edited by Cammie M. Sublette and Jennifer Martin, offer a collective exploration of representations of food in American culture. The contributors demonstrate that the study of consumption habits and ideas about food can yield a unique set of insights into the process of American identity construction. The contributors analyze materializations of culture ranging from public restaurants to literature to television and film to reveal the manifold ways in which, as the editors of the volume argue, "food communicates particulars of time, place, class, gender, race, trauma, agency, and ideology." This eclectic, rich, and thought-provoking collection fulfills the Food and Foodways series mission to explore understudied food stories as the authors search for and find food and meaning in a series of unexpected and intriguing places.

JENNIFER JENSEN WALLACH, *Series Editor*

ACKNOWLEDGMENTS

Creating a book is much like creating a delicious meal; it all hinges on the very finest and tastiest ingredients. We have been fortunate to find and collect here many exciting flavors to make a most enjoyable feast. It would not have been possible without many people along the way who helped make our recipe a reality. First, we are so appreciative of the brilliant scholars who added their knowledge and voices to our collection. It has been our pleasure to work with such talented researchers and writers. We also appreciate our editors at the University of Arkansas Press, who provided the guidance to bring the work from an assortment of interesting concepts to a book. Our sincere thanks also go to Jennifer Jensen Wallach, associate professor of history at the University of North Texas and the series editor for the University of Arkansas Press series Food and Foodways. Jennifer's direction and encouragement as we worked on the project were invaluable. The Popular Culture Association/American Culture Association and the food panels at the annual conferences in San Antonio, Boston, and Washington, D.C., gave us the seed of the idea to begin the project, and our wonderful English Department at the University of Arkansas–Fort Smith provided us the creative freedom to pursue our research. We also appreciate our incredible UAFS students who have allowed us to test our food ideas in the classroom and made us look at food in ways we had never before considered. We are indebted to the University of Minnesota Press for allowing us to publish Kelly Erby's "'Between Bolted Beef and Bolted Pudding': Boston's Eating Houses and Nineteenth-Century Social and Cultural Change," a version of which also appears in her book *Restaurant Republic: The Rise of Public Dining in Boston*. Cammie would like to thank the University of Arkansas–Fort Smith and the University of Arkansas system for allowing her a sabbatical to complete the project, as well as Elizabeth Klaver and Bob Fox from Southern Illinois University and Ruth Ellen Porter from Jacksonville State University, who mentored her as an emerging scholar. Jennifer would like to thank Bob Jackson and Grant Jenkins from the University of Tulsa for their encouraging guidance and Kedar Padhye, who has patiently listened to endless talk about books and food with a smile on his face. We both would like to thank our families who have shared in our food adventures at many a mealtime. This is your book, too.

ACKNOWLEDGMENTS

American Self-Fashioning and Culinary Consumption

Each pale yellow wrapper has a picture on it. A picture of little Mary Jane, for whom the candy is named. Smiling white face. Blond hair in gentle disarray, blue eyes looking at her out of a world of clean comfort. The eyes are petulant, mischievous. To Pecola they are simply pretty. She eats the candy, and its sweetness is good. To eat the candy is somehow to eat the eyes, eat Mary Jane. Love Mary Jane. Be Mary Jane.

—TONI MORRISON, *The Bluest Eye*

For humans, food is deeply invested with broad social meaning. While food has always represented the difference between starvation and life, between the possibility of establishing a flourishing civilization versus one plagued with death and suffering, food is also invested with deep personal meaning, with each meal potentially invoking elements of the political self, the moral self, the cultural self, and the aesthetic self. Our food preferences and aversions speak to how we see ourselves and how we wish to be seen, but also insinuate our desires to transform ourselves and the world around us. In Toni Morrison's *The Bluest Eye*, Pecola Breedlove desires, purchases, and imbibes the little white Mary Jane candies in an attempt to reconstruct her identity as one more beloved (or at least more socially acceptable) than her own black, lower-class, love-deprived self.[1] Her experiences contrast with the idealized happiness of little Mary Jane, and, in an innocent enactment of a consumptive ritual, Pecola consumes the other in order to transform the self. For

Pecola, what the Mary Jane represents transcends candy and links her to the cultural imagination of being privileged and cherished.

Our collection explores this power, contained not only in the food itself, but in the power and images the food represents. The chapters of the collection enrich, develop, and complicate one of the more recent turns in food studies: interrogation of how food consumption relates to identity and power, particularly, via American self-fashioning. Academic studies of food and foodways have flourished as food studies have expanded to include interdisciplinary approaches as well as varied methodologies, resulting in an increasingly robust body of foodways theory and literature. Enoch Padolsky notes that anthropologists have long been studying food and foodways but are now joined by sociologists, historians, philosophers, geographers, literary critics, and others, all of whom bring varied approaches "to the feast."[2] Furthermore, as Allison Carruth reports, "in the United States, the number of protests, activist groups, conferences, books, films, art installations, and websites devoted to food and food politics grows by the year."[3] Thus, now more than ever before, the academic interest in foodways aligns with a burgeoning popular interest in and activism related to culinary practices, representations, and ideologies.

The academic study of consumption, since the dawn of the twentieth century at least, has been largely preoccupied with the politics of consumer capitalism and its attendant social ills, most notably characterized by Thorstein Veblen's designation of "conspicuous consumption" as that which is consumed (either personally or vicariously, in the case of servants and wives of wealthy men) in order to demonstrate excess capital in the face of others' subsistence or deprivation and thus establish and maintain a social hierarchy.[4] Conspicuous consumption—and, indeed, all consumption undertaken in the neo-capitalist and eventual late capitalist world—is later redefined by Jean Baudrillard as a version of labor itself, wherein consumption trumps production of goods and services.[5] Thus, the theory goes, when it comes to the consumption of clothing, people invest their time and effort into consuming, not producing, the garments they wear and, in so doing, empty their clothing of personal meaning but sustain, rather, only a consumptive process.[6] Daniel Miller notes, "For the likes of Baudrillard, people are merely the mannequins who wear the clothes which ensure that the fashion system can continue to perpetuate its drive to constant profitability."[7] For his part, Miller wishes to challenge this understanding of consumption, writing, "Rather than seeing consumers merely as the passive end point of economic activity, I argue that they actively transform their world. They too see both the negative and the positive consequences of consumption and have their own critiques."[8] Likewise, the consumption of food involves potentially negative and positive consequences that diners are involved in sorting, considering, negotiating, and justifying. That many of the meals we consume involve us in some facet of food production further complicates a view of the food consumer as passive, for although there is consumption, typically, on both ends of the meal—in the supermarket as well as at the table—there is also the work of planning, storing, washing, cutting, combining, cooking, and plating food in between these two consumptive acts. No, food consumption is anything but passive, for even when dining out, the choices of where to dine, with whom to dine, what to order, whether or not to appropriate known dining etiquette, and when to stop eating all involve a number of active and potentially creative consumptive possibilities. All of these possibilities ultimately allow humans to engage in various forms of self-fashioning in their culinary experiences.

One of the most complicated of these constructions of self may be how to negotiate one's own consumption and enjoyment of food with what Carruth describes as "the troubling paradox of the modern food system: despite tremendous gains in the productivity of agriculture, nearly one billion people are hungry."[9] Raj Patel develops this paradoxical thesis of the ongoing global hunger crisis amidst a world of excessive food consumption in his book *Stuffed and Starved*. Patel informs that as of 2012, "a billion [people] are undernourished and 1.5 billion [are] overweight."[10] Assuming that not all diners enjoy the competitive and conspicuous consumption signaled by their own overly ample meals in contrast to people who experience food shortage, there must be other, more complicated explanations for how diners construct themselves positively or even neutrally within a known global food inequity. Isabelle de Solier argues that "many foodies are anxious about the morality of making a self through consumption" and thus negotiate their enjoyment of food and foodways through their selections of ingredients and recipes, often choosing those food-stuffs and preparations deemed most socially responsible, and by self-policing consumptive levels of expense as well as quantity.[11] De Solier urges theorists to develop ethnographies to study food consumption as a means to contradict and complicate a reading of consumption as inherently materialistic and glibly unconcerned: "When dealing with actual consumers and their everyday experiences, the interpretation of consumption in late modernity becomes a lot less black and white; it may be murky, messy, contradictory or ambivalent. It may involve pleasure and anxiety, spending and thrift, inclusion and exclusion. It is almost always complex, and not easily reducible to categories such as materialism or consumerism."[12]

Bruce Pietrykowski further complicates this explanation by turn-ing to the slow food movement and interrogating the prevailing social ethos of the movement as it combines with a doctrine of culinary pleasure.[13] Ultimately, Pietrykowski argues that through the "dual process of pleasure-seeking and politicization," slow food adherents transform Bourdieu's "cultural capital," largely the culturally exclusive practices and knowledge related to food quality and preparation and cultural foodways, into "social capital," something located more firmly outside the self and beyond a classed system of consumerism. The influence of slow food advocate Alice Waters, particularly her book *The Art of Simple Food*, and food journalist Michael Pollan, beginning with *The Omnivore's Dilemma: A Natural History of Four Meals* and continuing through *Cooked*, can be felt in the social ethos expressed by those foodies Pietrykowski describes, as they examine an alterna-tive way of approaching food focused both on culinary pleasure and social responsibility.

Several of the scholars represented in our collection interrogate the social ethos of various fictional food cultures and the imprint of the industrial food supply in the form of name-brand food-like prod-ucts such as a can of Coke or the ubiquitous Twinkie—including the apocalyptic landscapes of Cormac McCarthy's *The Road* and zombie films—developing theories that contribute to understanding American self-fashioning in the face of food shortages and exploring the ethics of consumption in the face of hunger crises. For instance, in "Consuming American Consumerism in *The Road*," Jennifer Martin ponders the problem of a non-existent natural food supply in an America that has suffered an apocalyptic disaster and the new moralities that become apparent in food choice. Martin explains, in Cormac McCarthy's *The Road*, the actions of the man and the boy are driven by the necessity to secure food sources in this post-apocalyptic landscape. The environmental disaster that has devastated nature, and the food scarcity which occurred in its wake, implicates the impending extinction of man and is a factor in the obliteration of America and American consumerism. As the man and boy scavenge for any remaining food in homes and stores along their route, Martin argues they are "consuming the end of American identity and American consumerism by consuming the last artifacts of symbolic American foods." That the man, in particular, highly values and wishes to pass on to his son some of the more iconic images of American food culture, such as the single can of Coke they find, suggests that his understanding of himself is deeply tied to American consumptive culture. As Martin illustrates, the man and boy must forge a new image of themselves and craft a new food ethos in this post-apocalyptic American landscape.

Similarly, Cammie M. Sublette's chapter, "The Last Twinkie in the Universe: Culinary Hedonism and Nostalgia in Zombie Films," explores food consumption in a post-apocalyptic landscape. Sublette's focus, however, is on zombie films, particularly American zombie films, such as George A. Romero's *Dawn of the Dead*, and zombie films deeply influenced by American zombie films and that have large American audiences, such as the British "zomedy," *Shaun of the Dead*. Sublette's chapter investigates how nostalgia functions in a food landscape punctuated, in many cases, by scarcity and the traumatic threat of zombie cannibalism. Sublette notes that modern zombie films often invoke Romero's extended metaphor of out-of-control American materialist spending and consumption via the hungry zombie horde. Sublette develops this metaphor of consumption, but she also interrogates the food consumed by non-zombies (human survivors) in zombie films. She writes, "In the imagined filmscapes of zombie apocalypse, humans often struggle for basic subsistence, but beyond the horizon of subsistence is the fantasy or ideal meal, the one talked about, sought after, debated, and, occasionally, consumed." As Sublette notes, many apocalyptic situations in both film and literature demand a certain degree of survivalist eating for mere subsistence, but characters in zombie films often enhance their sustenance eating with the pursuit of a culinary bliss infused with cultural longing, memory, and imagined past or future identities. Zombie apocalypse survivors often idealize or otherwise transform the past and seek to recapture a lost "homeland" via food consumption, much like the culinary nostalgia experienced by displaced immigrants, as described by Anita Mannur.[14]

Food can come to represent moral standing and nostalgia in times of scarcity, while in times of abundance food choice operates even more intently as a means of self-fashioning the individual's economic class, gender, race, and ethnicity, illustrating Leon Rappoport's claim that "there is hardly a significant social activity or emotional state to which food is irrelevant."[15] In their introduction to a food and literature issue of *MELUS*, Fred L. Gardaphé and Wenying Xu note, "Food often has an ability to last longer as a signifier for ethnicity than other markers, such as language and fashion," rendering food not only an important but also an enduring index of cultural identity.[16] Further, as folklorists Laurier Turgeon and Madeleine Pastinelli assert, "food is mobile, multivocal, and polysemic; it moves from one group to another, it expresses different voices, and it can take on different meanings depending on the intention of the consumers."[17] Thus, in its fluidity, food can be made to signify a nearly inexhaustible array of discursive possibilities.

The chapters collected here go beyond simply making connections between food and the ways that it can be made to signify, however, for each illustrates how closely connected to Americans' attempts at self-fashioning are foods and foodways. Importantly, for many of the contributing scholars in this collection, American culinary self-fashioning is about power. For example, in the section of our collection dealing with restaurant culture, the authors show that in the shared spaces of communal eating defined by the restaurant, there are a number of fissures, hierarchies, power struggles, and even pedagogies at play. Although the ubiquity of restaurants in America may make it seem as though "eating out" has always been a part of American life and culture, such that perhaps many diners fail to realize the power structures at play in any instance of dining out, the contemporary restaurant is a relatively recent and ideologically loaded phenomenon in American foodways. In a 2002 introduction to the food studies collection *Food Nations: Selling Taste in Consumer Societies*, Warren Belasco writes, "Food means power, power means food. And power means conflict, even violence. Many of the world's wars may be viewed as a series of colossal food fights."[18] In each of the chapters devoted to restaurant culture, the concept of food as a signifier of power is refined, complicated, and interrogated.

In her chapter "'Between Bolted Beef and Bolted Pudding': Boston's Eating Houses and Nineteenth-Century Social and Cultural Change," Kelly Erby examines the history of Boston eating houses and the implications of the social hierarchy established by these eateries. As Erby illustrates, the early 1820s marked a turning point in American cities' dining options. These early restaurants, or "eating houses," as they were called, attracted quite distinct groups of customers according to economic class and social class, sometimes connected to ethnic and racial distinctions. Furthermore, Erby illustrates an additional hierarchy operative in these early Boston restaurants, for they, like most eateries in America at the time, allowed access only to men, thereby precluding women from the experience of dining out.

Jessica Kenyatta Walker, in "Nervous Kitchens: Consuming Sentimentality Narratives and Black-White Intimacy at a Chicago Hot Dog Stand," moves the discussion of gender, race, and social class to the twenty-first century as she explores a restaurant culture that is a veritable ideological battlefield, in which white upper- and middle-class men frequent Chicago's The Weiner Circle (TWC) to exchange racist insults with, and demand sexual favors from, the Black women who work behind the counter. TWC is both popular and controversial, Walker contends, because of its commitment of "actively transgressing normalized scripts around race, gender, food service, and sensuality." Focusing on both the particulars of this restaurant culture itself and also Ira Glass's narrativization of TWC's nightly clashes as "scary" in the "Pandora's Box" episode of *This American Life*, Walker asserts that "food is an often over-looked terrain upon which bodies marked or constructed through difference engage in interactions of tension, nervousness, and possibility." Walker investigates the ways objectification of Black women's bodies at TWC speaks to historical mistreatment of Black women in domestic spaces and begins a conversation that is continued in Krystal McMillen's chapter, "From Aunt Jemima to Aunt

Marthy: Commodifying the Kitchen Cook and Undermining White Authority in *Incidents in the Life of a Slave Girl.*"

While restaurants can be scenes of deep ideological conflict, they can alternatively or simultaneously act as forums for learning. In "A Pedagogy of Dining Out: Learning to Consume Culture," Joe Marshall Hardin develops a framework for reading the pedagogical interactions in restaurants featuring ethnic or regional cuisine. Hardin's study enriches food studies, while simultaneously contributing to an area of sociology that investigates cultural omnivorousness.[19] Hardin illustrates that American ethnic restaurants employ a variety of pedagogical techniques to teach diners new to the cuisine what to expect and, ultimately, what they should consume—both in terms of comestibles and culture. One of the most interesting implications of Hardin's study is that diners may be resistant students to this pedagogy, that they will sometimes misinterpret or reject the pedagogy of ethnic cuisine and the proffered discourse of food consumption. Furthermore, Hardin interrogates the degree to which these "students" are able to access what Anita Mannur calls "culinary citizenship."[20] Ultimately, Hardin connects Mannur's theory of culinary citizenship to "glocalization," a phenomenon wherein corporations such as Starbucks attempt to provide "local" flavors, cuisines, and cultures, even as they export them to a global audience.

Laura Anh Williams's "Hunger Pains: Appetite and Racial Longing in *Stealing Buddha's Dinner*" also investigates the relationship of food to culinary citizenship. Williams's focus is on the ways that processed, industrialized American food comes to signify assimilation into American culture for a family of Vietnamese immigrants. Variously, Williams notes, the characters in *Stealing Buddha's Dinner* struggle between maintaining Vietnamese identity and adopting an American identity, and food is often the medium for conveying this ongoing struggle. Williams writes, "Bich Minh Nguyen's 2007 memoir *Stealing Buddha's Dinner* begins with a series of food images: boxed rice, egg noodles, half of an apple saved and shared on a refugee ship, a little girl's arm halfway engulfed by a canister of Pringles to retrieve a fistful of the thin crisps, the salty shards dusting her hands and the floor." As Williams notes, Nguyen's entire memoir is organized through a series of food memories. As a Vietnamese refugee relocated to Grand Rapids, Michigan while in infancy, Bich has no memory of her homeland. Surrounding Bich are the white children whose mothers bake Jiffy muffins and Nestle Toll House chocolate chip cookies that Bich longs to have, but she is denied access. These same white children take for granted the philosophical beauty of the Pringle and turn their noses up at "ethnic" cuisine. What emerges in this bifurcated world, argues Williams, is "a clearly defined culinary economy in which Bich invests her desires in her quest for belonging." At the forefront of Bich's culinary economy are the industrialized foods so closely associated with America, ranging from shelves of candy at the local gas station to the Twinkie.

In "Scenes from the Dialogic Kitchen: 'Thinking Culture Dialogically' in Italian American Narratives," James Cianciola, like Williams, explores the ways that food can be used to signify a culture as well as erase various ethnic origins. Cianciola investigates what Davide Girardelli terms "constructed representations of Italians and Italian food," noting that a number of popular culture depictions of Italian and Italian American chefs and kitchens have a caricatured aspect, often focused on hospitality and Italian food (such as the ever-popular spaghetti and meatballs) as it has been bastardized for American palates.[21] Interestingly, Cianciola finds some of the most complex portrayals of Italian American cooks and cooking in films like *The Godfather* and *Goodfellas,* films often criticized for their focus on *Mafiosi* and that run the risk of stereotyping Italian Americans as thugs. However, these films embrace the idea of eating as a ceremony and, like most ceremonies, contain potential moral quandaries, historical complications, and subtext expressed in each act of food preparation, presentation, and consumption.

Like Cianciola, Lindsy Lawrence focuses on the presentation of foreign cuisine and etiquette to American audiences. In "Consuming Pleasures: Nineteenth-Century Cookery as Narrative Structure in *Downton Abbey,*" Lawrence investigates how aristocratic British food preparation and consumption guide the narrative structure in *Downton Abbey.* She writes, "Numerous dinners, teas, and breakfasts work to structure a series about the intersections of an aristocratic family, their domestic servants, and the chaotic events of the first part of the twentieth century." In this hyper-focus on food and its corollary household management tasks, Lawrence finds a resemblance between this television period drama and discourse of nineteenth-century and early twentieth-century cookbook and domestic manuals, which "navigate between the practical, the aspirational, and the condemnatory." Lawrence analyzes Isabella Beeton's *Book of Household Management*, serialized in twenty-four monthly parts from 1859 to 1861 in association with her husband's *Englishwoman's Domestic Magazine* (1851–90), as one of several texts dispensing food and dining etiquette advice to the middle-class family. Turning her attention often to American audiences' consumption of *Downton Abbey*, Lawrence suggests that the show's transatlantic popularity has much in common with the popularity of the servants' memoirs and domestic manuals blueprinting it: middle-class people are entertained by narratives of upper-class household management. Moreover, some part of that entertainment may be related to American attempts at self-fashioning as upwardly mobile and excessively cosmopolitan. By foregrounding the work of the household in *Downton Abbey*, Lawrence argues that series creator Julian Fellowes "playfully blends issues of class and consumption."

That so many of the chapters in our collection highlight national identity as defined by food choices is no coincidence. National identity is closely related to food, as other food studies scholars have illustrated. Carole M. Counihan's *Food in the U.S.A.* examines food as it connects to a national, albeit nebulous, identity. One chapter in Counihan's book, "Eating American," by Sidney Mintz, suggests that America lacks a single American cuisine.[22] Instead, Americans borrow food from a multitude of cultures, all of them cohabiting on American soil, to create multiple food identities. This concept is reinforced by works in our volume such as those by Hardin, Cianciola, and Williams. Although this may seem counter to a national American identity, American identity is inherently multicultural. This does not, however, mean that Americans understand all foods prepared in America as equally American. As Keridiana Chez demonstrates in her insightful critique of Robert Sietsema's *The Food Lover's Guide to the Best Ethnic Eating in New York City*, an investment in multicultural eating or culinary touring within the United States "allows a member of the dominant group to self-fashion as 'modern,' elite, and cosmopolitan—a self-congratulatory construct that necessarily hinges on reproducing the 'ethnic' Other as inferior and un-American."[23] Thus, the act of consuming unfamiliar food and foodways provides many Americans with an opportunity to experience and sometimes appropriate the culture of the Other, while simultaneously providing a frame for self-fashioning the American self in contrast to the ethnic Other.

The consumption of the Other as a means of American self-fashioning is Krystal McMillen's focus in her chapter, "From Aunt Jemima to Aunt Marthy: Commodifying the Kitchen Cook and Undermining White Authority in *Incidents in the Life of a Slave Girl.*" Here, McMillen interrogates the stereotype of the mammy, seeking to tease out the relationship between this ubiquitous American stereotype, the American food that was marketed with the mammy image, and the white American fear and desire giving rise to the virtual consumption of Black American women via the figure of Aunt Jemima. McMillen insightfully points out that "types persist because in their shallow simplicity they offer a seductive solution to the complexity of humanity." McMillen's chapter explores how the figure of the mammy combines the artistic and revolutionary potential in texts such as Harriet Jacobs's *Incidents in the Life of a Slave Girl* with the deprivations of slavery and the exploitation of slavery and post-slavery commercial marketing. Indeed, as McMillen and others have demonstrated, the popularity of Aunt Jemima pancakes and syrup was largely based on the consumption of the figure of the mammy, Aunt Jemima. McMillen writes, "The figure of Aunt Jemima becomes fundamentally linked to the foods she cooks, making her simultaneously an industrious producer of goods (namely, breakfast) and an object for consumption herself." To consume Aunt Jemima was to consume plantation mythologies regarding the happy slave and was to consume, as well, Aunt Jemima's culinary expertise as well as her nurturing love. As McMillen illustrates, a white post-slavery American self-fashioning of amnesia, nostalgia, and forgiveness buttressed the marketing of Aunt Jemima foods. This self-fashioning, however, contrasts starkly against a Black post-slavery self-fashioning of trauma, triumph, and kitchen resistance, such as that found in *Incidents in the Life of a Slave Girl.*

As is evident with the mammy stereotype, food is resonant with gender identifiers. In *Kitchen Culture in America*, Sherrie A. Inness contends that millions of women "shop for groceries, flip through women's magazines for recipes, and prepare breakfasts, lunches, after-school snacks, and dinner for hordes of men, women, boys, and girls. I mention women, not men, because women still do most of the domestic cooking in the United States. It continues to be an activity coded as 'women's responsibility.'"[24] She continues, "The complex web of inter-relationships among women, food, and cooking must be untangled by anyone wishing to understand American culture."[25] In this collection, Rachel S. Hawley's chapter "Pie as Nostalgia: What One Food Symbolizes for Every Generation of Americans" looks at gender differences in perceptions of culinary nostalgia, using pie as a vehicle for the investigation. Hawley writes, "There is something about the idea of home-baked pie that makes people yearn with longing for something ethereal and nameless that can never be recaptured because that moment is gone. Pie is an American object of nostalgia." Arguing that pie is uniquely situated to help us answer the question of whether or not there is an American national cuisine, Hawley writes, "There is only one food that people *claim* to be so American that other American things are measured by its likeness. In fact, pie is so American that it is an example of one food that transcends region, race and class in its ability to create nostalgia." Hawley also explores the history of the term "nostalgia" as well as theories regarding nostalgia, ultimately finding that most of our American representations of pie summon Fredric Jameson's notions of unreliable memory and idealization, thus undermining the notion of pie as the American national cuisine except as an ambiguous and unattainable ideal. Hawley demonstrates along the way an American desire to self-fashion a national identity around pie and its consumption.

The chapters that follow explore the many ways that food and foodways serve as cultural indices of American self-fashioning. The authors in this collection combine the deep study of food and foodways with an array of cultural contexts and theoretical apparatuses but share an understanding that food acts as text and subtext, wherever it may be found. Collectively, the essays presented here investigate how food communicates particulars of time, place, class, gender, race, trauma, agency, and ideology and, therefore, how food and food consumption contribute to the fluid determination of cultural identity. This collection explores the manner in which food crafts identity for American individuals, regions, and cultures by examining the operation of food as a conveyer of identity, power, culture, and other aspects of self-fashioning in American restaurant culture and literature and in popular culture directed at and largely consumed by American audiences.

PART 1 ▪ Eating Out

How Restaurants Shape Cultural Identity

CHAPTER 1

"Between Bolted Beef and Bolted Pudding"

Boston's Eating Houses and Nineteenth-Century Social and Cultural Change

KELLY ERBY

In June 1832, the Journeymen Ship Carpenters and Caulkers of Boston demanded a ten-hour workday that stretched from 5:00 a.m. to 7:00 p.m. and included "an hour for breakfast, two hours for dinner, and half an hour for refreshments."[1] These men's concern about the amount of time their employers allowed for meals, especially dinner, reflected the recent assault of the emerging urban market economy on male workers' dining patterns.[2] The midday dinner had conventionally been the largest, most significant meal of the day in America, a legacy of agricultural work rhythms.[3] By the early 1830s, however, the demands of market capitalism had begun to seriously infringe upon this meal. Some employers refused to give their employees any dinner break at all; others allowed only a very short amount of time in which to eat. Even self-employed men, who had more control over their work schedules, began to demonstrate what some considered an "excessive devotion to business," which made them loath to leave their counting houses or offices for too long in the middle of the workday in order to dine.[4] These new time constraints on men's mealtimes had significant consequences for their appetites. First and foremost, men employed at any distance from their homes often found they did not have time to return there to eat. The eating house became a solution to this dilemma.

Men's commercial options for obtaining their midday meals grew and evolved throughout the century. Besides restaurants, there were the street vendors who had hawked oysters, roasted corn, sweets, and other foods to Bostonians of all classes since the colonial period. But beginning in the late 1820s a new kind of business increasingly began to address men's noontime appetites. Eating houses, open from late morning to late afternoon, specialized in dinner and quickly became the most prevalent type of eatery in nineteenth-century Boston.[5] These eateries focused on providing straightforward, affordable, and, above all, fast midday meals intended to satisfy hungry workingmen with little time to spare. A broad range of men—including craftsmen like those of the Journeymen Ship Carpenters and Caulkers of Boston, factory and dockworkers, bankers, merchants, and professionals— all increasingly sought to purchase their dinners, sharing the experience of buying and eating food away from home.

The eating-house trade was thus inspired by dramatic changes that occurred within American society and culture in the nineteenth century. The boundless growth of the market and consumption and the loosening of domestic ties altered how urbanites ate and gave rise to new habits and behaviors. The increasing segmentation and hierarchy of Boston society during this period was also reflected in the city's eating houses, with certain venues endeavoring to distinguish themselves in order to attract a more affluent clientele. And yet, although they were clearly divided along socioeconomic, racial, and ethnic lines, overall, the city's eating houses helped in the creation of a more market-driven society and culture. They also contributed to the construction of broad new notions of urban masculinity by emphasizing emerging male-gendered traits like efficiency and economic productivity and by excluding women. As they fed men day after day, the city's eating houses facilitated Bostonians in bridging the transition between traditional and modern patterns of living, working, and manhood.

Masculine Bastions

Except for the occasional female proprietor, the nineteenth-century eating house was a masculine bastion.[6] For the first half of the century, women's employment options did not lead them to seek a rushed dinner in a downtown eatery as men's occupations increasingly did. The number of women employed in this period grew, but the most typical type of job for women was domestic service, which entailed taking meals in the homes of their employers.[7] Women who did outwork—another common source of income for antebellum Boston women—in their homes while tending to children and housework could eat their dinners at home, too. The expanding shopping duties and reform activities of more affluent, non-employed women did lead them to seek commercial meals in the antebellum years, but they were not welcome in most eating houses (nor would they have wanted to dine there), which were imagined as masculine spaces and considered inappropriate for respectable women.[8] They instead sought more leisurely and refined meals in establishments earmarked especially for them.[9] Even late in the century, as working-class women began to dine out with increased frequency, they still tended to avoid male-dominated eating houses in an effort to safeguard their reputations.[10]

The Eating-House Genre

Hungry men in Boston knew where to go to find an eating house. Eating houses were densely clustered in the commercial heart of the city, which extended from the narrow strip of piers at the tip of the peninsula west of the waterfront to Washington Street and from Water Street north to Ann Street.[11] Here, in close proximity to the majority of the city's docks and factories, stores and counting-houses, offices and workshops, men found it most convenient to purchase and eat their dinners. Later in the century, pockets of eating houses also emerged in South and East Boston, close to the newer factories that developed in these regions as they became more industrialized.

There was very little regulation of eating houses in Boston for most of the century, and new ones opened all the time. Start-up capital was minimal. Proprietors were supposed to secure a license from the city, which required a fee, but penalties for operating without a license were only in place for those who sold alcohol in addition to food, and even then the rather stiff penalty, a one hundred dollar fine, was rarely enforced.[12] Many proprietors ran their businesses from their residential addresses, often enlisting the assistance of family members.[13] The domestic nature of such eating-house businesses was a bit ironic since it was the increasing separation of work and home that made the trend toward dining in an eating house popular in the first place.

While getting into business was relatively easy, staying in business was another matter. Historian Richard Pillsbury has estimated that only 2 percent of the restaurants operating in 1850 were still in business ten years later.[14] The quickly proliferating nature of the eating-house business meant that competition between eateries was stiff. Most eateries operated on razor-thin profit margins and did not have money to invest in marketing or frills. Few of Boston's eating houses had names more creative than their owner's or bothered with elaborate signage to announce their venue. Instead, one simple technique used to attract the attention of passersby was to attach bills of fare to string in the doorway, flapping in the wind. Other proprietors affixed chalkboards to their door on which they scrawled the day's menu items, hoping to entice customers inside.[15]

Boston's eating houses fed large, hungry crowds for low prices and in record time; a well-run venue could feed a man in under ten minutes. Their busiest hours tended to be between eleven and three.[16] Patrons came directly from their workplaces, hungry for their midday meals. Since bills of fare were costly to print and required time to distribute, many proprietors dispensed with them and simply called out available dishes to patrons as they entered. Once they received their orders, patrons ate as quickly as possible, taking only a short pause, according to one source, "between bolted beef and bolted pudding."[17] The meal was typically washed down with cups of hot coffee or, in those venues that sold alcohol, ale or whiskey.

Eating-house proprietors and customers alike dispensed with propriety. In fact, this became one of the main attractions of the eating house, where convenience and speed reigned. The most important objective was simply to fill one's belly and get on with the workday. Customers typically did not squander precious time or effort making conversation with their fellow diners, but focused instead on the main task at hand: eating. Indeed, first-time visitors to the eating house— especially critical English tourists—often expressed shock at the utter lack of sociability inside the typical American eating house.[18] When conversation did happen, it was made with mouths full of food, hands

Charles Stanley Reinhart, *The Lunch Counter*. This *Harper's Weekly* engraving from September 27, 1873, captures a frenzied, chaotic meal in a lower grade of eating house. *Courtesy of harpersweekly.com.*

gesticulating between bites. All pretense of decorum was abandoned. As one Boston newspaper explained later in the century, tongue in cheek, eating-house etiquette prescribed only that

> the hat shall not be removed, but shall be tilted
> on the back of the head, so that as the eater bends
> over to get his mouth nearer the victuals the hat may
> still retain an erect position.[19]

Eating-house fare likewise reflected this straightforward approach to dining. Proprietors avoided the French-influenced cuisine gaining prominence elsewhere in the city and stuck primarily, instead, to serving traditional Anglo-American dishes like roasted and boiled meats (most commonly beef, turkey, chicken, and ham), potatoes, baked beans, and sweet pastries. The standard eating-house dinner was built on a sturdy foundation of animal protein. Doctors at the time prescribed beef as the most efficient source of energy for working men. [20] Whether it was for health reasons or not, beef was certainly always in high demand at eating houses.

The well-managed eating-house kitchen precooked as many of the day's offerings as possible in large quantities in order to have any one of them ready the moment a patron ordered it. Slabs of boiled ham and corned beef, big pots of baked beans, piles of biscuits, and trays of pudding stood waiting to be portioned, dished onto a plate, and handed to a hungry customer. Griddles were kept piping hot so that meat sizzled immediately upon touching it. Vegetables like potatoes, peas, cabbage, and turnips were prepared in the morning and kept warm all day in steamer baskets or tepid oil. It is no wonder proprietors complained of having difficulty selling out their day's offering of vegetables; by noontime these vegetables would have all turned to greasy mush. Patrons ordered their food from the bill of fare à la carte (though they certainly would not have used that phrase). Today's convention of a fixed meal including a meat entrée, vegetable, and starch all listed together on the menu for one price and served on one plate (a "plate dinner") did not exist until the early twentieth century.[21] In the eating house, patrons instead ordered exactly what they wanted and as much or as little as they liked or could pay for.

Though there were undoubtedly eating houses that built a successful reputation based on their fare, overall, the quality of food was not what drew men to eating houses. Eating-house cuisine was routinely derided as some of the worst food in the city, and certainly far inferior to home cooking.[22] Only in jokes about the culinary inaptitude of newly married housewives did it occasionally emerge as superior. And yet men showed up at noontime day after day for their fill of it. For most customers, the convenience and speed of the eating house trumped any complaints they may have had about the taste of the food.

Distinctions among Eating Houses and Eating-House Patrons

The male-dominated, no-fuss eating house was thus a distinct genre of nineteenth-century commercial eatery. But there was also considerable variation within the genre. Subtle and sometimes not-so-subtle distinctions among eating houses set establishments apart and made some venues more appealing to certain occupation types, socioeconomic groups, races, and ethnicities. *Harper's New Monthly Magazine* in 1866 delineated for its readers the general taxonomy that had developed among eating houses in Boston and other US cities, explaining that prices for "low-class" establishments ranged from 6 to 10 cents per plate, 30 to 35 cents for "good class," and 25 to 65 cents for "best class."[23] Price, however, was only one of several factors that distinguished eating houses in Boston.

Location, surprisingly, did not play as influential a role in this regard in Boston as it did in other cities like New York.[24] Boston's docks, where predominately Irish day laborers found intermittent work cutting fish and unloading ships, attracted the lowest-end venues. The particular clientele of these establishments was likewise primarily Irish. But otherwise, downtown Boston was only rather slowly experiencing geographic differentiation among its commercial enterprises.[25] Retail shops, offices, banks, and other businesses generally mixed indiscriminately on Boston's streets throughout most of the 1800s.[26] This meant that different grades of eating houses, appealing to different workers' tastes and pocketbooks, also intermingled throughout the city's commercial hub.

There were wide variations, however, in the kinds of actual space Boston's eating houses occupied, and that variable did help to shape the character of a particular venue's clientele. For example, the lowest, cheapest class of eating house—the kind that attracted the poorest patrons—was often located in a space that was exactly that: low. These venues were frequently little more than a "subterranean," windowless room in the basement of a building or warehouse.[27] Kitchen and dining room were one and the same. These spaces tended to be cramped, as well as poorly lit and ventilated; indeed, their poor ventilation helps to explain the frequency of eating-house fires, a very common news item in Boston newspapers throughout the century. Poor ventilation also explains one of the most remarked upon characteristics of such venues: their smell. Discerning patrons again and again described the pungent aroma of grease and onions, mixed with acrid tobacco smoke and the unpleasant body odors of male patrons who had likely spent all morning performing some kind of manual labor.

As can be imagined, the dining ambience of these basement venues was far from fancy. Instead of sitting at tables, customers typically ate standing up along the counter behind which their food was cooked (see fig. 1.1). This helped to expedite service and eliminated the need for waiters. To accommodate more customers, some establishments also provided one or two communal tables, referred to as "boards," to which patrons could belly up, or at least try. According to one reluctant patron of a cheap eating house in 1844, "the back-less seats were nailed to the floor so far from [the tables] that the *epicures* who patronized the establishment dined at an angle of forty-five."[28] Silverware was rarely supplied, either because proprietors couldn't afford to purchase it or because they worried their patrons would abscond with it. Some customers brought their own utensils, but many preferred to just rely on their hands; pocketknives could also be useful tools for conveying food to mouth. Napkins were unheard of, though toothpicks, by all accounts, were in great demand and available for an extra charge.[29] (In a pinch, the pocketknife could do this job, too.) These venues were often quite dirty, and rarely was much consideration given to décor. Mismatched furniture and chipped plates and cups were used without embarrassment, presented to hungry men who were unlikely to notice or care.

The service in these eating houses was equally bare bones. Most proprietors could not afford to hire help with the cooking or waiting and so performed these jobs themselves or with the assistance of family members. Those who did employ additional help paid them very little; by the 1880s, the *Boston Globe* reported the average pay for male waiters of eating houses was just four to eight dollars a month.[30]

In spite of its low pay, waitering in these venues demanded considerable work. Eating houses—even the most "wretched" ones—could become extremely crowded during the busy noon hour, and most were undoubtedly understaffed as a strategy to keep overhead expenses as low as possible. Besides taking and delivering orders to hungry, hurried men, waiters in these venues were tasked with maintaining order among patrons. One Boston newspaper reporter interviewed a waiter who kept a "good-sized" stick of wood, "big enough to make a pretty big bump on a man's cranium," that the waiter referred to as his "persuader" behind the counter for just this purpose.[31] Refusal (or inability) to pay one's bill was one type of trouble waiters frequently confronted. General rowdiness and the occasional alcohol-fueled brawl were others. Sometimes, patrons came in already drunk and angry from work; other times the disagreement originated in the eating house itself, as was the case with one "savage fight" the *Boston Herald* reported in April 1857. A group of intoxicated men took to stabbing each other with broken glassware, and, as the newspaper concluded, "considerable bad blood was spilled."[32] Keeping order among such men was not an easy job, and it was not uncommon for customers to turn their violence on the waiters, as was the case when John Luckey attacked John Morse, his waiter, on October 13, 1854. Mr. Luckey, the *Boston Atlas* joked, was "lucky enough to get off with $10 and [court] costs."[33] The paper did not report how the waiter fared.

As a result of the low pay, stressful working conditions, and general servility associated with waitering in this period, native-born white men scorned jobs as eating-house waiters.[34] These positions instead went to the dregs of Boston society, those whose occupational options were strictly limited due to racial and ethnic discrimination and prejudice against them: African Americans and Irish immigrants. Indeed, 62 percent of Boston's waiters, according to the 1850 US census, were nonwhite or foreign-born.[35]

The significant proportion of Irish eating-house waiters in Boston imparted a distinctive flavor all their own to patrons' dining experiences. According to one bewildered patron, the Irish brogue alerting patrons to the day's menu items sounded something like this: "Haunchavenision, breastervealand-oysters, very nice; . . . rosegoose, legger-lamb an' sparrowhawks."[36] Further perplexing were the "restaurant calls," a kind of precursor to diner slang, that eating-house waiters used. "Boston strawberries" (baked beans), Cincinnati quail (pork), "sleeve balls" (fishcakes, authentically, a piece of fish between two potato slices), and "stars and stripes" (pork and beans) were some of the most commonly used in Boston.[37]

As for the actual fare in these basement eating houses, it is impossible to know for sure about its specific quality. It certainly received plenty of criticism, but, again, eating-house fare was generally maligned. One especially infamous eating-house specialty was hash, a dish of mixed chopped meat, potatoes, and onions.[38] In the cheapest places, hash was rumored to be composed of all the uneaten bits of food that had been left on patrons' plates and subsequently gathered up, reheated, and served again to someone else. Proprietors of the cheapest venues were also accused of purchasing and serving spoiled meat and rotten eggs because such products could, of course, be obtained at a discount, thus padding profit margins. In part, this suspicion toward eating-house food stemmed from disbelief at these establishments' rock-bottom prices. For example, at Carr's Eating House in the 1850s, a man could feast on roast pork, veal, lamb, or broiled beefsteak for just six cents.[39] When asked, proprietors vigorously denied resorting to any culinary chicanery to keep their prices this low, insisting instead that they shopped for inexpensive cuts of lean meat that could be cooked carefully to taste good and relied on high volume to turn a profit.[40] They were also careful not to waste parts of animals other Americans may have thrown away. Animal organs, flanks, and necks all found their way into eating-house fare, if only to help flavor stews and hashes.[41] In a candid interview with the *Boston Globe*, a proprietor of one cheap eating house acknowledged that his patrons were not necessarily concerned about the quality of the food they received: "Our trade is generally hungry. Folks that come in . . . ain't the kind that eats for fun or to kill time. They generally have a good appetite and are mighty glad to get something for it—be it ever so humble."[42] In this venue and in many others like it, food was food.

If a man was willing to spend more on his afternoon dinner— anywhere from just a few cents more to almost a dollar, depending on the venue and what the man ordered—he could dine higher up in the hierarchy of eating houses and enjoy certain improvements in style and service. In these venues, the dining room tended to be larger and aboveground; hence, light and air circulation were better. The kitchen and dining room were distinct spaces, with the kitchen frequently located in the basement below the dining room. For example, when Mr. A. R. Campbell remodeled his eating house on Wilson's Lane in 1850, separating the kitchen from the dining room was one of the primary improvements he made.[43] As a result of this arrangement, the whiffs of cookery were not so intense to patrons. Separate tables and booths replaced counters and "boards" to provide patrons with greater space and privacy. There were improvements in cleanliness as well; and, sometimes, there were even pictures hung on the wall or shabby curtains on the windows for decoration.[44]

EATING OUT

Wm. H. Ladd's Eating House, Boston, by J. C. Sharp after Fitzhugh Lane, lithograph, ca. 1840. The atmosphere of this eating house is clearly orderly and restrained compared to the venue in the first image. *Courtesy of the American Antiquarian Society.*

These eating houses further provided such dining accouterments as silverware and napkins. The "napkin rack" was one innovation that helped proprietors save money on laundry costs by reserving regular patrons' napkins to be reused several times between washes.[45] A customer simply retrieved his designated napkin from the rack each time he visited and returned it after his meal. Finally, waiters were more numerous and thus more attentive. Together, these enhancements served to justify higher menu prices and helped to draw a kind of clientele that could afford to pay them.

But even in these better-appointed and more expensive eating houses, men still ate in a rush, with little regard for decorum or sociability, intent on getting back to work as quickly as possible. In many cases, their patrons were still waged laborers like clerks and other lowly white-collar workers whose dinner breaks were limited in length. Even patrons who were self-employed would have learned by now that time was money. Overall, there was probably not much improvement in the quality of ingredients or cookery in these pricier venues. Instead, there seems to have been a general feeling among nineteenth-century diners that they just charged extra for more or less the same greasy dishes.[46]

So why frequent a higher-priced venue only to receive essentially the same food as that available in cheaper eating houses and when the meal was still a rushed, haphazard affair? What was the benefit, particularly if one was a clerk or otherwise still "on the make," with little extra income to spare? By choosing a superior class of eating house and paying more for their dinner, dining amidst clean-swept floors and well-arranged tables, middle-class and aspiring middle-class men asserted their economic superiority over those who ate in the lower sort. But more importantly, they asserted their cultural superiority. "Loafers" and "rowdies" ate in the lowest venues, kept in line (or not) by the threat of the waiter's "persuader," picking their teeth with their knives, and oblivious to the bad odors and filth surrounding them.[47] But in the nicer eateries, middle-class and aspiring middle-class men indicated they valued virtues like cleanliness, privacy, and the propriety of using a napkin and fork (and not a pocket knife, or worse, their hands) at the table.

Even if their social and economic positions were precarious, as

EATING OUT

they often were, even if they had yet to secure their economic independence, and even if they barely had time to pay attention to their enhanced surroundings before dashing back to work, dining in these venues instead of the cheaper ones became a kind of cultural capital, a way for a man to demonstrate that he possessed characteristics that prepared him for, and made him worthy of, opportunity, upward mobility, and, ultimately, success.[48] Though many patrons may have had to choose what they ordered carefully and eat less in order to be able to afford dinners at the nicer eating houses, the fringe benefit of the opportunity to distinguish themselves culturally from those who dined in the lower sort was worth the additional cost. Of course, the higher prices these eating houses charged also had the advantage of excluding lower-class, manual workers, the very people with whom many perilously positioned, lower-middle-class customers so desperately did not want to be confused (even though, economically speaking, they may not have been so very different from them).[49]

The Eating House as a Shared Experience

But though highly stratified, Boston's eating houses nevertheless also united Boston men in common experience. Precisely because there was an eating house to accommodate nearly every budget, frequenting an eating house became a daily occurrence for many men, resulting in significant changes in these men's lives. Instead of dining with their families, men in Boston became accustomed to eating among strangers, paying for the convenience with their hard-earned wages. Moreover, eating houses became an integral component of the city's blossoming commercial and market culture. Above all, these venues helped make it possible for men to fill their bellies and still submit to their employers' demands of their time.

There were other ways as well in which the city's eating houses helped to collapse and obscure the social divisions between Boston men. There is little doubt that at least some patrons moved back and forth between the different grades of eateries, perhaps dining higher up in the hierarchy of venues on some afternoons and pursuing meals in cheaper establishments on others. Indeed, the open, competitive nature of the eating-house business encouraged men to seek out and try different places for any variety of reasons. Perhaps one afternoon on his way to dinner at his usual spot, a man noticed a particularly enticing daily special chalked on the door of another venue and decided to step inside. Perhaps clerks favored one eating house when the boss was treating but went to another when dinner was on their own dime. Perhaps some men were willing to spend a bit more on dinner at the beginning of the week but then descended into the basement venues as their pocketbooks gradually emptied. Boston's dining landscape offered male diners the opportunity to make a social ascent or descent as they chose or could afford on any given afternoon.

Even nonwhite Bostonians—a category that included not just blacks but also Irish, Italians, and Jews—found that they were generally welcome in the city's eating houses. For European immigrants, it was often in an eating house that they tasted their first bites of "American" food. In many cases, this fare, purported, according to one source, to resemble "half-chewed tobacco," was probably not the most ideal introduction.[50] But for men from countries where meat was a luxury, the sight of broiled beefsteak, roast veal chops, and boiled ham all being dished up in plentiful quantities and bolted down by their fellow patrons—and for only a few cents—must have been a wonder.[51] In Boston, even the iconic baked beans were laced with bits of pork.[52] The immigrant patron of the eating house, lined up along a counter with men from various backgrounds, thus began to learn the ways of eating and living in America: abundance was possible, as long as one did not waste too much time on dinner and hurried back to work.

There were some notable exceptions to this policy of inclusivity, however, and they typically involved the city's black residents.[53] Frederick Douglass, for example, reported that he had experienced the early stages of Jim Crow segregation in 1846 when he was told at one eatery: "'We don't allow niggers in here.'"[54] But such strict racial intolerance does not seem to have been the general rule in Boston. As Walt Whitman exclaimed when he visited the city in 1856, "At the eating houses, a black, when he wants his dinner, comes in and takes a vacant seat wherever he finds one—and nobody minds it."[55] His surprise suggests Boston's eating houses were, at any rate, more welcoming in the antebellum period toward blacks than Whitman's native New York. In 1865, the Massachusetts state legislature was one of the first to pro-

EATING OUT

hibit discrimination based on race in public places, including dining venues.[56] Comments Frederick Douglass made as a dinner guest at the Parker House in 1884 indicated that the city of Boston did make real efforts to enforce its postbellum civil rights legislation. According to Elizabeth Hafkin Pleck, "no other northern state passed as many civil rights laws or was as inclusive in its coverage of discriminatory acts as Massachusetts." Nevertheless, there is no doubt that blacks in Boston continued to experience at least some level of discrimination and segregation in public accommodations like restaurants until well into the twentieth century.

Of course, not everyone in Boston experienced eating houses as patrons. For their staffs, eating houses were one of a limited number of racially integrated workplaces in the nineteenth century. As noted, because of the low esteem associated with working in eating houses, their employees tended to come from the polyglot assortment of migrants to the city, especially the African American and Irish populations with few other options.[57] There were instances throughout the 1800s when these inclusive workforces banded together to try to secure goals of shared self-interest. For example, waiters at different venues in Boston repeatedly joined together to strike for higher wages. Late in the century, they also formed the Waiters' Benevolent Association, an interracial mutual aid society. Perhaps even more noteworthy was the network of lookouts that white antebellum Boston restaurant employers and employees developed to warn black waiters—many of whom were fugitive slaves—whenever slave catchers were in the vicinity.[58]

Discrimination was more evident, however, among eating-house proprietors. While immigrants from across Europe opened dining venues in Boston (close to 14 percent of Boston's restaurant keepers were foreign born in 1850 and almost 30 percent were born abroad by 1880), black Bostonians were legally prevented from entering this trade until the 1840s.[59] According to British visitor Edward Abdy, "Even a license for keeping a house of refreshment is refused [blacks], under some frivolous or vexatious pretense, though the same can easily be procured by a white man of inferior condition and with less wealth."[60] Later, even once such legal barriers were removed, African American restaurateurs long continued to struggle in Boston. By 1850, the federal census listed just five black restaurant proprietors in the city.[61]

One of them was Joshua Bowen Smith, who operated an establishment at 16 Brattle Street in Cambridge.[62] Smith, known in Boston as the "prince of caterers," was, by far, the city's most successful black restaurateur. He was also a virulent abolitionist who advocated black pride and self defense and actively assisted fugitive slaves in Boston. Smith's political activities must have interfered with his professional interests since most white Bostonians denounced abolitionism. Perhaps this explains why Smith's business by the late 1850s seems to have been limited to catering to abolitionist organizations.[63]

Smith's race eventually hurt his business in other ways as well. In 1861, after feeding the Twelfth Regiment of Massachusetts Volunteers for a period of ninety days during the Civil War, Smith presented a bill for $40,378 to Governor John Andrew. Andrew, however, refused to compensate Smith, arguing the state legislature had failed to appropriate the funds with which he could legally pay. And yet, in anticipation of the legislature's later reimbursement, the governor had already paid the other proprietors—almost certainly all white men—who had provided similar catering services to soldiers.[64] The state's failure to pay devastated Smith. Though he later recouped a little over half of the total bill, he was nonetheless forced into bankruptcy. Historian Shane White has recently found that black nineteenth-century businessmen like Smith operated with the constant fear that their white customers would refuse to pay them.[65]

Racial discrimination also negatively affected black restaurant proprietors' access to credit. In the period before the founding of the national bank system during the Civil War, there was a chronic shortage of specie. Private banks freely printed and put into circulation paper money in an effort to meet this demand. The problem was that counterfeit and "broken" bank notes (notes issued by failed banks) were all too common.[66] As a result, the exchange of money for goods was an extremely fraught process that hinged largely on trust. Once again, black businessmen were at a distinct disadvantage in negotiating this process with white customers.[67]

The heterogeneity of Boston's eating houses, their racially and ethnically diverse spaces, could—and did—result in conflict. Racial and ethnic slurs were slung alongside hash. And, as described above, fights were not uncommon occurrences, fueled by a combination of racial and ethnic friction and alcohol. For example, racial tension was evident in an incident reported by the *Boston Globe* involving several Irishmen and an African American man at O'Connell's eating house at 163 Beach Street, a clash that resulted in three broken windows of the eating house and stitches for one of the men.[68] That time, no one was seriously injured, but these scraps could turn deadly.[69]

Tensions engendered amongst an interracial eating-house staff similarly ended in violence. The surprising frequency of knife and gun fights between interracial restaurant employees, as reported in Boston newspapers, hints at the status anxiety and conflict that often plagued these working relationships. For example, in April 1890, after a long and stressful afternoon of service, a black cook was accused of stabbing a white waiter with a knife, though the cook later insisted to the *Boston Globe* that his weapon had been a broken pie plate and that he had been motivated by self defense.[70]

Racial and ethnic distinctions, then, never broke down entirely within the walls of the eating house, though they were often transgressed. Thus, eating houses simultaneously—and paradoxically—helped to both define and blur differences between male Bostonians. While the range of eating houses became a vehicle for signaling and legitimizing difference, the common experience of bolting an eating-house dinner served to link the separate rhythms of patrons' individual lives to each other and to the city and its economic growth. Above all, eating houses facilitated the demands of a capitalist economy on infringing upon traditional patterns of eating. Eating houses helped their customers—standing elbow to elbow along the counter—come to a new understanding of what it meant to be a man living, working, and eating in the city.

CHAPTER 2

Nervous Kitchens

Consuming Sentimentality Narratives and Black-White Intimacy at a Chicago Hot Dog Stand

JESSICA KENYATTA WALKER

A hot dog stand in Chicago, The Wieners Circle, has this gimmick that you occasionally see in restaurants: the staff acts rudely, in sort of a playful way, and cracks jokes about the customers. Except at The Wieners Circle, late at night, the gimmick becomes more than just a gimmick. It becomes scary.

—IRA GLASS, *This American Life*, 2007

So, no one can describe what the mammy was, and only those can apprehend her who were rocked on her generous bosom, slept on her bed, fed at her table, were directed and controlled by her, watched by her unsleeping eye.

—THOMAS NELSON PAGE, *The Negro: The Southerner's Problem*, 1904

Multiple elements determine the success or failure of a restaurant. Most might consider the menu to be the most important factor, but pricing, ambiance, service, and clientele might also draw or deter customers.

In an incredibly competitive market, restaurants look to offer unique experiences and, generally, tailor supply to meet customers' demands. The Wieners Circle (TWC), like many other food service spaces, carves out a niche, altering and playing on the rules of good customer service in order to create a distinctive food experience. However, this is done not in terms of emphasizing delicious dishes, a romantic encounter, or nuclear family fun, but in terms of actively transgressing normalized scripts around race, gender, food service, and sensuality.

In 2007 an episode of *This American Life* called "Pandora's Box" featured a captivating seven-minute story about The Wieners Circle, a hot dog stand in Chicago's Lincoln Park neighborhood. The above epigraph from radio-turned-television-personality Ira Glass begins the episode with a promise of something disturbing. The show, originally a program on National Public Radio, features Glass as he explains that over the years the stand has become famous for two things: its charbroiled hot dogs and burgers and its mostly Black female servers. While the latter might not normally be considered noteworthy, at this restaurant, turned popular local attraction, the staff is known to regularly call customers motherfuckers and white bitches. In turn, the late-night, inebriated, mostly white, male patrons return the verbal abuse with racial slurs and sexual demands. In the midst of this back and forth, the customers put in orders for one of the stand's most popular items—the chocolate milkshake. This menu item calls for the women behind the counter to lift up their shirts, expose their breasts, and bounce up and down.

Through the performance of the chocolate milkshake, these Black women are re-imagining the fast-food kitchen space by engaging with scripts that offer a counternarrative to normalized and racialized representations of food services and Black womanhood. As with any act that paints a space anew, the women of TWC unsettle multiple discourses and, in doing so, create and embrace tensions for the viewer, whose expectation of food service at a hot dog stand might not involve sexist and racists slurs.

The version of TWC represented on *This American Life* is indeed ripe for critique. Although there are many discourses that shape the interactions at TWC, most fascinating are the narrative elements that frame the servers at the hot dog stand as victims and the kitchen space as a site where the "scary" clashing of tensions, desires, and expectations interact. I argue for the centrality of the kitchen space in transgressing the boundaries of intimacy between white men and Black women. Furthermore, I suggest that when reading these interactions we cannot underestimate the extent that the kitchen space foregrounds how people interact inside TWC.

Finally, by identifying the tensions between sentimentality and hypersexuality in TWC, the space becomes a nervous kitchen. "Nervous kitchens" is a phrase that works to do two things: (1) it highlights the wealth of interpersonal interactions that determine the hegemonic rules and behaviors of the space, and (2) it reveals the unpleasant feelings, histories, and performances that often interact in kitchens, where food is used to express identity, intimacy, and desire. In short, the nervous kitchens as an analytical frame redirects our attention in a text like TWC away from the sensation of the story and toward understanding the narratives that make the scene legible through raced histories of intimacy, food, and Black womanhood, narratives that continue to resonate in the show *This American Life*.

Nervous Kitchens: Disturbing the Familiar

Local foodscapes provide a common ground upon which bodies marked by difference can often engage in unlikely interactions, creating sites of tension and nervousness through consumption.

Aspects of nervousness from which I would like to draw the most come from the work of Denis R. Byrne. He brings attention to the spatial consequences of racial segregation that leave unmarked and marked borders. Drawing on colonial spatial systems in Australia that restricted Aboriginal communities into fenced-in reserves, Byrne argues for a framework of spatial nervousness where a minority group transgresses colonial systems of racial segregation. The term "nervousness" enables us to think of racial segregation not so much in terms of physical infrastructure but in terms of how it's a "spatial order governed primarily by behavioral convention and coercion."[1]

The nervousness that I nervously attempt to develop is understood as a type of anxiety, but not just in spaces. As an analytic tool it embraces the interplay between discourses, taking into account, in the instance of TWC, modes of representation. Nervousness, as I take it up, has no negative or positive connotations and allows for a reading that can color consumption habits, spaces of food production, and subjective relationships to food as contradictory to normative ideas. I do not wish to argue whether or not nervousness can be read from the viewers or participants in TWC video clips, but rather how can we use the structures and conditions of nervousness (anxiety, fear, transgression, tension, agitation, uneasiness) to order and put into conversation the multiple discourses that are engaged/performed in that space. In the following analysis, nervousness illustrates how nourishment or satisfaction can look violent and uncomfortable for the Black female servers at TWC.

The Narrative Frames: What We Do and Do Not See

Glass makes certain narrative choices that erase the structural and everyday racism that these women potentially face outside of the workplace and suggests that these interactions are isolated events occurring in a vacuum. Clear examples of these sensationalized and decontextualized interactions include the following dialogues between employee Shawanna Smith and belligerent white male customers: Interaction 1:

Customer 1: Nice headband, you fuckin' whore!

Customer 2: Fuck you, you sagging slut.

Shawanna: You gonna keep waiting bitch, pop your thumb and sit down, you fuckin' slut.

Interaction 2:

Shawanna: Grab that dick!

Customer: Get your hand on it! You fuckin' Ninja-Turtle-looking bitch![2]

Speaking to the camera, Roberta (nickname Poochie), the segment's most interviewed employee, reflects on the nature of her workplace interactions:

Roberta: Yeah [I] will get like one or two that come in and, you know what I'm sayin'? [They say,] "Do you all have monkeys back there? Coons back there?" You know what I'm sayin'? Then that make . . . that make us . . . that'll piss a mutherfucker off.

These are prime examples of the "gimmick" that has nearly doubled the business of TWC and attracted thousands of people to YouTube clips showcasing the over-the-top behavior of the employees. The episode of *This American Life,* however, is more deliberate in how it depicts TWC. As the show progresses, it seems to be concerned or, better yet, fascinated by how this *abnormal* behavior started with one of the two middle-aged, white, male owners, Larry, who started yelling at drunk customers who stumbled through orders. The show further elaborates on how the environment is sustained by owners who find the unique style of their hot dog stand to be mostly about fun and letting off steam. But Glass and his fellow reporters are primarily interested in how Black women like Poochie and her coworker Shawanna feel, for example, when they tell one customer to "lay those bitches" because they are "horny" or how they feel when customers decide to fight back.

Adapted for Showtime from a popular Chicago Public Radio program, the premise of *This American Life* is to travel the United States collecting "true stories that are dramatic, emotional, and often funny."[3] Indeed, the scenes depicted in TWC's episode evoke a range of emotional responses, and as the stories build, so do elements of drama. Showtime gave the creators of the show a lot of room to develop a film-inspired series that did not have to dumb down content. In wanting the "images themselves [to] carry the story forward," the show uses the compelling coupling of cinematic visuals and efficient narration that, as one critic notes, allows Glass to "take the wheel of stories" when his informants aren't saying "exactly what the producers want them to."[4] I investigate the narrative choices that Glass makes in order to "take the wheel" of how we are reading the representation of Black women's subjectivities in relation to TWC. More to the point, I argue that Glass narrates the Black women servers as racial martyrs who exchange their dignity for monetary compensation. The following exchange provides a clear example in which Glass foregrounds the story's climax (the chocolate milkshake) by describing an eruption of violence and bigotry quelled only by a story of class mobility:

Roberta Jackson: It supposed to be fun, a lot people take it beyond the extreme, calling me "nigger." . . . It's really not no worse thing that you can say to me.

Ira Glass: When The Wieners Circle suspended the normal rules of how people should treat each other they accidentally unleashed a lot of pent up feelings, that were probably pent up for good reason. This free for all honestly changes how you feel about everybody, you really wish you never saw it (begin ominous music and rapid cuts showing TWC employees performing the chocolate milkshake). The tips are great, everyone says that, people stay here 10, 20 years. One woman raised three kids, got her daughter into Northwestern.

Roberta Jackson: You have to do what you have to do, point blank. If you gotta keep food on the table for your kids, for yourself, however it go . . . you ain't never had a high school diploma get out there and make your money.

The above framing of Roberta's reaction to and justification of a racist and traumatizing work environment uses sentimentality in order to make her difficult reality a legible narrative for popular consumption. In *The Suffering Will Not be Televised,* Rebecca Wanzo argues that African American women can only gain political power by deploying the logics of sentimentality in storytelling. Sentimental storytelling is "the narrativization of sympathy for purposes of political mobilization."[5] Wanzo argues that there are five conventions of suffering through which African American women are seen as appropriate objects of sympathy. These conventions, used to structure a narrative, rely on African American women's abilities to garner affective reactions to their suffering narrative in order to bolster political agendas.[6] The specific conventions I see at work in the above narrative about and by Roberta include using progress and self-transformation as the best response to structural inequality. Both of these narrative conventions "[treat] feelings as the end of political change, encouraging a mode of individualist, self-transformation endemic to U.S culture," where "you need only change yourself, and in so doing you change the world."[7]

Wanzo uses the life story of Oprah Winfrey to explain how narratives of self-transformation are packaged as pre-formed routes toward empathy, excusing the realities of pain African American women must endure as a result of structural power relations. Sentiment, or constructed affective response, intersects with race in specifically American stories of racial sentimentality, joining feeling and freedom. And while not bad or good, these narratives tend to be "politically effective but insufficient means of political change."[8] In the case of Oprah, this narrative manifests itself in how she fashions her own struggles with sexual assault, poverty, and familial alienation as stories of "personal suffering as a path to citizenship in the United States," where citizenship is inclusion by way of feelings of liberation that characterize slave narratives of the nineteenth century. Although not selling hot dogs, Oprah conflates "suffering citizens" with self-transformation through her book club selections.[9] Toni Morrison's *The Bluest Eye*, a story about one Black girl coming to terms with abuse and living up to white standards, had its political potency evacuated through Oprah's facilitated book club conversations. As Wanzo puts it, Oprah makes Morrison's novel consumable by downplaying the "political scope . . . in order to privilege the strand of the narrative concerned with self-transformation," something her audience can relate to. When and if a story of Black women's suffering finally does become visible for consumption by a larger public, it is within these expected forms, stories of tensions or conflict sold as an "issue of self-determination for women."[10]

While one woman is transformed through her ability to pay for a secondary education for her child, Roberta reminds us that TWC is still a place where Black women get routinely harassed and are also victims of social injustices. For instance, Roberta reminds us of structural inequalities around education that make getting a high school diploma a challenge, coercing her to resort to tolerating abuses to make money and survive. Glass's narration uses the language of feeling but also of triumph to both soften the blow of the racist and sexist images we witness and, perhaps more importantly, erase their structural underpinnings.

Women like Roberta Johnson reflect that constantly being called the "worst" name possible gets resolved and makes the story consumable through engagement with progressive narratives of sentimentality. We are directed to feel sorry for people like Roberta, but not too sorry because she actually makes good tips, good enough, it turns out, to send her daughter to Northwestern University. Ultimately, we are made to feel that the Black women who staff the hot dog stand transform themselves and are able to push past their suffering. Yet, the danger of relying on affective understandings of suffering is that "sentimental evocations of history and progress depend on affect as an organizing principle and not on a discussion of structural inequality."[11] When Glass "wishes" he never encountered the verbal violence of TWC, when he "feels" like it changes how he views everyone, and when he describes the hostile scenes as a "free-for-all," we now understand that what we see is isolated to this one space and is an amorphous and uncontrollable situation, lacking rationale and structure. Even when Glass mentions that Chicago is so racially segregated that demographers invented the term "hyper segregation" to describe it, there is a way in which this only serves to reify the borders between Black and white actors. Hyper segregation becomes a justification for the behavior instead of a way to contextualize the behavior within sometimes fetishistic ethnic food tourism, or processes of gentrification that continually rewrite the lines and terms of hyper segregation. Still, at the end of the show, even if we are to believe that TWC is a unique business model of fast-food service, we are also aware that these Black women are victims who also are generally okay with their treatment because they get money to better themselves and their families.

As the episode moves forward from the scene above, we see a long shot of the hot dog stand at night as some of the worst insults are played, transcribed in subtitles so that we can hear and see every word. Although we never see any of the white customers' faces, a move to protect their identities, we hear, "Hey, everyone, they're on their crack break! Don't come for a while; they're gonna smoke crack in their fucking car." We see the transcription as Roberta and her coworkers are referred to as "slaggin' sluts" and "tits." Hearing the vitriol with which these faceless figures mercilessly attack the servers at TWC supports Glass's observation that this hot dog stand accidently unleashes "a lot of pent up feelings." However, the sensationalism of these moments distracts from the everyday nature of racial violences that, depending on the social location of Glass's audience, can either seem like a phenomenon or business as usual. The environment of the kitchen spaces of restaurants, for example, is notoriously racist and sexist, translating to lower pay, constant workplace humiliation, and physical objectification, especially for women of color.[12] The language of unleashing makes one think these faceless white men are uncontrollable animals, not responsible or liable for any action or utterance. It also reinforces workplace abuses that occur in restaurants as inconsequential to a customer's behavior in that space.

Although we may think that this behavior would not be acceptable outside of this space, the nervous kitchens analytic also asks how discourses that seem to be exceptional in kitchen spaces might reveal everyday imaginings. In this case, all we can do is speculate that while these dramatic utterances are business as usual at TWC, they may indeed be a mundane characteristic of how customers imagine interactions with Black people every day. This makes statements like the following, uttered by a white male customer and directed at one of the Black female workers at TWC—"It's like an abortion bitch, I'm eating your babies and you love it!"—smack of so much sensationalism it almost seems fictional.

Far from fictional, however, are recent and historical experiences of Black women's forced sterilization and the routine misrepresentation of Black girls as hypersexualized, coloring the comment with a disturbing truth. From the early twentieth century to as recently as 1974, women of color, especially Black and Latina women, were forcibly sterilized sometimes through non-consensual major surgery or even as a prerequisite to receive welfare benefits. Many women were lied to, as these dangerous and painful procedures were often done under the guise of less invasive ones. These practices "purge black women or men of their reproductive possibilities," relegating the bodies of women of color to that of lab rat.[13]

What appears a fascinating statement to one person can be a haunting reminder of the ordinariness of racist practice when framed in the right historical context. These racist and sexist interactions are not "unleashed" in one grand moment of crisis but have always existed in a consistent simmer through racialized discourse of Black women's hypersexuality informed by tropes of Black women in food service.

The Chocolate Milkshake: Black-White Intimacy

Part of what allows Glass to identify TWC as a "free-for-all" is that the stand has suspended the normal rules of how people treat each other. Yet what happens next in the segment, as the camera pans across what seems like an infinite sea of blurred-out, white male faces, pushes back against normative expectations of fast-food service. The stand itself, an important part of Chicago's urban history of immigration and industrialization, is a vernacular structure missing the familiar uniformity of a McDonald's franchise but containing the graffiti and the informal ordering of a local joint grounded in the community.[14] At the root of the narrator's discomfort with the behavior in TWC is that the standardized image of a courteous and efficient approach to fast-food service is thrown out the window as women yell at customers. Moreover, the Black women who work at TWC are not just hawking food but become, at a certain point of the night, items on the menu themselves.

As the soundtrack turns to low, ominous pulses, the camera pans to approximately thirty to thirty-five inebriated customers chanting, "Chocolate milkshake! Chocolate milkshake!" The three women on the other side of this mob, Poochie included, stand with arms folded, preparing to satisfy the demand. Suddenly, the lights flicker in the kitchen and one woman lifts up her shirt and jumps up and down while others bang pots and utensils to a 1-2-3 rhythm. The blurred faces lose it with excitement, ravenously taking in the sight of bare, black breasts at their local hot dog stand.

Moving beyond the Gaze

The ordering and serving of a chocolate milkshake goes beyond blurring the lines between consumable bodies and food to reveal a more complex set of communications about race, desire, and intimacy. Within a scene that looks like the objectification of Black female bodies, for instance, there is the possibility for reading both the zealous chanting by the white men and the topless performance by Black women in the space as communicating each subject's relation to power, racialized sexual desire, and food.[15] Indeed, food is not incidental to this space but is in fact the basis for its operation, with its products grounding it in Chicago's ethnic food traditions. And although one could link the accessibility of cheap drunk food to the accessibility of a sexual performance named after a dessert item, a critique of the exchange must delve deeper into the logics of this conflation. While on the one hand we can read this exchange as one in which the consumer wields power over the consumed, there are historical resonances that frame the interaction in, if not a more equitable balance of power, certainly a more dynamic one.

The performance of the chocolate milkshake is an unnerving encounter between historically racialized sexual desires. The Black female body has served seemingly contradictory purposes in the Western imagination. Her body has been the site for eroticization, hypersexuality, and a mysterious sensuality, while it is also figured as brutish, embattled, and menacing.[16] Although these are ostensibly contradictory traits, scholars like Sheri L. Parks argue that Black womanhood is often charged to contain these contradictions—her body is often expected to negotiate between many different subject positions.[17] An oversimplification of Black women's subjectivity reinforces stereotypes that limit the extent to which Black women are allowed to self-define outside of extremes. Subject to oppressive disciplining in public and private circles, Black women often have no control over how they are represented popularly. Patricia Hill Collins argues that tropes like mammies and the jezebel are technologies of control "designed to make racism, sexism, poverty, and other forms of social injustice appear to be natural, normal, and inevitable parts of everyday life."[18] Narratives like *This American Life* "take the wheel" of the representation and, by doing so, explain Black women's lives through images that find confluence with historical intimacies between Black and white bodies.

One cannot help but point to the historically persistent trope of the mammy figure in the sexualized exchanges of the food service space.[19] Mammy's roles, both imagined and in real life, were around caretaking and food preparation, and thus her presence shaped a certain set of interracial relationships, overdetermined by dependence. Micki McElya explains how mammy letters (letters written to southern heritage organizations venerating a romantic ideal of an enslaved woman) written in the 1910s and 1920s made "claims of intimate and satisfying bodily contact between Black women and whites in the private sphere of the white home" and described "white southerners' allegedly indescribable or 'unspeakable' longing for the black mammy."[20] McElya points to a longing that creates a tension between a need "for sanctioned physicality between Black women and both white women and men" and the structural realities of segregation that seemingly limit access to this physicality.

So while segregation emphasized the spatial separation along lines of race, the rationales behind this very separation contained a "profound nostalgia" for an antebellum South where everyday intimacies between Black women and white men, women, boys, and girls was sanctioned. The realities of reminiscing on formal modes of integration belie the very informal and consensual modes through which Black women's bodies remained accessible to all kinds of violence even after formalized segregation.[21]

Framing the mammy in terms of intimate longings and desires helps us understand the racial discourses that order and give provenance to the actions of the white men who demand chocolate milkshakes. In an attempt to break open the concealing forces of structural segregation, these white men use sexual language and aggressive behavior to regain access to Black women's *privates*—her bosom, in particular.[22] This intimate access was seemingly taken away with the end of slavery, but through nervous spaces we can see how it is still allowed and perpetuated.

Nervousness disrupts the extent to which we can impulsively name the Black women behind TWC counter "mammies." The women who perform the milkshake are large-breasted Black women, a common physiological norm of depicting the mammy, which means that referent will always "be in the frame." Still, the conventions of the mammy trope, like her constant accessibility, as well as the contradictions of white desire for her dehumanized body, are enacted and performed in this space while at the same time being violently transgressed. This transgression occurs through the use of the chocolate milkshake for Black women's strategic self-definition and survival, where accessibility to the white male gaze does not equal powerlessness or wholesale victimhood.

Looking at other sites where Black women let their bodies be consumed for desirous audiences sheds more light on how we can read the chocolate milkshake as a dynamic conversation about race, desire, and consumption. For example, M. Miller-Young writes on a similar tension involving Black women in the pornography industry. These Black women often deal with an industry that treats them as both hyperaccessible objects of Black fetishization and super disposable objects of marginalization. However, Miller-Young argues that these women put their hypersexuality to "work for their own interest in survival, success, and sexual autonomy."[23] Miller-Young's argument is necessary to provide nuance and a language of autonomy for Black women whose agency is often thought to disappear in the pornographic entertainment industry. However, I do not want to make the same arguments for autonomy and survival as she does for her informants. Rather, by making the connection between the chocolate milkshake and Miller-Young's subjects, I re-think the performative expectations of Black women in each practice and the ways these performances of sensuality (taste, touch, smell, etc.) are necessarily packaged within racialized sexual desire.

Specifically, Miller-Young's framework opens the door for a niche sexual fetish, racial Bondage Domination Sadomasochism (BDSM), that I find resonates with interactions at TWC. Racial BDSM is a category of sexual role-playing, in which, for example, white men scream racial slurs at Black women to satisfy a sexual desire.[24] The "play" with racial discourse in order to satisfy a desire is certainly a part of the ordering and performing of the chocolate milkshake. Play here in both practices is not meant to signify escapism from the familiar but is, in fact, used to show how these performances delve deep into the interconnectedness of race and the erotic.[25] However, those who practice racial BDSM are quick to note that the racial play presupposes a certain type of psychological and protective care, an element missing in the representation of TWC. Still, what racial BDSM offers is another site of interracial sexual performances where the erotic is necessarily undergirded by histories of racial intimacy where there is a strategic deployment of Black hypersexuality and fetishization. In TWC the hypersexuality of the Black female body is at once being exploited and consumed, sometimes violently.

A critique of the episode must also be open to a reading of the chocolate milkshake as a potentially strategic moment for Black women to express success, experience pleasure, gain survival through monetary exchange, and perform autonomy through what has become an infamous event. When asked what her mother thought of her caustic verbal exchanges with customers, Poochie smiles and says, "That's my baby!"—indicating the extent to which pride, creativity, and thick skin are highly valued in a Black woman who has to succumb daily to racist micro-aggressions in and outside of work. More importantly, these characteristics are incredibly nuanced traits represented in the text.

The representation leads us to believe that the hypersexuality of Black female bodies is at once being exploited and consumed, sometimes violently, but that Black women leverage their presumed hypersexuality for financial stability (or even pleasure?). Poochie does like her job and has gained a type of celebrity. I note this not to assign these Black women "agency," but rather to problematize my impulse to do so. Indeed, an aspect of these narrative conventions is to propel the Black female subject toward "affective agency" or "the ability of a subject to have her political and social circumstances move a populace and produce institutional effects."[26] Although agency cannot be prescribed in these moments and is not utilized here as the possibility for empowerment so much as the means through which subjugated Black bodies must sell their stories of suffering, there are opportunities within the confined structures of the representation to read certain exclamations about self, suffering, and power as counter narratives within the episode.

Applying critical race theorist Richard Delgado's notion of "counter storytelling," Wanzo considers what narratives that can check the dominant conventions around suffering might look like for African American women. Although Wanzo is focused on the medical industry, I find her definitions of counter stories helpful in conceptualizing Roberta's self-named positionality of being "a Black bitch in a hot kitchen." Counter stories should attend to the ways that histories of identity "shape the meaning of pain," how power influences both the infliction of pain and how it is communicated and experienced, and that those experiences can count as evidence.[27] Roberta provides this bit of evidence to the viewers:

> **Roberta**: It's just like this: I'm a Black bitch in a hot kitchen and for you to come in and say that I look like a monkey or some— you know what I mean? That'll make me fuck you up, point blank. Then again, that my job, I can't leave behind here to go whoop nobody's ass.

You can see the inner turmoil and contradictions that swirl in the nervous kitchen space as Roberta negotiates raw frustration with realities of sustaining life. Her expression of pain is in two parts, the second part of this statement, privileging employment over expressing her *true* feelings, might belong to the larger goals of the show's progressive narrative that serves to quiet Roberta's anger again with the promise of financial security. The first half of the statement stands out as a counter narrative position. Indeed, Roberta reminds us "point blank" of the consequences for underestimating her Black bitch self. This fails to properly "sell" her story of pain and instead accentuates it on her own terms and, therefore, fits awkwardly into a narrative convention of progress and self-transformation that, while perhaps making her pain understandable, is not translatable. How can we read Roberta's exclaiming that she is a "Black bitch in a hot kitchen" through the lens of a counter story? Her Blackness, the very thing that instigates some of the worst names one can be called, is claimed by her in concert with the kitchen space—whose stereotypical image of comfort and nourishment is resisted by naming it "hot." The old adage, "if you can't stand the heat, get out of the kitchen," advising people to remove themselves from intense and perhaps uncomfortable situations juxtaposes Roberta's phrasing of the kitchen space as indeed hot but necessarily inescapable. The kitchen and she are co-constitutive, not a compulsory association, as she is not simply a Black bitch; she is also in the heat of the kitchen. In this utterance she reminds us that while she is hard at work in a hot kitchen, a type of heat or kinetic energy gets launched at her through hate speech and vitriol. However, unlike the adage, she is neither getting out of the kitchen nor remaining in it, passive to the insults launched at her. Instead her "point blank" self-definition of being a Black bitch reminds us that her gendered and raced subjectivities are intersecting, converging to form a statement of strength and determination. These are counter stories because they allow her to claim how she's experiencing pain, and in explaining how she can "fuck you up," she takes control of how that pain gets communicated.

These exchanges expose the tensions of the nervous kitchen space's inner workings. I am not claiming Roberta's exclamation as a bright point in an unfair representation, but instead use the nervous kitchens analytic to productively trace how discourses interact in the space. Namely, those between dominant conventions for making Black women's suffering legible and those counter moments within the scene that eschew convention in favor of statements that highlight the intimate entanglements of power, race, and gender in the articulation of Black women's discomfort and pain. But all of these formations are contingent upon the presence of the kitchen's main product—fast food.

Finally, at the crux of this formulation, standing as the translating object between white and Black bodies, is the food. As a vernacular fast-food joint, TWC exists on a low position on a hierarchy of culinary capital, where fine dining is defined through ornate spaces with formalized language and service. When Black women are working in a low-wage-earning occupation within a devalued food service space, we know that their labor is similarly devalued. Aside from structural racisms and persistent stereotypes of Black women and food in popular culture, the space of TWC itself presents as a safe space to make the unspeakable desire for interracial sexuality speakable.

Between Narrative and Desire: Nervous Kitchens

We pass through and interact with many kitchens in our daily lives. We enter into and use products from kitchens in our homes and workspaces, and in the process we engage with friends, family, restaurants, food trucks, fast-food drive-thrus, airplanes, community kitchens, and hospitals. These spaces are a lynchpin for how we physically and socially navigate and nourish our everyday existence. Our reactions and interactions in these spaces can lie in a vexed and tenuous relation to what we imagine to happen in these spaces. And because our expectations of what happens in a space like The Weiners Circle are informed by histories of race, food service, and gendered work, social locations can be expressed through how and what we consume from the kitchen. The nervousness that I theorize in the kitchen space is often but not always a direct result of seemingly conflicting social locations and desires.

Nervousness allows us to read these aspects of the text as concurrent and transformative—it compels us toward new questions and considerations. For example, when we normalize these types of events, or at least place them in frames that don't render them sensational and the bodies within them spectacles, we are more open to considering, or at least approaching, ways of life (subjectivities) that differ from our own as important. This importance lies in a reading of food services spaces that don't nourish or comfort in the traditional sense as reframing our notions of consumption. The interracial relationships that the chocolate milkshake displays frame consumption in terms of violence, violations, slurs, suffering, and pain to satisfy. In what ways has the Black woman embraced these nervous concepts in her idea of nurturing, and in what ways do we as readers and scholars of food studies, critical race theory, and gender and women's studies rely on language of sympathy, nurturing, and sentimentality to describe the relationship between Black women and food work?

Although the creators of *This American Life* claim to depict "true stories," we know better. There is a tension within the representation between the consistent engagement with sentimentality narratives that obscures the realities of structural racism and the claims to true depictions of the realities of structural racism via sexual transgressions. The reliance on sentimentality to portray Poochie and others as bodies worthy of victim status because of their potential to self-transform pushes up against a consideration of the chocolate milkshake as a transgressive performance that has the potential to express Black women's unique subjectivity, a feat that is rarely allowed in the disciplining structures of representation that too often rest on tired mammy tropes.

CHAPTER 3

A Pedagogy of Dining Out
Learning to Consume Culture

JOE MARSHALL HARDIN

We now take for granted the common trope of the "globalized" world, a somewhat unfortunate phrase that generally signals the necessity of crafting policies, products, and messages so that they can be mobilized and remain functional across national, ethnic, and regional boundaries. In 1983, Theodore Levitt, head of the marketing area of the Harvard Business School, sounded a call for businesses to "globalize" in response to the "powerful force" of technology. He reasoned that since communication, transportation, and travel were becoming "proletarianized," that people in every culture would begin to want "all the things they have heard about, seen, or experienced via the new technologies." His article, entitled "The Globalization of Markets" and published in the *Harvard Business Review*, trumpeted "the emergence of global markets for standardized consumer products on a previously unimagined scale of magnitude."[1] Corporations operating with a global strategy would be different from the standard multinational: "The multinational corporation operates in a number of countries, and adjusts its products and practices in each—at high relative costs. The global corporation operates with resolute constancy—at low relative cost—as if the entire world (or major regions of it) were a single entity; it sells the same things in the same way everywhere."[2] Selling "the same things in the same way everywhere" required that corporations create sites of high-context communication, where cultural, physical, socio-relational, and perceptual features would create a pedagogical complex designed to teach consumers how to respond positively to the global brand through a variety of signals, linguistic and otherwise, that would work on a global scale.

Between the push to globalize and the desire to preserve local cultures and promote ethnic and cultural difference, there is, as we know, a confusing tension. This is a world in which Dennis Rodman promotes the largely American sport of basketball behind the nearly impenetrable walls of North Korea and in which the "locavore" movement threatens to become a global sensation, at least among the global elite. As such, we currently experience an interesting dialectic between the forces of globalization and localism. In "Globalization and the Experience of Culture: The Resilience of Nationhood," Wimal Dissanayake writes, "A new world space of cultural products and national representation, which is simultaneously becoming more globalized and more localized as capitalism moves across borders, is also producing coalitions and resistances in everyday life."[3]

As with globalizing movements, localizing movements also employ high-context communication to teach a sense of identity and purpose. In addition to the complex communicative and cultural structures designed to support localizing movements in their quest for self-identity, these movements also create structures and messages that contextualize the localizing movement within the global network. To describe the simultaneous growth of both of these seemingly contradictory movements and their expression within the same brands and marketing concepts, some now use the term "glocalization." According to sociologist Roland Robertson,

> talk about globalization has tended to assume that it is a process which overrides locality, including large-scale locality such as is exhibited in the various ethnic nationalisms which have seemingly arisen in various parts of the world in recent years. This interpretation neglects two things. First, it neglects the extent to which what is called local is in large degree constructed on a trans- or super-local basis. In other words much of the promotion of locality is in fact done from above or outside. . . . Even in cases where there is apparently no concrete recipe at work—as in the case of some of the more aggressive forms of contemporary nationalism—there is still, or so I would claim, a translocal factor at work.[4]

In other words, the production of the local, whether in terms of ethnicity, nationalism, or regionalism, always comes in terms that require its contextualization within the global.

Walk through the door of any modern restaurant, especially in globalized America, and you enter a liminal place where the high-context pedagogical processes of glocalization are readily examined. Such pedagogy is designed to accomplish two things, and the first is to create a site where consumers of all kinds might find themselves "at home." In fact, one will find at least two kinds of consumers in most restaurants. First, a diner might be one who comes from the surrounding neighborhood. This is the diner who appreciates how the restaurant and its aesthetics and cuisine have been localized for the area in which he or she lives or works. The second type of diner might be the traveler from beyond the neighborhood who recognizes that this restaurant will contain familiar aesthetics and cuisine that he or she will recognize and respond to. In other words, any particular McDonald's or any Chinese restaurant will be populated by at least two groups of diners: people from the area who appreciate the way "fast-food" or "Chinese" cuisine and aesthetics have been localized to their particular neighborhood and people from beyond the neighborhood who appreciate that these cuisines and aesthetics are available wherever they find themselves. Diners in the Chinese restaurant might also be those who have some distinct connection to China because of their identification as members or inheritors of Chinese or Chinese American culture.

In "Culinary Nostalgia: Authenticity, Nationalism, and Diaspora," Anita Mannur describes how the preservation of culinary practices from the homeland allows immigrants and even the children and grandchildren of immigrants to "yoke national identity with culinary tastes and practices." While this form of culinary citizenship encourages a "nostalgic longing" for a homeland, the presentation of this cuisine and the associated aesthetics often serve more as a "placeholder for marking cultural distinctiveness and as a palliative for dislocation."[5] As such,

> discursive and affective aspects of food are valued over
> their symbolic or semiotic meaning in nostalgic narratives that

negotiate the parameters of "culinary citizenship," a form of affective citizenship which grants subjects the ability to claim and inhabit certain subject positions via their relationship to food.[6]

The emphasis on the discursive and affective aspects in so-called ethnic restaurants is also what allows diners with no relation to the homeland cuisines represented in these restaurants to claim their own relationship to the cuisine. By receiving and responding positively to the pedagogy of these high-context scenes, diners can, in effect, claim their own culinary citizenship even if they have no direct relationship to the home culture from which the cuisine and aesthetic are drawn. All one needs to do is to open oneself to the pedagogy apparent in these spaces, learn the appropriate lessons, and then pass the citizenship tests by consuming these cuisines and cultures accordingly. If I frequent the local curry shop enough times so that I learn to negotiate whatever tests there are—ordering correctly from the menu, pronouncing words correctly, adding the table sauces and spices correctly, negotiating the specifics of manners and personal interactions—then I gain some level of culinary citizenship, at least in that particular site. I might also be able to use what I have learned from that pedagogy as a sort of "passport" with which I can enter and establish at least a partial and temporary citizenship in other curry shops.

One of the most obvious pedagogical methods employed by restaurants is to establish a familiar context for the consumer and then to build on that knowledge to introduce the unknown. Entering into my local Vietnamese restaurant, The Green Papaya, we recognize various signs, language, and conventions common both to restaurants in general and to other Asian restaurants. Inside, high-context design, décor, signage, and fixtures will encourage us to reference other types of Asian restaurants in both the décor and the menu—there is a statue of Buddha and a playful Hello Kitty waving from beside the cash register. A large tank full of goldfish dominates the back wall. Here, on the menu, are the already familiar fried egg rolls and fried rice. These familiar markers point to other less-familiar items, spring rolls, bubble tea, pho, and báhn mì sandwiches, alongside curries and stir-fries. These elements of high-context communication serve as pedagogical processes by which we are invited to consume a glocalized version of the culture and cuisine of Vietnam. Over time, we learn to pronounce the word "pho" correctly, and if we are committed to become culinary citizens, we work up the nerve to order it ourselves instead of ordering the familiar Chinese-influenced dishes such as stir-fry and fried rice. By watching other diners and making educated guesses based on context, we learn to perform the tasks of adding the proper herbs and sauces to the soup. Now we have effectively used our skills at negotiating these high-context markers to gain at least a nominal culinary citizenship.

High-context cultural markers are generally easily identified, especially where the markers correspond to actual or perceived geographic, national, or ethnic difference. Restaurants that at first seem to be without these obvious national or ethnic markers—we might think of McDonald's, Subway, Dunkin' Donuts, Applebee's, Sonic, Dairy Queen, Red Lobster, and Denny's, for example—still actually require diners to negotiate a variety of quasi-cultural conventions, genres, and lexicons specific to their sites. To the casual American diner, these restaurants and their cuisines may not appear "marked" in the same way as the Mexican or the Vietnamese restaurant, but we know that they, too, contain high-context signs indicating great variation in dining experiences and representing various cultural perspectives. Diners coming from cultures that have yet to encounter these restaurants would, of course, probably mark them as "American." Even for the American diner, though, these restaurants represent a wide variety of different cultural and regional perspectives on the American experience.

For example, fast-food restaurants generally teach a specific cultural lifestyle through a set of shared features, including a particular design aesthetic, a shared lexicon, and specific conventions of behavior. Décor for the fast-food restaurant generally focuses on some exciting blend of orange, red, and yellow, and the conventions of ordering and picking up food are fairly standard so as to appeal to and encourage an on-the-go, fast-food culture. Even if the specific brand is unfamiliar, most diners can spot a fast-food restaurant by its design and architectural features. In this way, fast-food cuisine has been glocalized, as well. One can get fries and shakes and combos at almost all fast-food restaurants, and most allow some form of "drive-thru" ordering and food pickup. If you frequent fast-food restaurants regularly, then visiting one you have never been to before would probably not present many cultural challenges, as you would easily recognize the global features as they have been glocalized to the brand. If somehow you had never been to any fast-food restaurant before, these same features would act as high-context pedagogy to instruct you how to become a culinary citizen of the fast-food culture and to fully experience and consume the product. Foods that we might consider American, or at least fully Americanized—steaks, hamburgers, apple pie, hot dogs, fried chicken, pizza—have been further glocalized for specific regions (Kentucky-fried chicken, Chicago- and New York–style pizza). The culinary citizen of the fast-food culture will most likely be aware of the subtle differences in these presentations and cuisines. For the fast-food culinary citizen, Burger King and McDonald's are very different, although the subtlety of that difference might be lost on diners who do not frequent fast-food restaurants. Most "American" restaurants are actually representative of certain cultural values or aspects of American culture: fast-food places, diners, family-style restaurants, steak houses, barbeque and hamburger joints, seafood houses, supper clubs. Each of these present high-context, localized versions of regional or "lifestyle" approaches to American culture that its culinary citizens have been taught to recognize and respond to.

Starbucks, the American coffeehouse founded in Seattle, is a site where the processes of glocalization and the formation of culinary citizenships are readily apparent. In their article, "The Starbucks Brandscape and Consumers' (Anticorporate) Experiences of Glocalization," Craig J. Thompson and Zeynep Arsel develop the concept of "brandscape" in order better to theorize the processes of glocalization specific to Starbucks: "We reconfigure the consumer-centric definition to encompass the hegemonic influences that global experiential brands exert on their local competitors and the meanings consumers derived from their experiences of these glocal services-capes." Brandscapes, they write, are structured to provide "discursive, symbolic, and competitive relationships" to the dominant brand. Brandscaping allows corporations like Starbucks to overcome possible anxieties about the "power wielded by transnational corporations" by masking a corporate strategy that seeks domination of one entire section of the global market. Thompson and Arsel "reconfigure this consumerist definition [of glocalization] to encompass the hegemonic influences that global experiential brands exert on their local competitors and the meanings consumers derive from the experience of these glocal servicescapes." The brandscape of Starbucks establishes hegemony over other independent and chain coffee shops because all competitors must now establish their identities "in relation to Starbucks."[7] The high-context features of Euro-American Northwest modern décor, the expressive lexicon, the international products, and the globalized corporate ambiance allow Starbucks to set the level of expectation for all other coffee shops. Even the oppositional discourse about Starbucks signals that, for good or ill, all other coffee shops must be measured against the Starbucks brand and experience.

Upon entering a Starbucks, we are presented with a high-context environment in which design, signage, aesthetic, ambiance, and lexicon work to provide us with both familiar global and local features. These same features offer just enough pedagogy so that unfamiliar customs, language, and products may be quickly learned and normalized. In fact, the first time in a Starbucks we might be seized with a bit of trepidation about making a "cultural" misstep. One cannot simply order "a cup of coffee." However, if we are attuned, we can find fairly clear directions and suggestions for how to best experience the brand built directly into the design, the signage, and the aesthetics.

According to Starbucks' website, each individualized location has been specifically designed for the community in which it is located. Starbucks, the website points out, employs "design studios located around the globe so that our designers can fully understand the communities they serve. The mission of each designer is to create a spectacular Starbucks café experience that is steeped in the local culture and designed to reflect the unique characteristics of each neighborhood."[8] Nevertheless, each Starbucks also references at least two globalizing cultures, which must also be learned in order to enjoy the full Starbucks experience. The first is drawn from the "hipster" culture of the American Northwest, and the second is imported from the bohemian European intellectual culture. Within the hipster culture of the American Northwest, two ideologies are paramount: sustainability and, not coincidentally, a glocal perspective. In this regard, Starbucks focuses some of its pedagogy on persuading us that these two ideologies are positive and represent a responsible feature of globalization.

Sustainability, at least as Starbucks presents it, is the ultimate glocalizing force, and their website emphasizes the way the corporation's global activity supports and helps to protect the local communities in which its individual stores operate and the economies and cultures from which it sources its coffees, teas, foods, and merchandise. Starbucks is, according to the website, "interested in the way design can connect us all to sustainable building practices and provoke thoughtful questions and engagement within the built environment. In addition to reducing energy and water consumption, we incorporate reused and recycled materials wherever possible and often use locally inspired design details and materials in our stores."[9] Under the "responsibility" menu on their website, Starbucks offers a report on its "global responsibility." In that document, we learn that Starbucks is committed to ethical sourcing, to helping its suppliers with investments in their operations, with reducing its environmental impact around the globe through sustainable models of business, to investing in renewable energy, and to community involvement.[10] Only the most skeptical consumer would charge that these projects are merely designed to increase Starbucks' market share, but they are certainly a part of Starbucks' high-context glocalizing pedagogy.

Coffee shops are also, of course, linked historically to European intellectualism, which expresses itself in a certain warmth and edginess that one finds inside every Starbucks. The music is slightly outside the mainstream, magazines devoted to arts and leisure are offered, and there are the inevitable newspapers scattered on the tables. These days, however, one is just as likely to find a business meeting going on at one of the tables as to find a philosophical or intellectual conversation. Still, the mood is relaxed and consumers are encouraged to interact and to stay as long as they like.

The specialized lexicon of Starbucks is also an apparent glocalizing pedagogy. When we have snaked through the line, past the bakery goods, the CDs, and the brand-specific merchandise, we are ready to place our order. A "barista" will encourage us to demonstrate an almost immediate knowledge of this specialized lexicon, which is hybridized from a multitude of global languages. If we order a "small" coffee, we may be corrected: "small" is "tall" in Starbucks (one cannot help but think of George Orwell here). A medium-sized drink is a "grande," and a large-sized drink is a "venti." The lexical globalism only begins with sizing. For instance, ordering a "venti chai frappé" in an ordinary coffee shop in Italy, India, or France will certainly produce a confused look from the person behind the counter, although in Starbucks this is a possible order that contains an Italian, an Indian, and a French word. "Venti" is the Italian word for the number twenty (used by Starbucks to signify a twenty-ounce drink, a large), "chai" is an Indian black tea made with "masala" spices, and "frappé" is a French term for "beating" or blending liquids. The culinary citizen of Starbucks need not know the origin of any of those words or even recognize that they have specific meaning in another culture to order and enjoy the venti chai frappé. Many of today's consumers, especially those who live in larger cities or who travel often, are largely fluent in the glocalized culture of Starbucks. For even the casual or first-time consumer, though, Starbucks is a highly contextualized space where we are quickly instructed in how best to have the Starbucks' "experience."

Almost anyone can recognize the globalized structures, aesthetics, and language common to all coffee shops and employed by Starbucks: visual art, non-mainstream background music, high-end bakery goods and epicurean foods, magazines and newspapers focused on art and global politics:

> Accordingly, a selection of arts-oriented media and news-papers, including prestigious dailies such as the *New York Times*, are standard coffee shop accouterments. The edifying reading materials connect coffee shop patrons to the broader worlds of art and community events. . . . A sense of worldliness is also con-veyed through signifiers of the international coffee trade—such as maps of the major coffee-growing regions, images of indig-enous coffee farmers, and bulk coffee displays, often in archaic burlap bags.[11]

In the end, Starbucks' achievement as a glocalizing institution is larger than its simple victory over the coffee shop market:

> Starbucks' cultural influence extends beyond the confines of its corporate Web site, catalogs, and 6,500 retail outlets. The Starbucks revolution has crystallized and propagated a partic-ular kind of third-place experience (coffee shop patronage): it

has shaped expectations and ideals about what a coffee shop should be.[12]

Through its high-context, glocalizing pedagogy, Starbucks has now become the standard for American coffee shop culture.

The idea that restaurants are sites of cultural difference subject to glocalizing forces is, of course, even easier to see when the restaurant is also marked by national, ethnic, or regional difference. Only the least cosmopolitan diner will expect that the cuisines and atmospheres of Panda Express or Chipotle have much more than a distant resemblance to what the average person in China or Mexico actually eats or to the environment in which "authentic" Chinese or Mexican foods are generally prepared and served. Restaurants that feature these kinds of difference do tend to "flatten out" and homogenize the different cultures they represent so that they may be easily consumed, blending the familiar with the new so as to construct the now-familiar high-context pedagogy.

For example, if we venture into our local "Mexican" restaurant, we can expect that there will be tortilla chips and salsa on the table and a menu full of familiar words like "amigo," "casa," "beinvenidos," "verde," "queso," "guacamole," "tortilla," "carne," "relleno," "salsa," and "pico de gallo." While the restaurant may be staffed by people who represent any number of Meso-American cultures, we have been taught to expect the same homogenous representation of Mexican culture to accompany our burritos, enchiladas, tacos, tamales, quesadillas, nachos, and fajitas, some of which are specific only to certain of the broad range of Meso-American cuisines. The décor features lush browns, bright oranges, reds, greens, and yellows. On the walls are sombreros, serapes, and pictures of Mayan or Aztec ruins. Furniture and doors are of heavy wood (real or simulated), and wrought-iron fixtures are apparent, as are tiled surfaces. Some wall finishes mimic adobe and others present murals of mariachi bands and sunlit courtyards. Those experienced in Meso-American and Spanish culture might notice the subtle differences hidden behind these normative features, but most casual diners will read a unified theme they have been taught by frequenting other Mexican restaurants.

We experience a similar pedagogy upon entering the local

Chinese restaurant, of course, which features murals of the Forbidden City and traditional Chinese landscape paintings. Paper lanterns and fans adorn the walls, and dragons or foo dogs guard the entrance and sit at the end of wooden railings, which are painted red and black to mimic traditional shellac wood finishes. Gold metallic wallpaper features scenes of the imperial court, and there is, of course, a jade statue of Buddha (is it actually plastic?). The metaphoric buffet of the eight major cuisines of China—Anhui, Cantonese, Fujian, Hunan, Jiangsu, Shandong, Szechuan, and Zhejiang—has become, in our glocalized version of Chinese cuisine, a literal buffet or a vast array of dishes available for "take-out."

These familiar glocalizing features of Mexican and Chinese restaurants, which culinary citizens of all sorts have been taught by frequenting other like establishments, are infinitely scalable to the independent and the chain restaurant alike, and like all successful messages in the glocalized world of the contemporary restaurant, they are also malleable and portable and available for culinary citizens of all types. Edward Said famously asserted that regions such as those indicated by these types of terms were a "human product" of "imaginary geography."[13] The culinary citizens of these imaginary geographies will find inside—whether they are neighborhood locals, travelers who recognize the global signs and stop because they know what to expect, or those who bear an actual physical relationship to the "homeland" of the cuisine being offered—a constructed and glocalized place where they can feel at home.

While restaurants that feature ethnic, national, regional, and "lifestyle" cuisines serve to glocalize their product for a variety of culinary citizens, the truth is that most national, ethnic, and regional cuisines are already, of course, the result of ongoing globalization brought about by centuries of exploration, colonization, and war. For example, Vietnamese cuisine, even at its most "authentic," is a glocalization of French, Chinese, and even Eastern European cuisines because of the area's encounters with these cultures during centuries of colonization and war. Chinese cuisine, as we have noted, is itself a blend of many regional cuisines brought together as the modern country was formed. The national cuisine of India, at least as it is recognized globally, represents over two dozen regional cuisines and is also influenced by Chinese, Singaporean, Malaysian, and Pakistani cuisine. Perhaps it is only natural that foods and foodways are among the first features of any culture to respond to globalizing and glocalizing forces.

As we have seen, the mixture of food, language, semiotics, folkways, costume, color, and convention encountered in glocalized restaurants creates a dazzling and often confusing array of representations whose individual sources are often cloudy or ambiguous. For example, restaurants that purport to offer "Chinese," "Vietnamese," "Thai," or "Japanese" cuisine all generally offer fortune cookies at the end of the meal. The origins of the fortune cookie are murky, with various claims made that trace the cookie to an American or Japanese source or tradition, although most people probably think that being presented with fortune cookies is a Chinese culinary convention (it certainly is not). Whatever its origin, the fortune cookie represents an interesting case of how the cultural traditions of one nation or culture are reinvented in another.

Most likely, the fortune cookie followed a Japanese tradition that "jumped" in the early twentieth century from Japanese cooks on the West Coast of the United States to the growing numbers of restaurants that served chop suey and chow mein, which might be run by either Japanese or Chinese proprietors or chefs. Chop suey and chow mein are also both complex blendings of various dishes from the Eastern Hemisphere that were Americanized by Japanese and Chinese restaurants in California during that time and that only appear as Chinese American dishes. Now, most Americans expect that any menu in a Chinese restaurant will include chop suey and chow mein and that the meal will end with a fortune cookie.

In the end, the simple act of successfully moving a corporation, an institution, or a cultural cuisine into the global marketplace has grown increasingly complex, but it may have been inevitable that restaurants would lead the way in glocalizing movements. For culinary citizens and locals of all types, glocalization has proved to be a way to learn and then experience an array of international cuisines, foodways, and cultures while doing nothing more than being willing to enter into a restaurant and encounter its high-context pedagogy. Through these experiences, we learn not how to become citizens of other cultures, but how to become culinary citizens of a glocalized and imaginary culture that we might consume and enjoy.

PART 2 ▪ Consuming Literature

Food and Identity in Writing

CHAPTER 4

Hunger Pains
Appetite and Racial Longing in *Stealing Buddha's Dinner*

LAURA ANH WILLIAMS

Food provided a large part of the culture that bound a Vietnamese family together, but there was nothing new about the idea of encouraging one's children to ingest foods that would change their life opportunities.

—Erica J. Peters, *Appetites and Aspirations in Vietnam*

I grew up hardly thinking about my "real" mother at all.

—Bich Minh Nguyen, "How I Found My Mother"

Bich Minh Nguyen's 2007 memoir, *Stealing Buddha's Dinner*, begins with a series of food images: boxed rice, egg noodles, half of an apple saved and shared on a refugee ship, a little girl's arm halfway engulfed by a canister of Pringles to retrieve a fistful of the thin crisps, the salty shards dusting her hands and the floor. Nguyen builds her narrative of a childhood relocated from Saigon to Grand Rapids, Michigan, through food memories—from generic staples to brand-name snacks, from her grandmother's Vietnamese cooking to her public school lunches. It is through these culinary encounters that elementary-school-age Bich navigates the cultural demands that discipline her appetites and her identity. Reckoning with influences from her white classmates and teachers, steeped in 1980s' American popular culture, and navigating among pressures by her grandmother, father, and sister, her Mexican American stepmother and stepsister, and the unarticulated absence of her birth mother, Nguyen's child protagonist is confronted with a wide spectrum of food choices and conflicting desires that shape her complex, racialized subjectivity. What is at stake for Nguyen is not simply an appetite for different foods, but existence and viability as a Vietnamese American subject in the contemporary United States.

Stealing Buddha's Dinner lays out a clearly defined culinary economy in which Bich invests her desires in her quest for belonging. The ways different foods are valorized by the text suggest the limited degree to which its racialized subjects have been accepted by their white American community. Anthropologist Mary Douglas, writing about the cultural significance of foodways, suggests, "If food is treated as a code, the messages it encodes will be found in the pattern of social relations being expressed. The message is about different degrees of hierarchy, inclusion and exclusion, boundaries and transactions across the boundaries."[1] Indeed, the history of exclusion in US immigration legislature has left the residual mark on Asian Americans as perpetual foreigners to the body of the American nation, even as different Asian foods have increasingly been embraced as cultural commodities. Making ethnic difference "palatable" often functions as a survival strategy that requires a self-awareness of the limits of how much difference is tolerable. In *Ethnic and Regional Foodways in the US,* Linda Keller Brown and Kay Mussell acknowledge the power dynamics involved in consuming and assimilating the ethnic Other:

> Mainstream Americans frequently use foodways as a factor in the identification of subcultural groups who find in the traditional dishes and ingredients of "others" who eat differently from themselves a set of convenient ways to categorize ethnic and regional character. Most Americans, however, encounter ethnic and regional foodways in attenuated situations, tinged with commercialism.[2]

For Brown and Mussell, the commercial "tinge" suggests for the ethnic "other" that difference be downplayed or even eliminated for the comfort of mainstream white Americans. They write:

Ethnic Americans (Mexicans or Chinese, for example) who consume highly spiced foods in their homes and communities may find it advisable to minimize the tang of foods served for the public at large. In addition, the most exotic foods, or those with ingredients that are unusual in American foods, may not appear on menus for fear of offending customers. Some Chinese menus, for example, have a separate section of the menu written in Chinese for ethnic patrons, including specialties with those ingredients mainstream Americans might define as exotic or "not food."[3]

Here the "public at large" alludes implicitly and exclusively to white American eaters. Moreover, the negation of the "tang" of exotic ingredients or food as "not food" carries the troubling association of the racialized or "exotic" subject as a negated subject or non-person. Success or survival of the ethnic other, therefore, necessitates finding the balance between making one's own difference visible and discernable and making it palatable and inoffensive (i.e., consumable) to the unmarked, white American.

In her influential, critical text *Reading Asian American Literature,* Sau Ling Cynthia Wong argues that the narratives and, indeed, food motifs of first-generation Asian immigrants in the United States "symbolize Necessity—all the hardships, deprivations, restrictions, disenfranchisements, and dislocations that Asian Americans have collectively suffered as immigrants and minorities in a white-dominated country."[4] In contrast, the American-born children of "Necessity" are second-generation Asian Americans whose narratives and appetites are marked by treats: "Staples are Necessity; candies, snacks, and fancy foods from stores and restaurants are Extravagance, going beyond what is needed for survival."[5] Perhaps because of its protagonist's status as an "in-between" or 1.5-generation immigrant (born abroad, but immigrating at a young age), *Stealing Buddha's Dinner* engages with different territory in the realm of Asian American food narratives and disrupts binaries typically associated with the immigrant story. I suggest Nguyen's memoir complicates food motifs, associating abundance and excess with emotional hunger and rejection of foods as a self-affirming practice. *Stealing Buddha's Dinner* critiques the romance of the American dream offered through the consumption of cultural commodities, even as it celebrates the aesthetics of these commodities. This dream of belonging to the nation is offered through the text's obsessive imagery from television commercials; specific name-brand, processed foods; frozen dinners; and, of course, treats. *Stealing Buddha's Dinner* ultimately suggests the damage that an investment in the promises of belonging and acceptance offered through these can have on the psyche of a Vietnamese American girl.

Nguyen's memoir traces her family's experiences—including her father, Grandmother Noi, older sister Anh, and three uncles—from their escape from Saigon through their resettlement and Bich's early childhood years in Grand Rapids, Michigan, and her father's remarriage to her Mexican American stepmother, Rosa. The narrative highlights the complexity of the relationship between the diasporic Vietnamese refugee subject and the nation-state that represents both "rescue" and exile, whose citizens demand, "Don't you people know how to speak English?" and "Why don't you go back to where you came from?"[6] Nguyen hints at this contradiction when she describes her initial impressions of Grand Rapids in the early 1980s, populated largely by German and Dutch descendants with last names like Jansen, Vander Wal, Heidenga, and Doornbos and dotted with looming billboards covered in "rippling flags, proclaiming 'An All-American City.'" She writes, "As a kid, I couldn't figure out what 'All-American' was supposed to mean. Was it a promise, a threat, a warning?"[7] Committed to fitting in, young Bich invests herself fully in the project of becoming all-American through following the cues suggested by her environment: "In school hallways blonde heads glided, illuminated in the lockers creaking open and slamming shut, taunting me to be what I only wished I could be. That was the dilemma, the push and pull. The voice saying, Come on in. Now transform. And if you cannot, then disappear."[8] These cultural cues create tension between an inclusion that is predicated upon transformation or racial erasure and a racialized abjection that threatens complete erasure. Although she cannot literally transform herself into a blonde white girl, Nguyen's protagonist rehearses her own racial erasure through fantasies of belonging projected by ever-present commercials for food commodities.

The alimentary landscape of Nguyen's memoir offers up what I refer to as different culinary registers. As sociolinguists Douglas Biber and Edward Finegan define the term, "broadly conceived, a register is a language variety viewed with respect to its context of use."[9] In "Toward a Psychosociology of Contemporary Food Consumption," Roland Barthes alludes to a similar idea of "situationally defined" culinary varieties when he discusses the "polysemia" of foods by differentiating between a snack bar and a business lunch, "two very closely related work situations, yet the food connected with them signals their differences in a perfectly readable manner."[10] While an endless variety of registers is possible, each context implies clearly defined patterns of foods. Likewise, the distinct classes of foodways in *Stealing Buddha's Dinner* demonstrate a clear sense that Bich has learned "situations for which appropriate patterns are available."[11] As she is socialized by US public school lunches and interpellated by American popular culture, Bich is intuitively aware of which food practices and products are appropriate for which environment and which further ostracize her. I classify Nguyen's distinct culinary registers not by the specific situation (sociolinguists differentiate between registers in sports reportage versus baby talk, for instance), but rather through grouping and defining classes of foods as objects of varying degrees of desire in the text. Nguyen's different culinary registers include "Home" foods, which are Vietnamese foods like *pho,* and *canh chua* as well as Rosa's sopa and holiday tamales, and "Approximation" foods, which include a Burger King dinner, when Bich's father is treating the family but all she wants is a Big Mac from McDonald's, as well as many of Rosa's grocery choices, governed by frugality, "sensible, no-waste foods."[12] While these culinary registers mark the foods Bich consumes primarily with her family, these are not the foods of her fantasy life that she imagines her classmates or housewives from commercials consume. The culinary register that occupies the majority of the text, "Real" food, is characterized by brand-name candies and processed meal starters by Shake n' Bake and Noodle-Roni, home-baked goods like Nestle Toll House cookies and Jiffy blueberry muffins, and family dinners like pot roast and pork chops—the fantasy foodways sold to Bich through television commercials and programs—that she believes are her avenue for assimilation to white Americanness: "I was still in the stage of longing: all I wanted was to sit at the dinner table and eat pork chops the way my friends did. Because I could not, because our household did not, I invested such foods with power and allure."[13] The text is filled with catalogs of product names, grocery lists for a preadolescent subject with a sweet tooth that stand in for a deeper sense of longing and loss.

In *The Melancholy of Race,* Anne Anlin Cheng discusses the formation of racialized subjectivity through the psychoanalytic structure of melancholia, in particular, noting the alimentary images Freud used to conceptualize this idea: "The melancholic cannot 'get over' loss. . . . The melancholic eats the lost object, feeds on it, as it were. He or she is stuck—almost choking on the hateful and loved thing he or she just devoured."[14] Cheng argues that melancholia can be used to describe American racial dynamics because of the way "the racial other is in fact 'assimilated' into—or, more accurately, most uneasily digested by—American nationality. The history of American national idealism has always been caught in this melancholic bind between incorporation and rejection."[15] The American ideal of "whiteness" functions in the text as Bich's lost object, whose unattainable status cannot be fully acknowledged. Her struggle to attain what she calls "realness" is articulated through a disciplining of her appetite. She literally feeds off of pop cultural cues that define legitimate personhood as well as womanhood, motherhood, family—in television commercials, neighbors' dinners, and peers' lunchbox contents. She writes,

> To me, life lived in commercials was real life. Commercials were instructions: they were news. They showed me what perfection could be: in the right woman's hands. . . . Commercials had a firm definition of motherhood, which almost all of my friends' mothers had no trouble filling.[16]

For Bich, Real foods constitute not only realness and Americanness, but also socioeconomic status, as well as traditional motherhood and family. Of her classmates, we learn that Jennifer Vander Wal's mother plays the piano and makes chocolate chip cookies and Kool-Aid pops. Holly Jansen's mother bakes Jiffy muffins and packs pizza lunches and thermoses of Campbell's chicken noodle soup. At school, Nguyen notes, "a student was measured by the contents of her lunch bag, which displayed status, class, and parental love."[17] Nguyen is drawn to the romance of the United States that she sees through the commodities consumed by classmates and neighbors, in grocery stores, gas stations, and commercials:

At home, I kept opening the refrigerator and cupboards, wishing for American foods to magically appear. I wanted what the other kids had: Bundt cakes and casseroles, Cheetos and Doritos. My secret dream was to bite off just the tip of every slice of pizza in the two-for-one deal we got at Little Caesar's. The more American foods I ate, the more my desires multiplied, outpacing any interest in Vietnamese food. I had memorized the menu at Dairy Cone, the sugary options in the cereal aisle at Meijer's, and every inch of the candy display at Gas City: the rows of gum, the rows with chocolate, the rows without chocolate.[18]

Nguyen devotes the remainder of this long paragraph to further elaborating on the confectionary products on display at Gas City, naming forty-nine specific brand-name products and seven additional categories of sweets (including hamburger- and hot dog–shaped gum, gummy worms, candy cigarettes, popsicles, and chocolate- and nut-coated ice-cream drumsticks). This cataloging of specific products reflects not only her ravenous appetite for belonging, but her belief that consuming the right products will grant access to Americanness as well as her coveted status of belonging: realness. Timothy August characterizes Nguyen's writing about valorizing these foods as a transformative act that works to situate her within this symbolic order:

Nguyen bestows the food with a meaning that far exceeds what the marketers may have imagined or the regular users of these products might experience. She is excessive with her hoarding and pleasure seeking. She invests the object into a new imaginative constellation or economy, which changes the givenness of the product.[19]

Contrasting her obsession with Real foods to her relationship to the Home foods her Vietnamese grandmother prepares, Nguyen writes, "But now I knew what real people ate. And in my mind I used that term: real people. Real people did not eat *cha gio*. Real people ate hamburgers and casseroles and brownies. And I wanted to be a real person, or at least make others believe that I was one."[20] In an interview with Deborah Kalb, Nguyen racializes this distinction overtly: "I thought that if I consumed Americanness then I would become it.... Food also marked a sharp difference between my life at home, where we mostly ate Vietnamese food, and my life outside the home, where I wanted to be as white American as my friends."[21]

While Real foods remain the object of Bich's desire, her Vietnamese Home foods—like her own Vietnamese refugee body—stand as objects of scrutiny under the gaze of her classmates and teachers. The chapter entitled "Green Sticky Rice Cakes" centers around the 1981 Tet festival held in her Michigan elementary school. Bich and her sister Anh are put on display, along with one other Vietnamese girl, Loan, in front of the entire school in the gymnasium. Bich's grandmother has prepared a special platter of *banh chung*, banana-leaf-wrapped rice cakes stuffed with marinated pork, for the assembly, and an extra platter for the girls. As Bich and Anh prepare to share their tray among themselves, a teacher takes them away, saying simply, "Oh girls, . . . these are for everyone."[22] Nguyen writes, "We knew then that they would be going to the Land of Sharing, of white people looking and declining. The cakes would grow crusty and stale under the recoiling gazes of our classmates. They would be ruined by the staring."[23] The teacher's reproach, "these are for everyone," describes and delimits an "everyone" as a community the girls themselves are outside of. An allegorical reflection of the Vietnamese diasporic condition in Grand Rapids—that of ambivalent inclusion—the green sticky rice cakes stand as an offering that is politely accepted and simultaneously rejected. Likewise, the Tet assembly as a whole puts the Vietnamese students on display, just as it disavows the white community's ambivalence to their presence.

This sense of ambivalence, feelings of simultaneous inclusion and rejection, continues to be articulated through Bich's relationship to foods. Brand-name foods are invested with magically transformative power, but Bich's access to this transformative potential is always simultaneously offered and foreclosed. Having known only prepackaged cookies like Oreos and Chips Ahoy, Bich is introduced to the idea of homemade cookies, specifically, Nestle Toll House chocolate chip cookies, by her next-door neighbor and classmate Jennifer Vander Wal. Bich marvels not only that such treats can be made from scratch at home, but that they "name [their] cookies."[24] While Bich covets the Vander Wals' pot roast and Macaroni Helper dinners, Jennifer is suspicious of all of Noi's food and politely rejects everything offered to her. Bich understands the deeper implications of these rejections, "the funny looks, the polite no-thank-yous that signified, *You're different. You're strange.* You *people.*"[25] Jennifer is permitted to enter and walk around in the Nguyen home, but Bich, while allowed in the Vander Wal house, is confined to a path of plastic runners from which she cannot stray. She is forbidden from setting foot into many of the rooms in the house, including Jennifer's. When Bich sneaks into her neighbor's home when they are on vacation, she grabs two Toll House cookies from the Vander Wal's kitchen and eats them in secret. Although she is caught and forced to formally apologize, no one ever learns about the stolen cookies, and their taste is what lingers with Bich and persists as a reminder of how hungry the young protagonist still is for what these cultural commodities signify:

> I knew the cookies would stay with me forever, echoing with each successive one I might eat and learn to make, each chocolate chip a reminder of the toll, the price of admission into a long-desired house. How I wanted such entrance through cookies, through candy and cake, popsicles, ice cream, endless kinds of dinner. I wanted all of it, and hated to be hungry.[26]

In this moment Bich's hunger is articulated overtly and juxtaposed with not only the abundance and belonging suggested by the endless variety of American foods, but also the unarticulated emotional cost this hunger has on her psyche. While Bich's American classmates share her disciplinary culinary economy of "realness" and normalcy, Rosa, one of the text's other major, racialized characters, offers a critical perspective on this investment. When Bich says for the first time, "You're not my real mother" to Rosa, Rosa spends the next three days wordlessly cleaning the house—vacuuming, mopping, scrubbing—and cooking. Rosa's silent protest enacts the domestic labor glamorized in television commercials and demonstrates to Bich what it would *really* be like if, like Bich's friends' mothers, she were a homemaker. Rosa provides plates heaped with

> Kraft macaroni and cheese and chicken nuggets.... For dinner, large portions of Noodle Roni. ... Chef Boyardee, frozen pizza, scalloped potatoes from a box. But we could not enjoy it. My sisters glowered and Rosa spoke to no one. The food itself

began to feel heavy, slicked with the artificial flavorings and colorings promised right on the packages. I didn't know how much more I could take of such silence and abundance.[27]

The disjunction between the fantasy promised by these Real foods' commercials and their processed flavors and appearances—not to mention the distinction between commercial homemakers and Rosa's lived experience—begins to weaken the transformative potential of the commodity. Although the standoff ends as quickly as it begins, it marks a turning point for Bich's valorization of commercial homemakers and complicates her desires for these Real foods.

At another point the fantasy of the name-brand commodity similarly fails her. Learning that Holly Jansen's mother uses Jiffy baking mixes, Bich coerces Rosa into letting her buy these to make the same blueberry muffins. At first, Bich feels relief and satisfaction, "a little mean gladness that I was finally able to have what Holly had every day."[28] But to her, they taste different from Holly's, ordinary rather than phenomenal. The Jiffy muffins' transformative potential eludes Bich, forcing her to reckon with what she and her family might lack: "missing the element no one in my family could supply."[29] Nguyen juxtaposes this scene with a rare moment of racial panic. Years later, she is visiting from college and passing the Jiffy grain hotel in Chelsea, Michigan:

> It towered, monstrous, creamy white, surrounded by a wisp of chain link fence. As I crossed the empty lot toward it the word "Jiffy," bright blue and serifed with its trademark quotation marks, expanded. I remembered so clearly the taste of those blueberry muffins, of Mrs. Jansen's banana bread, and I stopped walking. I didn't know where I was going. I imagined the grain hotel filled with muffin mix, all those dried blueberries stifled in flour and sugar. . . . Something about the moment filled me with fear—as if the grain hotel would fall down, smother and erase me.[30]

August describes this moment as a confrontation with insurmountable lack in the face of indeterminate whiteness, noting, "This is not merely a personal disappointment or neurosis, but rather something structural and material. . . . The idea that she could disappear speaks to her feeling of impermanence in the US; even in Nguyen's advanced college years, someone like her could still be dragged down and smothered by these impersonal structures of whiteness."[31] Like the tiny, dehydrated blueberries in the towering grain silos, Nguyen feels stifled by the overwhelming and sustaining presence of the building complex's literal whiteness and the promises of whiteness never realized through the consumption of this commodity.

As name-brand foods begin to lose their luster, the narrative begins to acknowledge that those foods symbolize not "reality" for Bich, but rather fantasy, specifically, a racialized fantasy promised by the popular cultural media she is steeped in. When Real foods do not transform her lived reality into the quintessentially American life she longs for, Nguyen contemplates her own reality in contrast to these pop culture fantasies. Late in the text, Bich travels to Boston to see her birth mother for the first time since their separation in 1975, and the reality of the event is juxtaposed against narratives of reunion in pop culture:

> On soap operas I had seen people reuniting with great cries and splashing tears. They would run at each other at full speed across a giant meadow or parking lot or airport. I never imagined this for myself. . . . I had always known that whoever my mother was, she was not the stuff of fantasies. She was, on the contrary, the stuff of too much reality. And I had avoided that reality—my whole family had—for years.[32]

Elsewhere, Nguyen describes the dramatic value inherent in this moment of reunion: "It is uncomfortably dramatic—and yet, people always want it to be more dramatic."[33] This concession suggests the overdetermined nature of soap operatic narrative desire as well as the impossibility for Nguyen's own individual narrative ever to satisfy that narrative desire. In a sense, she articulates a familial narrative fantasy that ultimately remains unfulfilled. Nguyen suggests the link between the centrality of the culinary fixations of her memoir and its unspoken cliffhanger:

> When I was growing up much of the world seemed steeped in mystery. The minor mysteries—how exactly did Pringles get their shape?—weighed almost as much as the major mysteries—what had happened to my mother? The subject of her life was shrouded in secrecy—no one in the family wanted, or dared, to talk about

her. The structure of the book mirrors my experience of not knowing, and not even really allowing myself to think about her.[34]

This avoidance and silence surrounding the separation from Bich's mother brings us back to Freud's structure of melancholia. In her short essay, "How I Found My Mother," Nguyen writes, "What does it mean when you forget how you found something? It means you want to have had it all along. It means you don't want to think about the loss that precedes the finding."[35] The magnitude of the loss and the inarticulable nature of their separation, compounded by the family's silence, create such a yawning emotional absence that Bich's ravenous desires to satiate herself with fantasy foodstuffs can also be read as an emotionally compensatory impulse.

That is not to say these longings are for any one thing, for Nguyen's narrative moves from a value system characterized by a singular investment in the rhetoric of all-Americanness toward an acquiescence that Real foods do not bestow the happy fantasy promised in commercials any more than they fill in the emotional void left by her family's separation from her mother. The memoir closes with a food catalog of another sort, when Nguyen visits Vietnam for the first time after her family's relocation. In Hanoi, a feast is prepared for Bich and Noi that includes

> crepes stuffed with vegetables, fish heads and herbs floating in sweet and sour broth, beef stewed with eggs, shrimp dipped in *nuoc mam* spiked with lime and pepper, chicken tossed with cellophane noodles, fresh spring rolls bursting with bean sprouts, shrimp, and coriander, and always, for the American girl, a plate of fresh French fries. We sat in a circle on the floor, spreading the dishes out in front of us between our rice bowls and glasses of 7Up and Tiger Beer.[36]

Bich's plate of French fries suggests the paradox of the contemporary Vietnamese American subject—her successful transformation into an American girl now differentiates her from her Vietnamese relatives. She admits in an interview, "I have learned from Noi how to cook some Vietnamese foods, like *cha gio* and *pho*. I crave these dishes now, but somehow they never seem to turn out exactly the same, or nearly as good, when I'm on my own."[37]

Of course, Bich's 1980s tastes and longings are not the only discourses interrogating the "realness" of foods. Many, such as journalist and "foodie intellectual" Michael Pollan, have written volumes submitting to readers the value of eating "real foods." Julie Guthman, a scholar who calls into question the disciplinary rhetoric of popular food writers, maps a common structure to that rhetoric that includes "discuss[ing] the ubiquity of fast, junky food in order to make their points about what constitutes 'real' food."[38] An irony of *Stealing Buddha's Dinner* is that the processed and packaged foods that young Bich valorizes as Real foods can, in fact, also easily be described as junk foods—mass produced and with high caloric and marginal nutritional value. Even Nguyen, writing for the *New York Times* in 2012 about the Hostess brand filing for bankruptcy and the potentially looming extinction of the Twinkie, offers a different perspective on these commodity fetishes. She writes, "'Junk food' is a phrase at once grotesque and appealing. We know it's bad, and that's why we want it."[39] Nguyen positions Hostess Twinkies, like much of the popular and material culture of the 1980s, as evidence of the ways gustatory and aesthetic tastes are constructed as inversely related, in ways recognizably similar to Susan Sontag's 1964 discussion of the aesthetics of "Camp": "it's good *because* it's awful."[40] The instant gratification promised by the "snack cake" signals its cultural lowness; and, having developed a more sophisticated palate, Nguyen's description demonstrates the artificiality of the Twinkie, discernable through gustatory taste, stripped of her previous racial investments. She is met with "the smell of sugary, fake, buttery-ish vanilla.... and it tasted like what it was, a blend of shortening and corn syrup, coating the tongue."[41] Although she discusses her Proustian remembrances conjured by the Twinkie, she does so firmly in the context of wishing the commodity a fond farewell.

In an interview, Nguyen distances herself from the 1980s popular culture her narrative evokes. She characterizes the era in terms of its "intense materialism," "good badness," and "excess and indulgence and synthesizers" that served as her "first (if perverse) lesson in aesthetics."[42] August argues that Nguyen's discursive "relegating [of] this wonderment to the past disavows the overpowering lure of the commodity and suggests that perhaps she has understood, moved past, and overcome aspects of this symbolic order."[43] Speaking openly about the ways she coveted American commodities and her childhood desire for American foods to transform her from the inside out, Nguyen critically acknowledges that for Asian Americans now, "to be a twinkie is to be a sellout; yellow on the outside, white on the inside."[44] She actively demonstrates the progression of her aesthetic tastes: "I'm happy to report that my tastes and desires have evolved since that time. I still love candy, but now I mostly look for things like single-origin chocolates and handmade sweets (though, I confess, a box of Nerds once in a great while is very satisfying)."[45] She now evinces a new form of disciplining of her appetites, this time governed by more highbrow aesthetic, dietary, and culinary expectations: "After all, we're not supposed to eat like this anymore. Michael Pollan would not approve. Mr. Pollan, I swear that I have not tasted a Twinkie in years. I would not feed them to my kids."[46]

Nguyen's literary appetite complicates any facile sense of cultural assimilation, as she is able to construct a hybrid, racialized identity with complex tastes as well as complicate any easy alignment of the racialized subject with exoticized foods. Like other ethnic American food memoirs, for example, Linda Furiya's *Bento Box in the Heartland* (2006) and Diana Abu-Jaber's *The Language of Baklava* (2005)—in addition to many Asian American novels, including fictional narratives of Vietnamese refugees, such as Monique Truong's *Bitter in the Mouth* and Nguyen's novel *Pioneer Girl—Stealing Buddha's Dinner* suggests the perils of growing up in a "multicultural" society in which positive or successful articulations of racial difference are associated largely with either erasure or the ability to offer one's culture to be consumed by (or rejected by) another. Ed Schiffer suggests that "'personhood' in capitalist culture . . . is tied to, if not located in, one's ability to be a consumer. . . . It is no accident that aspirations of emergent classes are so often figured as a desire for 'a place at the table.'"[47] Nguyen's memoir offers a narrative of subject formation that extends beyond simply appealing for a place at the table and contributes to a growing body of Asian American cultural production that works to disrupt the consumption and erasure of the racial other, while affirming its own quirky, hungry, complicated "realness."

CHAPTER 5

Consuming American Consumerism in *The Road*

JENNIFER MARTIN

The idea of an apocalypse has appeared as a theme in literature from the Christian Bible to contemporary science fiction and zombie movies. Cormac McCarthy's *The Road* explores the destruction of nature through the lens of a family, a man and his son. As the two struggle through their post-apocalyptic world where all of nature has been devastated, they must find food sources in order to survive. The scarcity of food in *The Road* suggests the possibility of the extinction of man unless the earth begins the process of rejuvenation. As the two journey southward on the road, they must also navigate a new moral code of consumption involving the taboo of cannibalism. The crux of the man and boy's struggle is finding a moral food supply as they journey down the road toward the southern oceanfront and what the man hopes will be a more hospitable climate. Both the man and the boy remain close to the brink of starvation throughout the novel, yet, because of the boy's strict adherence to his belief system that the consumption of human flesh is wrong, they never participate in the new, immoral consumption of the post-apocalyptic world. McCarthy shares the man's thoughts: "Mostly he worried about their shoes. That and food. Always food."[1] The consumption featured in the novel interrogates the contemporary American practices of consumerism. The cannibals of this dystopian world resemble the voracious consumers of contemporary society as they discard old moral codes in their incessant search for items to consume. McCarthy offers a dim hope of the birth of a new, non-consumeristic ideology with the boy, who has never experienced the lifestyle of consumerism, to replace the diseased philosophy of consumerism in contemporary America that lies in his father's memory and dies with him alongside the road.

In McCarthy's post-apocalyptic world, the food web, consisting of a diversity of food chains, has been destroyed because the earth's environment is damaged beyond the point of immediate rejuvenation. McCarthy gives a brief description of the disaster without revealing if it was man-made or natural: "A long shear of light and then a series of low concussions."[2] Ben De Bruyn says of the disaster, "Significantly, the devastation that destroyed the world has not simply returned us to an unkempt garden. The novel does not simply evoke the ruin of human stewardship, but the ruin of nature itself. This is more surprising than may appear at first sight.... [I]t may be difficult to imagine the destruction of the human world, but it is even more difficult to imagine the annihilation of the earth itself."[3] Later that evening, in the only description of a meal with his wife, the man remembers, "They sat at the window and ate in their robes by candlelight a midnight supper and watched distant cities burn."[4] A few days later, his pregnant wife gives birth to their son. Approximately ten years later, the young boy and his father travel on the southbound road in hopes of finding a more hospitable place to live. The long-term destruction to the lower species of the food web has been realized in the ten years since the disaster, allowing McCarthy to examine the extinction of all plant and animal life and the chaos this presents for constructing ethical food choices.

In the novel, McCarthy investigates man's reliance on the food web for survival and the implications of the destruction of the lower branches of the food chains constituting the larger food web. Food webs concern the transfer of energy from one organism to the next. Michael Pollan, journalist turned food guru, says, "Food chains are systems for ... linking us, through what we eat, to the fertility of the earth and the energy of the sun. It might be hard to see how, but even a Twinkie does this—constitutes an engagement with the natural world. As ecology teaches ... it's all connected, even the Twinkie."[5] In McCarthy's world, the original source of energy to any food chain, the sun, is no longer an effective energy source. While it is unclear what caused the destruction to the earth's ecosystems, McCarthy does make it clear that there is a large layer of ash blocking the radiant heat of the sun from providing energy to any living thing on the earth. The disaster has created "nights dark beyond darkness and the days more gray each one than what had gone before."[6] Without the sun, plant life on earth is compromised and ultimately dies. All of the natural world that surrounds the man and boy is dead: "Along the shore a burden of dead reeds."[7] As they enter a gas station early in the novel, "the weeds they forded fell to dust about them."[8] Without the sun or vegetation, not only do the lower-order organisms die, but organisms higher in the food web also die. As the man and his son look at a manmade lake behind a dam the boy asks, "Do you think there could be fish in the lake?" The man answers, "No. There's nothing in the lake."[9] The humans remaining on earth are the only live organisms in the food web.

As the man and the boy continue on their southerly journey, the rest of the food web is examined. The man recalls a memory from a time closer to the disaster: "Once in those early years he'd wakened in a barren wood and lay listening to flocks of migratory birds overhead in that bitter dark. Their half muted crankings miles above where they circled the earth as senselessly as insects trooping to the rim of a bowl. He wished them godspeed till they were gone. He never heard them again."[10] In a town along their route they hear a dog bark. The boy, who was born in the days after the disaster, has only seen a dog once, and his father must explain to him what the sound of the bark actually is, since it is a foreign sound for the boy. The boy, who realizes that in this world anything beneath them on the food web could be dinner, says, "We're not going to kill it, are we Papa?"[11] His dad says, "We wont hurt the dog. . . . I promise."[12] Jonathan Safran Foer in *Eating Animals* explains the American ideas on consuming dogs: "Despite the fact that it's perfectly legal in forty-four states, eating 'man's best friend' is as taboo as a man eating his best friend. Even the most enthusiastic carnivores won't eat dogs."[13] McCarthy challenges every form of American social eating taboos in the novel. He begins by admitting that the domesticated dog could be supper. McCarthy later hints at the dog's demise: "They never heard the dog again," just as the man never heard the migratory birds again.[14] In the entirety of the man and boy's journey down the road, the dog's bark is the only indication of another live mammal.

When the man entered a barn to scavenge for food he noticed

that "there was yet a lingering odor of cows and he realized they were extinct. Was that true? There could be a cow somewhere being fed and cared for. Could there? Fed what? Saved for what?"[15] The unlikelihood that anyone remaining on earth has a food supply to keep an animal alive is evident as the man ponders extinction. Cows are herbivores, and with the lack of energy transferred from the sun to vegetation, there is no renewable food source available to keep a cow alive. Extinction is a difficult term to grasp, and as the man ponders the lingering odor of the cow, he has a difficult time coming to the realization that there are no cows left on earth. He must imagine the unimaginable. The use of the word "extinct" in this passage is McCarthy's only direct mention of the term; it serves as a warning for his examination of consumerism.

Unlike the cows, humans are omnivores and are placed at the top of any food chain due to their ability for sentient thought, adaptable diets, and their tools and technologies for killing other animals. With no renewable food source available, humans are forced into two distinctive categories, those who only scavenge for food and those who are willing to eat other humans for nutrition. For the man and the boy, this division is deeper than just a food choice; it marks the difference between good and evil. Morality in this world is simplified to black and white. The little bit of moral gray area revolves around selfishness, many times mixed with self-survival. Those who do not eat humans but refuse to help their fellow survivors or share food with others occupy this gray area. The boy, who is the voice of a new morality, struggles to remove his father from the moral gray area by extending goodwill to others they meet. Randal S. Wilhelm, in "'Golden chalice, good to a house god': Still Life in *The Road*," asserts, "In *The Road* ... the presence of evil is palpable and serves as a primal force in the world with which the characters must in some way contend."[16] For the man and the boy, evil presents itself in the form of the cannibals: the immoral humans of their world who have resorted to hunting and eating each other in order to live. McCarthy creates a platform in the novel to explore the ultimate American dining taboo, cannibalism. Thus, food choice takes on great significance as it is not just for subsistence, but a marker of the morality of the individual. Brad Kessler, in "One Reader's Digest: Toward a Gastronomic Theory of Literature," says, "Food in fiction signifies. It means more than itself. It is symbolic. It opens doors to double and triple meaning."[17] Kessler adds, "Certainly shame and eating have a long-linked history in Western culture."[18] Never has the old idiom, "You are what you eat," taken on such moralistic baggage.

In desperation to find food, the man and boy come to a house off the road and search it for anything edible. The man pries the lock off a door in the floor of the pantry and uncovers a group of people in the cellar being held as food. "Huddled against the back wall were naked people, male and female, all trying to hide, shielding their faces with their hands. On the mattress lay a man with his legs gone to the hip and the stumps of them blackened and burnt. The smell was hideous. . . . Then one by one they turned and blinked in the pitiful light. Help us, they whispered. Please help us."[19] As the man and boy turn to escape, they see the cannibals "coming across the field toward the house . . . four bearded men and two women."[20] The boy realizes the gravity of the situation as he later reflects on the encounter with the cannibals with his father:

> They're going to kill those people, arent they?
> Yes.
> Why do they have to do that?
> I dont know.
> Are they going to eat them?
> I dont know.
> They're going to eat them, arent they?
> Yes.
> And we couldnt help them because then they'd eat us too.
> Yes.
> And that's why we couldnt help them?
> Yes.
> Okay.[21]

The boy struggles with the moral implications of withdrawing their help from the cannibals' prisoners. He repeatedly tells his father that, regardless how hungry they get, they will not eat people. The boy's beliefs are similar to those of moral vegetarians—those who refuse to consume items of animal origin. Paul Rozin, Maureen Markwith, and Caryn Stroess explain this process of moralization. They say, "The significance of moralization is that it converts preferences into values. Values are more durable than preferences, more central to self, and more internalized."[22] For the boy equipped with the notion of moralization, food choice is not about preference or availability, but about the moral standing of the consumer. He is the voice of the new morality by insisting that he and his father will never eat people regardless of how desperate they become for nutrition. The boy demands that they choose starvation over a breach in their morals. The boy, who was born in the wake of the disaster, is better able to comprehend the new moral order than his father, who still remembers the old ways where there was a large gray area between the binary of good and evil. While the boy and his father choose the moral high ground, the cannibals become the other side of the binary and stand on the moral low ground. Erik J. Wielenberg, in "God, Morality, and Meaning in Cormac McCarthy's *The Road*," asserts, "The cannibals of *The Road* may survive, but they have paid a heavy price for doing so. By turning their back on morality, they have cut themselves off from genuine human connections forever."[23] The man and the boy have a genuine connection with each other due to the mutual trust they carry that they will not kill each other or others they encounter for food. This morality provides them strength to face the seemingly impossible along the road. The cannibals lack the connective strength that comes from this trust and morality, and the loss of their humanity is encrypted in their immoral actions.

This new food chain creates a new social hierarchy that escapes the social moralities of the old world and pits the strongest and best armed against the weak. Since humans are now the only live source of food, there are very few children left in this world because they are at the bottom of the new food web since they are weak and unable to protect themselves. Ely, the lone man they meet along the road, is surprised to see a little boy and says, "I never thought to see a child again. I didnt know that would happen."[24]

The fragile standing of children in this world is reinforced when, shortly after a very pregnant woman and her escorts pass the pair on the road, the man and boy see a cook fire in the woods. Driven by hunger, they investigate it. The group abandons their campfire when they hear the man and boy approach: "They'd taken everything with them except whatever black thing was skewered over the coals."[25] The man and boy realize it "was a charred human infant headless and gut-ted and blackening on the spit."[26] The father can only say "I'm sorry" to his distraught son following this bleak revelation that children are indeed food.[27] Wielenberg notes, "Horrifying as it is to contemplate, the fact is that the baby constitutes food. Others killed and cooked the baby; not eating it is not going to bring it back to life. But there is never any question that they will not eat the baby; they are good guys, and good guys don't eat people."[28] The boy and man follow the rules of moralization that they have established, despite the fact that they are literally starving to death. The roasting baby is left over the coals, and they continue their quest for a moral food source.

When the boy's father dies, a man comes upon the boy standing in the road. The man and his wife have been watching the pair and were aware that the father was ill and that the boy would be left alone. The man invites the boy to join him. The boy has been directed by his dying father to find the "good guys" and his only measure of goodness is in food choice. He interrogates his potential protector:

> Do you have any kids?
> We do.
> Do you have a little boy?
> We have a little boy and we have a little girl.
> How old is he?
> He's about your age. Maybe a little older.
> And you didnt eat them.
> No.
> You dont eat people.
> No. We dont eat people.
> And I can go with you?
> Yes. You can.
> Okay then.[29]

When the boy establishes that the man is not a cannibal, he willingly goes with him. He has judged the man with the only moral marker he understands. The boy is introduced to the maternal presence, who "when she saw him put her arms around him and held him. Oh, she said, I am so glad to see you."[30] In the brief passage where the boy meets the new family, McCarthy indicates the passage of time, noting the woman, who is concerned with the intellectual life of the boy, would "talk to him sometimes about God."[31] There is promise that both the intellectual and physical needs of the young child will be nurtured with this new family that has the potential to shelter the boy to adulthood, allowing him to carry forth his peaceful ideology of moral food consumption. McCarthy's ending leaves the boy with protection so that he has the potential to lead a new world order of humans that are more prudent and moral consumers.

With the extinction of both plant and animal life, except for humans, there is not a way to replenish the pre-disaster food supply. This forces some serious survival issues on the non-cannibals who remain in the world. Pollan, in *The Omnivore's Dilemma*, says, "Some philosophers have argued that the very open-endedness of human appetite is responsible for both our savagery and civility, since a creature that could conceive of eating anything (including, notably, other humans) stands in particular need of ethical rules, manners, and rituals. We are not only what we eat, but how we eat, too."[32] Those who choose not to consume human flesh in McCarthy's world must then scavenge for food among what remains of the processed food prepared before the disaster since it is not possible to grow or gather food from natural sources. This becomes problematic for the survivors as the amount of processed food available is finite, and the more time that lapses from the disaster, the more dangerous that food supply becomes since even processed food does not have an eternal shelf life. Each can of food could be spoiled and laden with bacteria that could leave the consumer very ill or dead. McCarthy demonstrates the deadliness of the food supply when the boy becomes ill from eating tainted food. After days of fatigue while watching his child fight a deadly infection, the man "checked all the foodtins but he could find nothing suspect. He threw out a few that looked pretty rusty."[33] With a finite and gradually spoiling food supply, long-term survival for humanity seems bleak without a renewal of the natural world. The survivors are in the ironic position of consuming the end of unhealthy American consumerism with each rusty tin of food that is eaten. McCarthy draws a parallel between this desperate consumption and the enthusiastic contemporary American consumption. The consumerism celebrated in America defiles the natural world and leads to confusing and conflicting moral choices.

There are times when the man must make difficult decisions about what to eat: "In the pantry were three jars of homecanned tomatoes. He blew the dust from the lids and studied them. Someone before him had not trusted them and in the end neither did he and he walked out with the blankets over his shoulder and they set off along the road again."[34] Much like the consumers in American culture today, the homegrown is rejected and the industrial food sources are preferred. The man fears consuming tainted food and believes the industrial, consumer-driven choices are safer for his small family. He knows that sickness caused from eating spoiled foods, such as the home-canned tomatoes, could render him and his son weak and helpless prey for the other group of eaters left in the world.

The cannibals also face the issue of a diminishing food supply. There are a limited number of people remaining in the world and many of them are sick or dying. Human reproduction cannot happen quickly enough to replenish the supply of humans to feed everyone and also allow for the continuance of the species. The chance for survival of the species depends on the renewal of nature. The boy asks his father, "So how many people do you think are alive?" The father finally answers, "I dont know how many people there are. . . . I dont think there are very many."[35] There are several indications in the novel that the cannibals are attempting to extend their food supply by breeding women to give birth to food. When the "army in tennis shoes" passes the man and the boy on the road, it becomes apparent that the cannibals are using women as broodmares.[36] "They passed two hundred feet away, the ground shuddering lightly. Tramping. Behind them came wagons drawn by slaves in harness and piled with goods of war and after that the women, perhaps a dozen in number, some of them pregnant."[37] The woman as broodmare is reinforced in the novel when, after seeing a group traveling along the road earlier in the day with a pregnant woman, the man and boy later that evening stumble upon the human baby roasting over the fire pit. In this new world order of the cannibals, women fall below the men who are physically able to force the weaker individuals to do their bidding.

The man's wife realizes the futility of her life and commits suicide rather than attempt to live through the drama of relocation. She lost her vision in the time between the disaster and their decision to relocate, and she understands her weakened condition makes her easy prey for the cannibals. She knows the fate of women in this new world order and refuses to submit to it. In her mind, death is preferable to the doom of the women walking down the road behind the army as slaves to the hungry men who are willing to use the women as food and food producers. She is also realistic about the fate of the weak. She tells her husband before she commits suicide, "They are going to rape us and kill us and eat us and you wont face it."[38] She knows she is at the bottom of the food web and has no desire to be a cannibal's meal. Despite the cannibals' attempts to renew their food supply by forcing women into a form of sexual slavery, both types of eaters in the novel face an end to their food supply unless the earth is able to renew itself so that the environment is living again instead of dead.

In this world where life and death hinge on securing the next meal and moral standing is based on the choice to eat or not eat people, an interesting paradox emerges. Those, like the man and boy, who desire to remain on moral high ground must choose to eat dead food. Don Colbert, in his book *The Seven Pillars of Health,* says dead food will "make you disease-prone [and] will cause degenerative diseases such as diabetes, cardiovascular disease, and arthritis."[39] He defines dead food as "living foods that have fallen into human hands and have been altered in every imaginable way, making them last as long as possible at room temperature and to be as addictive as possible to the consumer."[40] He continues, "Dead foods hit our bodies like a foreign intruder. Chemicals, including preservatives, food additives, bleaching agents, and so on, place a strain on the liver. Toxic man-made fats begin to form in our cell membranes and become incorporated in our bodies or stored as fats."[41] He calls the diet of dead food the "standard American diet."[42] The man realizes that not only are he and his child starving, but they are also starving for proper nutrients which have been lost in the processing and in the age of the packaged goods they must consume to survive. At one of the stores that they find along the way, he looks for vitamins to supplement their diet, but the vitamins are long gone, picked up by other scavengers also seeking nutritional supplements.

Pollan elaborates on this same concept of dead food in *In Defense of Food: An Eater's Manifesto*: "For while it used to be that food was all you *could* eat, today there are thousands of other edible foodlike substances in the supermarket. These novel products of food science often come in packages elaborately festooned with health claims."[43] Ironically, the only "live" food left in McCarthy's world is the food source of the cannibals, human flesh. Therefore, those who choose the moral low ground for subsistence are consuming the only live food available. Whereas, those who have taken the moral high ground and choose not to consume other humans have no choice but to consume dead food unless the quality of the food supply changes with the renewal of the earth. The good guys will not be able to maintain a long-term existence with the dead food supply available to them. Ultimately, the disease and decay that Colbert proclaims follow from consuming such a poor diet, along with the scarcity of the supply, will cause those on the moral high ground to perish. The cannibals, who have access to the only live food source, face the issue of a diseased and dying food supply; and, ultimately, they too will not be able to subsist on the limited food available on the planet.

Prior to the disaster, not only had Americans reached a critical point in the composition of the food supply, but they had also reached a perilous state due to the manner in which food was consumed. Food consumption that is devoid of pleasure is hazardous to the mental well-being of the population. Pollan explains,

> I contend that most of what we're consuming today is no longer, strictly speaking, food at all, and how we're consuming it—in the car, in front of the TV, and, increasingly, alone—is not really eating, at least not in the sense that civilization has long understood the term. Jean-Anthelme Brillat-Savarin, the eighteenth-century gastronomist, drew a useful distinction between the alimentary activity of animals, which "feed," and humans, who eat, or dine, a practice he suggested, that owes as much to culture as it does to biology.[44]

In *The Road*, food becomes more associated with survival than with the rituals of social interaction that had slowly been extracted from the American dining experience, leading up to the disaster. Therefore, when the man and the boy eat, they are depicted in the animalistic activity of "feeding" rather than in the more human-like activity that Jean-Anthelme Brillat-Savarin refers to as "dining." Maguelonne

Toussaint-Samat, in *The History of Food,* says, "If we must eat to live, then naturally the pleasure of eating must also be preserved; it is more than the beginning of happiness. First comes a certain sense of well-being, both physical (of course) and psychological. In general, that is a sign of good health. Today, no one can ignore the fact that our health depends on what we eat."[45] The man and his son are therefore missing an important component in the consumption of food: pleasure. McCarthy examines the American ideal of "eating to live" that is prevalent in the busy, consumer-driven, contemporary culture, instead of the more holistic approach of living to eat. Without the pleasure that comes with dining, the health and well-being of the man and boy are at stake.

Food consumption in *The Road* by the man and the boy is usually furtive and without ceremony. Before the pair entered the mountain pass, "they squatted in the road and ate cold rice and cold beans that they'd cooked days ago. Already beginning to ferment. No place to make a fire that would not be seen."[46] Far from being a social ceremony, this meal speaks about the desperation of the man to find food for the child, to keep hidden to avoid capture by cannibals, and to escape the cold temperatures of the north. They squat in the road to eat, and as with all their meals along the road, they eat in silence. Conversation is saved for other times but is not brought on by the sharing of food. Instead of celebration, food becomes a drudgery: "He [the man] piled wood on the coals and fanned the fire to life and trudged out through the drifts to dig out the cart. He sorted through the cans and went back and they sat by the fire and ate the last of their crackers and a tin of sausage."[47] The road does not offer hospitable areas for roadside picnics, instead, "they were all day on the long black road, stopping in the afternoon to eat sparingly from their meager supplies."[48] No longer do the meals have titles such as breakfast or lunch, it is just a feeding time, similar to the ways non-human animals feed. The man and the boy are more involved with the act of staying alive by feeding like animals on anything they can scavenge than they are about the ceremony of coming together at the table for communion with family and friends.

The farmhouse bunker that they find is the only point where food becomes a ceremony instead of mere survival. Upon entering the bunker, they both are willing to let down their guard against the terror of the outside world and indulge in the luxury of food and sleep. De

Bruyn says of the bunker, "The only paradise truly accessible to the protagonists is an abandoned fall-out shelter."[49] To celebrate the new-found paradise, the boy requests pears for their first dinner in the bunker; the man says, "These will be the best pears you ever tasted. ... The best. Just you wait."[50] The boy has had pears before, but these pears will be eaten in a safe, warm place that becomes an escape from the reality of the road for the pair. "They sat side by side and ate the can of pears. Then they ate a can of peaches. They licked the spoons and tipped the bowls and drank the rich sweet syrup. They looked at each other."[51] For the first time in the novel, McCarthy shows the man and boy enjoying food together. He describes the "rich sweet syrup" and their desire to savor every bite as they lick the spoons and drink from the bowl. Nowhere else in the novel is food described as a delight except in the bunker.

The only feast scene of the novel occurs in the bunker as the man prepares a memorable meal for his child. The boy awaked to the sound of coffee being ground, and then the man

> dragged a footlocker across the floor between the bunks and covered it with a towel and set out the plates and cups and plastic utensils. He set out a bowl of biscuits covered with a handtowel and a plate of butter and a can of condensed milk. Salt and pepper. He looked at the boy. The boy looked drugged. He brought out the frying pan from the stove and forked a piece of browned ham onto the boy's plate and scooped scrambled eggs from the other pan and ladled out spoonfuls of baked beans and poured coffee into their cups. The boy looked at him. Go ahead, he said. Dont let it get cold.
>
> What do I eat first?[52]

The event is so monumental to the boy that he does not want to eat it without thanking someone. Instead of a prayer of thanksgiving to the gods for the bounty, the boy says a prayer of thanksgiving to the people who stockpiled the food but died before they could eat it. In his mind, these people are like gods because they have left a bounty for the man and boy who partake of the food in a ceremony akin to communion.

McCarthy continues to use peaceful, descriptive language to describe the food the two eat in the bunker: "They ate a sumptuous meal by candlelight. Ham and green beans and mashed potatoes with biscuits and gravy. . . . They ate peaches and cream over biscuits for dessert and drank coffee."[53] Food takes on a new meaning in the bunker. Pollan writes, "We forget that historically, people have eaten for a great many reasons other than biological necessity. Food is also about pleasure, about community, about family and spirituality, about our relationship to the natural world, and about expressing our identity. As long as humans have been taking meals together, eating has been as much about culture as it has been about biology."[54] Foer likewise notes, "Sharing food generates good feeling and creates social bonds."[55] On the road, the man and the boy lose some of their humanity, as displayed in the lack of community associated with their meals while they struggle just to stay alive. However, in the bunker, they have the leisure of rediscovering their lost humanity and partaking of food as a ceremony of pleasure and bonding instead of an act of pure survival.

The peace and pleasure of the bunker follow them onto the road for a period of time. Their initial meal after the bunker involves conversation for the first time on the road. "They nooned in the middle of the road and fixed hot tea and ate the last of the canned ham with crackers and applesauce. . . . Do you know where we are Papa?"[56] The man and boy are united over the food that they have found together in the bunker and in a sense of community they gained from sharing the food with each other. This meal is still pleasurable even though they are back on the road.

The serenity of the pair dissolves when they meet Ely on the road. The boy, who maintains high morality in his food choice and actions, immediately wants to share all that they have with Ely, and the father does not want to even stop and speak with the man. The father realizes the danger of sharing their limited supply of food and the danger of conversing with a man who could be a decoy for a larger group. The boy convinces his father to share a meal with Ely, and begrudgingly the father does. The magic of the bunker is gone and McCarthy's sparse language once again describes the meal: "They ate."[57] The next day, after they part from Ely, their meal once again takes on the desperation of the road. "In the early afternoon they spread their tarp on the road and sat and ate a cold lunch."[58] They have returned to feeding instead of dining, and any magic and peace they found in the bunker is erased by the severity of the road.

Food also works as an agent to define place within this post-apocalyptic world. As the novel begins, the landscape is so ravaged and unidentifiable that it is difficult to determine where the man and boy are located. It is through artifacts that it becomes apparent that the duo is indeed on American soil. The first mention of artifacts is combined with the first mention of food: "He [the man] pulled the blue plastic tarp off of him and folded it and carried it out to the grocery cart and packed it and came back with their plates and some cornmeal cakes and a plastic bottle of syrup."[59] A grocery cart, blue plastic tarp, plastic bag, and a plastic bottle of syrup are all artifacts that define place, and the place they most readily describe is consumer-driven America. Kessler avers, "Food in fiction engages all the reader's senses (taste, touch, feel, sight, and smell). So putting a meal up front, early on, might very well stimulate the salivary glands. Food also lends a concreteness, a specificity, a round tactile feel like an apple in hand."[60] McCarthy's opening passage sets the tone for the bleakness of the novel. Kessler continues, "A writer is forever trying to get his reader to taste. Taste my world, he says, smell it, ingest it. A novelist involves himself with the raw materials of the world just as a cook does with an onion, a carrot, an egg."[61] McCarthy pulls the reader into his dystopian world by making him taste the cold cornmeal cakes laced with syrup, and the reader is immediately struck with the distastefulness of the food that the man and boy must eat in order to survive. This passage also marks the beginning of McCarthy's examination of American consumerism in the novel, and how food is linked to Americans' drive to consume.

As the two travel down the road pushing their grocery cart, which Americans used for years to collect their capitalistic purchases, they find a supermarket, another commercial icon. "By the door were two softdrink machines that had been tilted over into the floor and opened with a prybar. Coins everywhere in the ash."[62] American consumerism is linked with money, yet in this new world the extinction of American consumerism is evident in that the money is ignored, and the only things of value in the supermarket are things that are useful to survival. A country that had been ruled by commercialism no longer has that basis to define itself. The previous looters to the grocery store were well aware of the end of commercialism and, thereby, the end of the old definition of America. They left the money sitting in the ash and instead looked for food or items they could recycle for survival. In the new world that the man and boy inhabit, the prized commodities are food, shoes, and warm clothing.

The man and boy also ignore the money and the American system of capitalism it represents and instead search for food. The man "sat and ran his hand around in the works of the gutted machines and in the second one it closed over a cold metal cylinder. He withdrew his hand slowly and sat looking at a Coca Cola."[63] McCarthy chooses one of the best-known commercial icons in the world to represent the American commercialism that is now only a memory to the man and unknown to his son. He firmly establishes the two in America with his nod to the well-known consumer product. The boy, however, realizes that it is a relic of a past world that will not be again. The father offers the drink to his son. When the man refuses to split the drink with the boy and insists that the boy enjoys it himself, his son says, "It's because I wont ever get to drink another one, isnt it?"[64] De Bruyn notes, "Just as the burnt effigies of trees remind the reader of the earth's former fecundity, the novel's many ruins hint at the functional civilization that has disappeared. . . . Unavoidably, this collapse erodes human institutions such as 'states.'"[65] Both the boy and the father in this moment acknowledge the death of America and American consumerism through the consumption of this drink that is possibly the last of its kind on earth.

McCarthy creates a sense of the ironic as the two literally consume the end of America and American consumerism in the novel through the consumption of the last artifacts of symbolic American foods. In addition to the Coca Cola, the other food choices available to them embody the country and the land of the time before the disaster. The first meal described in the novel consists of cornmeal cakes. Corn is a grain that is indigenous to America. It was a novelty to the first European settlers to the country and is symbolic of the land. Additionally, the syrup they consume with the cornmeal cakes is also indigenous to the North American continent. Maple syrup is only produced in North America because it has the proper winter temperatures to create the sap used to make the syrup. Wilhelm further analyzes the meal, "The image [of cornmeal cakes] lends a subtle nod to the generations of humanity who have come before, but this positive connection is undermined through its linkage to the billowing clouds of ash that blow incessantly across the now blighted landscape and from which they protect themselves with face masks."[66] The food choice invariably links the pair to the land and their past, but with the breakdown of the capitalist machine, the two are consuming the end of an American way of life.

Later in the novel, the man finds an apple orchard, and he harvests ten-year-old, dried apples from the dead grasses under the trees. The image of the apple is also linked to America. Apple pie is the ubiquitous symbol of wholesome American goodness. As the two eat the dried apples, they are consuming the end of wholesomeness of American life, which at this point is as old and withered as the apples they eat. McCarthy uses the physical consumption of food representing America as a means to demonstrate the final consumption of America and American consumerism. The implication is that contemporary American consumption is as final and destructive as the destruction faced by the boy and man. American society is consuming itself to death as the industrialization of the food supply ravishes the natural resources of the earth. The final fruits of the consumeristic practices of America are offered up as a sacrifice to guarantee the survival of the boy so that he is able to herald in a new morality to a world ravaged by consumption-driven cannibals.

McCarthy begins the novel with an allusion to a new beginning. The man dreams of "a creature that raised its dripping mouth from the rimstone pool and stared into the light with eyes dead white and sightless as the eggs of spiders. It swung its head low over the water as if to take in the scent of what it could not see. Crouching there pale and naked and translucent, its alabaster bones cast up in shadow on the rocks behind it."[67] This surreal description implies that a new morality that is innocent and fragile like the "pale and naked" creature will emerge and evolve.[68] The boy represents this new innocence—one untarnished by American consumerism—as a foundation for humans to band together, to step into the light of simplicity without voracious consumption. The man's dream serves as a premonition of the possibility that a new future will be innocent of the faults found in the current consumption patterns. The boy's union with the "good guys" as the novel ends provides a limited hope that the consumption by the cannibals can be halted and a new peace prevail on an earth that begins to heal under the same sunlight that the creature feels arising from the rimstone pool.

The final passage of the book also takes on a surreal, dreamlike quality not found elsewhere in the novel and thus alludes back to the man's dream, which opened the story:

> Once there were brook trout in the streams in the mountains. You could see them standing in the amber current where the white edges of their fins wimpled softly in the flow. They smelled of moss in your hand. Polished and muscular and torsional. On their backs were vermiculate patterns that were maps of the world in its becoming. Maps and mazes. Of a thing which could not be put back. Not be made right again. In the deep glens where they lived all things were older than man and they hummed of mystery.[69]

The trout represent the cycle of new life sprouting from the old life. The novel ends with hope that the earth may be able to recover from this environmental disaster and a new cycle of life will rise from the ashes of the earth's destruction. The new "maps of the world in its becoming" imply a new moral code must prevail that unites man and nature in a common cause instead of man as a consumer and abuser of the natural world. Consumerism is the "thing which could not be put back. Not be made right again."[70] The boy embodies this new worldview that could contribute to creating a healthy world in the wake of such destruction. The rimstone pool from the beginning of the novel is connected to the streams in the mountains where the trout live. Water is a cleansing and restorative natural feature in both visions. The trout hold the promise that nature can and will cleanse itself and that life will again take its place on the earth, as noted in the "evolution printed on their [the trout's] backs."[71] The novel ends with hope that the circle of life will not fail and that, ultimately, life on earth will begin again. It is encrypted on the trout that a new food web will spring forth, allowing the boy, as a leader of the good guys, the opportunity to introduce a new morality devoid of the dangers of rabid consumerism.

CHAPTER 6

From Aunt Jemima to Aunt Marthy

Commodifying the Kitchen Cook and Undermining White Authority in *Incidents in the Life of a Slave Girl*

KRYSTAL MCMILLEN

Aunt Jemima pancakes without her syrup is like the spring without the fall. There's only one thing worse in this universe. That's no Aunt Jemima at all.

—Classic Aunt Jemima Commercial, 1967

In April of 2012, David Pilgrim, vice president for Diversity and Inclusion at Ferris State University, opened a museum with an ambitious mission. The goal was to utilize the incendiary relics of the Jim Crow era in order to open a dialogue about race relations.[1] While the Jim Crow Museum of Racist Memorabilia boasts thousands of objects, it was a single item—a mammy saltshaker figurine—that Pilgrim cites as the inspiration for his archive of knick-knacks.[2] This particular saltshaker does not appear in the museum, though there are multiple other culinary artifacts in the exhibit. It is not in the collection because it no longer exists—Pilgrim destroyed it.

In an interview with Jennie Rothenberg Gritz of *The Atlantic*, Pilgrim explained that he broke the figurine because "on a gut level, I just didn't like them. . . . [A] lot of people, including blacks, had those sorts of objects in their homes, and I hated them."[3] It is not insignificant to my argument that the trinket to begin Pilgrim's work was an item that belonged on a dining table. Pilgrim's visceral reaction to the object, as well as his observation regarding the ubiquitous nature of these cultural artifacts, reveals a curious intersection between race, dining, and objectification.[4] Here, the table becomes not only a site of communion and camaraderie but also a site of racial categorization and commodification.

This chapter will examine the complicated and contradictory depictions of the mammy—the archetypal figure of the beloved, female, domestic slave—in the American imagination. Most specifically, this argument revolves around, arguably, the most identifiable and iconic mammy figure, Aunt Jemima. As the commercial jingle from the 1960s demonstrates, Aunt Jemima was more than a brand— she became a figure, a constant entity in the commercial landscape of the United States. But she also became intrinsically linked to the product, the comestible good that she symbolically produced through her pancakes. Aunt Jemima pancakes, while perhaps delicious in their own right, are incomplete without the syrup. Yet, "the only thing worse in this universe" is the absence of the person, Aunt Jemima herself. As such, the figure of Aunt Jemima becomes fundamentally linked to the foods she cooks, making her simultaneously an industrious producer of goods (namely, breakfast) and an object for consumption herself.

This dual role of the Aunt Jemima icon belies a greater legacy regarding racial representation in US culture, one revolving around and evolving from the kitchen.[5] By examining the power dynamics demonstrated in the archetype of the mammy, I forward that this figure becomes an icon at once idealized by white representations for her ability to create feasts from a scarcity of resources and also a potentially subversive, threatening presence due to her powerful ability to acquire respect as a result of her culinary delights. As such, the gastronomic propensities of the mammy figure demonstrate the unique ways that food aligns with identity and power. To possess skills over that which is consumed is to procure authority (sometimes threatening authority) over those whom we feed. In the history of the mammy, especially as seen in figures such as Aunt Jemima, I contend that white fascination with rendering the black kitchen cook as a friendly "family figure" belies a concern with the intimate proximity these culinary figures have to the lives of white American families.

Creating the Myth of the Kitchen

The trajectory from kitchen slave to the beloved family figure in the kitchen might seem peculiar at first blush, yet it stems from a long-standing practice of subjugating and categorizing black women. This convention extends well beyond the kitchen, for certain, but an examination of representations of black women from the antebellum era to the present reveals, in the words of scholar Trudier Harris, that "whether victims of sexual exploitations during slavery, or tragic mulattoes who tried to escape their blackness by passing, or extremely dark skinned women who suffered inter- and intra- racial prejudice, . . . black women have [always] been treated as types."[6] Harris's observation that representations of blackness function as modes of existence would seem to demonstrate that these identities are static and fixed. However, Harris's examination of the "types" that the white imagination casts blackness into reveals an overlap and a blurring of boundaries rather than a rigid adherence to a one-dimensional identity. Implicit in the examples that Harris offers is a subtle, yet contradictory, emphasis on the way these categories shift—from slave to free, from mixed race to black, from white racism to black bigotry. This movement, nominal as it may seem, demonstrates the failure of fixed categories to capture the fluidity of identity. Types persist because in their shallow simplicity they offer a seductive solution to the complexity of humanity. They render the whole of a human into one controllable unit that neutralizes the unwieldy reality of identity. Yet this presentation is a fiction, one that only belies the impossibility of situating the dynamic human character within stable boundaries.

It is the type of the kitchen slave, therefore, that becomes a problematically one-dimensional figure. Relegated to the kitchen to produce culinary delights, the cook of the meal is obscured from her master's sight. It is not the cooking that is apparent, but rather the final product of the meal. As Mary Titus contends, the master's "pleasure in the elaborate meal rests on his ability to ignore its origins."[7] With the process of production entirely separated from white enjoyment, the final product of the meal becomes embodied with near mythical elements—the mystery of kitchen work creates the magic of a meal. This magic necessarily reflects back upon the slave cook who has been kept just out of sight until the meal is prepared. Alice Deck, in her study of slave cooks from the antebellum South, describes this quintessential slave type, the kitchen slave, as "a very large, dark earth mother who represents fecundity, self-sufficiency, and endless succor."[8] She is a type who can produce and manifest sustenance and nourishment, one who creates the meal that creates communion.

No figure exemplifies this culinary magic more successfully than Aunt Jemima, still a predominant advertising icon in the twenty-first century. Aunt Jemima's long-lasting fame is an indication of the obsession with the abilities of the slave cook. What started as a marketing campaign in 1889 took on a life of its own when, in 1890, the R. T. Davis Milling Company "envisioned a living Aunt Jemima to advertise [its] wares."[9] The marketing ploy swept the nation over the course of a century, and Quaker Oats still manufactures the Aunt Jemima label to this day. Yet even in the iconic fame of Aunt Jemima lies the dormant contradictions of southern civility, which depended upon systems of slavery and racial inequality in order to establish categories that determined power and privilege. The marketing decision to make a friendly human being the face of an entire product line transports Aunt Jemima into the consumer's home. She is warm, welcoming, and, most importantly, nonthreatening; however, this action also necessarily transforms the human into an object, one that can be purchased and controlled.

One of Aunt Jemima's most significant abilities, captured in the iconic advertisements of the late nineteenth century, was her capacity to move from the slave quarters and the plantation kitchen to the tables of middle-class, white America. As one advertisement from the 1920s stated, Aunt Jemima had become "the cook whose cabin became more famous than Uncle Tom's."[10] Aligning Aunt Jemima and Uncle Tom serves at once to unite these two racial types into a fictive family—a black community commodified by middle-class America. Yet, as Aunt Jemima surpasses Tom's fame, the product serves to distinguish the active kitchen presence of the female cook from the passive male presence of Tom.

A substantial component of the mystery behind the slave cook came from her apparent ability to make abundance from lack. As Doris Witt writes in *Black Hunger*, "the 'lived blues experience' of hunger would . . . derive from its lack. . . . [H]er blues experience would perhaps derive from the fact that she was at work in the kitchen . . . making gravy to cover the absence of meat."[11] Latent in Witt's statement is a paradox: hunger is most keenly experienced only through the demonstration of its absence. That is to say, obscuring the reality of famine is a mark of the artistry of the African American cooking experience. Such an artistry, through the process of cooking, creates abundance from the absence of sustenance. However, by ascribing the slave chef as such, white perceptions of this fetish figure render her only within the domestic kitchen. Thus, the "mammy . . . exists to do nothing but prepare and serve food."[12] And yet, with Harris's comments revealing the failure of such one-dimensional types in mind, the notion of a mammy existing solely for the purpose of providing victuals is rife with binary impossibilities.

Whereas the passivity of an Uncle Tom–type served to alleviate white anxiety regarding fears of rebellion and violence, the activity of the kitchen cook depends upon a mastery of knowledge and ability absent in the white vocabulary. The anxiety caused by this unknown power is allocated outside of the scope of white attention. As the master chooses to see only the finished product—the orderly array of edibles on an orderly southern table—rather than the combustible activity taking place in the kitchen, cultural renditions of the black cook subjugate culinary power through physical markers. Alice Deck, in her assessment of the variety of nineteenth- and twentieth-century depictions of black cooks, writes,

> An integral part of the Mammy's attire is the broad smile displaying clean, even, white teeth because it suggests not only a cheerful personality but also pleasure in what she does. This cheerful aspect actually works to counterbalance the potentially aggressive signals contained in the pointed ends of her bandanna and the sharp angles of her elbows and hands.[13]

Latent in these descriptions of Jemima-like mammies is an unstable evaluation of power and authority. Slave cooks ought to be cheerful, as it indicates they enjoy their work. As Deck's assessment entails, enjoyment is necessary to counteract the potential for aggression. As the southern table was indicative of prosperity, a subversive act from an unhappy slave in the kitchen would easily rend the plantation asunder.

Rather than aligning the master's home with culture and prestige through the acquisition of such an impressive slave, the entire perception of the culinary magician is rendered suspect. It would appear, instead, that whites' fascination with their absence of knowledge (particularly, culinary knowledge) leads to the desire to capture the agent of such unfamiliar knowledge within a safe and approachable figure. Underlying this categorical captivity of the slave cook as the master of the kitchen is the unspoken anxiety of the white citizenry consuming the product of her domain.[14] If the ability of the slave cook to make much of nothing was her power in the kitchen, it was both a coveted skill and a perceived threat by her master; it was the proficiency that moved her from the field and into the home and the talent that put her in direct control over the nourishment and sustenance of her master's family.

Food, Power, and White Authority

The array of cultural products and icons that exhibit the kitchen slave's experience demonstrate the anxiety bound up in foodstuffs. There is a power that is attributed to both the kitchen slave and the master that echoes Michel Foucault's power dynamic as he articulates in "The Subject and Power." Foucault writes, "A power relationship can only be articulated on the basis of two elements which are each indispensable if it is really to be a power relationship."[15] In this sense, both the slave and the master are sources of power, or mastery, *but* they are also at the mercy of the other. The slave is not free as a result of her master's position. The master, however, cannot run his home without the abilities of his kitchen slave. It is this relationship that creates the need for the master to relegate his slave at once to a position of power, while simultaneously inscribing the slave into a position innocuous enough not to pose a threat, for, as Foucault writes, "faced with a relationship of power, a whole field of responses, reactions, results, and possible inventions may open up."[16] Therefore, in this context, the master configures the kitchen slave as a mammy figure, for if the master were to recognize the elements of dominance that the kitchen slave exerts over the home, the threat of her presence would be too great.

In order to establish the kitchen as a place that problematizes issues of dominance within slave-owning properties, it is necessary to examine the way food is manifestly a tool of power. To accomplish this task, I would like to utilize a case study, the slave narrative *Incidents in the Life of a Slave Girl*. Written by Harriet Jacobs in 1861, this text chronicles the trials Linda Brent (Jacobs's pseudonym) faced while she was enslaved. The text records her youth, a time of joy until she is given to the abusive and cruel Dr. Flint. As the property of Dr. Flint, Linda faces sexual assault and unthinkable cruelty that ultimately prompt her to flee to her grandmother, Aunt Marthy. Linda hides in the attic of her grandmother's home for seven years, after which she escapes north, where she is ultimately purchased by a kindly figure, Mrs. Bruce, who serves as her employer at the close of the tale.

In many ways, Jacobs's text functions in a polemical fashion common to many slave narratives. Yet distinct to Jacobs's work is the powerful role that food plays. Linda Naranjo-Huebl and Anne Bradford Warner have addressed the prominence of food imagery in Jacobs's text. Naranjo-Huebl establishes, in "'Take, Eat': Food Imagery, the Nurturing Ethic, and Christian Identity in *The Wide, Wide World, Uncle Tom's Cabin,* and *Incidents in the Life of a Slave Girl*," a system of oppositional distribution with regard to food, slaves, and masters. She writes, "Evil is depicted in acts of withholding food, failing to feed the hungry, or in its most despicable form, devouring those one should be feeding."[17] Certainly, this is a more than apt assessment of the Flints' behavior in Jacobs's account. Upon introducing the Flint family in her story, Jacobs writes: "Little attention was paid to the slaves' meals in Dr. Flint's house. If they could catch a bit of food while it was going, well and good."[18] However, in Jacobs's anecdotes, the Flints' ambivalence toward their slaves' meals seems relatively tame. It is the descriptions of the slaves' response to starvation that accost the reader's ear more fully. On several occasions, Jacobs outlines incidents that result in dire punishment. On one occasion, Dr. Flint spends a night issuing "hundreds of blows . . . in succession, on a human being."[19] While the slaves are unaware of the cause of such an atrocious punishment, many speculate that the master had accused the slave of stealing corn. Jacobs reveals in her narrative the true reason for Flint's retribution, yet the mere revelation that the slave population could find a night of dire whippings a credible punishment for acquiring much needed sustenance signifies the intense fear that food could inspire on the plantation.

The Flints are not the only slave owners whom Jacobs indicts in her evaluation of improper food management. In a chapter that addresses the variety of atrocities committed by "neighboring slaveholders," three of her five accounts are food-related events. Two involve the slave owner "Mr. Litch," who, much like Dr. Flint, if a "pound of meat or a peck of corn" was stolen from him, would take recourse by putting the slave "in chains and imprison[ment], and so [he was] kept till his form was attenuated by hunger and suffering."[20] Another incident of theft led Mr. Litch to use a club upon the suspected slaves and "[fell] them to the ground."[21] While these responses of Litch indicate the retributive power food is embodied with, a variety of the punishments Litch and others resort to serves to transform food from a nourishing item to an item of destruction. Anne Warner comments on Litch's methods of recourse as a mode of inverted cooking: "Perversions of cooking and eating, equations of human with animal flesh abound in the sketches which Jacobs uses to show the fate of other slaves."[22] Litch's crimes most clearly illustrate the perversions Warner addresses, as Jacobs relates:

> Various were the punishments resorted to. A favorite one was to tie a rope round a man's body, and suspend him from the ground. A fire was kindled over him, from which was suspended a piece of fat pork. As this cooked, the scalding drops of fat continually fell on the bare flesh.[23]

Litch's sadistic use of food as punishment illustrates the punitive properties food acquired on the slave estate. The irony that food can be both the crime and the punishment invests the deprived with a forlorn sense of their own gastronomic deficiencies. In order to survive, the slave must acquire food, yet, if caught, the mission will be in vain as it results either in death or in an act that inscribes the food with a horrifying power.

Jacobs also relates the story of a runaway slave who, when caught, is brutally whipped and left between the planks of a gin press. Food and water were placed within reach of the press for several days, until finally the slave was discovered dead and partially eaten by rats and vermin. Much as Litch's punishment of burning slaves with scalding fat demonstrates the use of comestibles to punish, the attention to this gin-press punishment by Jacobs establishes what Warner describes as a complex system of devouring. In using the much-coveted object of food to injure his slave, Litch asserts his power and authority through the sign of food. As such, the food item and the one controlling that food item are inscribed with incredible amounts of power. Litch's use of the pork fat to scald his slave at once suggests that Litch has suffi-cient amounts of food to supply his workers and that it is only out of choice that he starves his slaves. Further, by inverting the process of cooking—thereby using the food to cook his slave—the desired objec-tive of the theft is transformed into a tableau of demonic proportions.

This inversion of sustenance with annihilation is further carried through in the punishment of the slave in the gin press. While Jacobs never explains precisely the reason for the slave's attempted escape, the final result of his punishment functions in much the same way that Litch's torture device does. Food, yet again, is kept out of the hand of the slave. While the bread that sits beside the gin press continues to disappear, it is the vermin, not the imprisoned slave, who are consum-ing it. Furthermore, that very same vermin that keep the food from the slave eventually begin to consume the slave, transforming food from a provider of life to, quite literally, the representation of death.

Jacobs's accounts of these two atrocities are distinct from the types of atrocities she experiences regarding food. Early in her narrative, Jacobs describes Dr. Flint's ability to transform daily meals within his home from "shared family ritual" to a monstrous demonstration of authority.[24] In order to have time alone with Jacobs, occasionally Flint would complain of the heat within his own dining room and "order his supper to be placed on a small table in the piazza."[25] There, Jacobs recounts, he would

> seat himself . . . with a well-satisfied smile, and tell me to stand by and brush away flies. He would eat very slowly, paus-ing between the mouthfuls. These intervals were employed in describing the happiness I was so foolishly throwing away, and in threatening me with the penalty that finally awaited my stubborn disobedience.[26]

This disturbing scene merges the basest appetites in Dr. Flint, aligning the "gratification of physical hunger" with the "assertion of illicit sexual appetite."[27] While Warner examines the larger implications of Flint's "appetites" in order to undermine the ritual communion of hospitality within the southern home, the anti-hospitality demonstrated at the Flint's table furthers the inscription of power upon dining in general. Jacobs's reflection on Flint's "well-satisfied smile" and the pauses taken between "mouthfuls" of food serve to make his mouth the site of his improper indulgences. Jacobs, as one who is forced to service these oral indulgences, at least at the dinner table, becomes victim to sexual advances through food.

Moving into the Kitchen

While Dr. Flint is the epitome of epicurean indulgence, it is Mrs. Flint's regulatory behavior in the kitchen that ultimately reveals the significance of Jacobs' kitchen characters. Mrs. Flint, according to Jacobs, "would station herself in the kitchen, and wait till it was dished, and then spit in all the kettles and pans that had been used for cooking. She did this to prevent the cook and her children from eking out their meager fare with the remains of the gravy and other scrapings."[28] Mrs. Flint's involvement in the kitchen directly contrasts the white plantation diner who is completely unaware of the occurrences in the kitchen. Unlike the type of the ignorant master, Mrs. Flint actively seeks to discover the comings and goings of her kitchen staff. Jacobs uses Mrs. Flint's obsessive activity to demonstrate the horrifying isolation a domestic slave faces. The Flints' control over their staff extends to every corner of the house.

It would be a simplification of Jacobs's account, however, to merely say the Flints have discovered a method of ultimate mastery unknown to other slave owners at the time. Much as the caricatures of the nineteenth-century slave cook embody a symbol of white anxiety, Mrs. Flint's actions are problematically complex:

> The slaves could get nothing to eat except what she chose to give them. Provisions were weighed out by the pound and ounce, three times a day. I can assure you she gave them no chance to eat wheat bread from her flour barrel. She knew how many biscuits

a quart of flour would make, and exactly what size they ought to be.[29]

Jacobs's assessment of Mrs. Flint's attempts to control her slave's comestible intake ironically reveals that her attempts may be failing. Why would flour need to be weighed three times daily if the power structure in place within the Flint home was exempt from recalcitrant efforts from the staff? Furthermore, the syntactical choices in Jacobs's statement are striking when compared to Witt's conception of the black cook's ability to make abundance from lack. By measuring by the pound *and* ounce, Mrs. Flint is attempting to thwart the consumption of even the tiniest amount of flour, something she might not fear if she thought it impossible to create food from the meager amount. Jacobs's text alludes to the magical transformation of inedible to edible as she writes that wheat bread might come from a flour barrel. The syntax of the sentence indicates that Mrs. Flint's obsession with flour is an effort to prevent the kitchen staff from metaphorically reaching into the barrel of unrefined product and pulling out finished loaves of bread.

Mrs. Flint has ample reason to be anxious. While she knows "how many biscuits a quart of flour would make, and exactly what size they ought to be," she is missing the knowledge of how to create the final, savory result. Mrs. Flint, while supervising the actions of her slaves, is not the individual executing the tasks at hand. In fact, Jacobs writes, she is a rather sickly woman in body, "deficient in energy" and lacking strength to "superintend her household affairs."[30] This weakness, typical—Jacobs attributes rather acerbically—of "many southern women," is mated with a potent cruelty of spirit.[31] Mrs. Flint's body might have been weak, but her "nerves were so strong, that she could sit in her easy chair and see a woman whipped, till the blood trickled from every stroke of the lash."[32] In this way, Jacobs's assessment of Mrs. Flint leaves her excluded from active participation in the feminine domestic sphere of the kitchen and the home and situates her within the passive realm of observing the execution of punishments.

The happenings in *Incidents in the Life of a Slave Girl* paint Mrs. Flint outside of the realm of sisterly communion. She is married to a vicious man with licentious habits, and her efforts to control and punish her domestic slaves demonstrate an insecurity regarding her status in her own home. As a result, she is alienated from the women she encounters in her residence as well as from her own femininity. Not only do her violent outbursts and rages of jealousy serve to masculinize her temper, but her complete inability to identify with the trial Jacobs narrates establishes her as incapable of recognizing her own connections with the larger feminine corpus. Regardless of Mrs. Flint's desire to extricate nutritional possibilities from her slaves' lives, Jacobs provides women in her narrative who actively demonstrate the agency presented within the realm of the kitchen space. The contrasting status of the Flint's kitchen slaves and the status of "Aunt Marthy" serves to indicate the ultimately liberating and empowering possibilities of the kitchen.

Mrs. Flint's desire to maintain a close relationship with her kitchen locates white anxiety regarding domestic servants within the realm of the kitchen. If, as Titus argues, the "kitchen was a place where black women could establish an authority that potentially [threatened] the white household," that threat was directed at the household's very center, "the dining room and its rituals."[33] The perceived menace stems from the precarious position in which both black and white women are placed. Wealthy slave-owning women relinquished control over the center of their domestic realm, offering the nerve center of the house to their kitchen slaves. The result of this exchange led, potentially, to an unstable set up of power: the coveted kitchen slave became a puissant, independent figure, yet this figure only had access to this power as a result of the shackles of slavery. Through the depiction of Aunt Marthy and her life, Jacobs demonstrates this duality of a kitchen existence.

Jacobs, admittedly, owes a great deal of the comforts she has to her grandmother. Unlike many of the Flints' other slaves, she does not go hungry, for, as she writes,

> On my various errands I passed my grandmother's house, where there was always something to spare for me. I was frequently threatened with punishment if I stopped there; and my grandmother, to avoid detaining me, often stood at the gate with something for my breakfast or dinner. I was indebted to *her* for all my comforts, spiritual or temporal. It was *her* labor that supplied my scanty wardrobe.[34]

The insight Jacobs offers into her grandmother's actions serve to demonstrate the ways in which Aunt Marthy has been able to evade the most imprisoning structures of slavery. Her actions are directly opposed to the desires of Mrs. Flint, yet they are actions situated in the magical abundance of the kitchen slave. Jacobs's mention that "there was always something to spare" depicts her grandmother's house as a location of abundance. Unlike the stingy kitchen of Mrs. Flint, Aunt Marthy's hearth overflows with nourishing goods. Furthermore, Aunt Marthy's delivery mechanism of this abundance overtly evades Mrs. Flint's grasp. By waiting at the gate, Marthy is able to transfer the efforts of her kitchen outside the scope of her home. As Linda Brent consumes the comestible goodies Marthy supplies for her walk back to the plantation, the comforts of her grandmother's kitchen infiltrate the isolated cooking space the Flints provide.

Yet undermining Mrs. Flint's punitive efforts in the kitchen is only the beginning of Marthy's capabilities. Heralded as "Aunt Marthy" by the entire community, Jacobs's grandmother has, in many ways, become her own local brand name. Much as the Jemima label functioned to bring the delicacies of the African American kitchen to the white consumer, Marthy's product serves to enamor the former kitchen slave within the hearts and minds of the white townspeople. The development of this brand name is indicative of the displacing realities of being the master of the kitchen. Marthy's sweetmeats have landed her in a position of power within the black *and* white communities, yet in many ways this is the direct result of her condition as a slave. Under the rule of her first owners,

> she became an indispensable personage in the household, officiating in all capacities, from cook and wet nurse to seamstress. She was much praised for her cooking; and her nice crackers became so famous in the neighborhood that many people were desirous of obtaining them. In consequence of numerous requests of this kind, she asked permission of her mistress to bake crackers at night, after all her household work was done; and she obtained leave to do it, provided she would clothe herself and her children from the profits. Upon these terms, after working hard all day for her mistress, she began her midnight baking, assisted by her two oldest children the business proved profitable; and each year she laid by a little, which was saved for a fund to purchase her children.[35]

The rhetoric Jacobs uses to establish her grandmother's past experience as a slave is deliberately empowering. Marthy is established as having been "indispensable" to the household in "all capacities." Jacobs's rendition of her grandmother's abilities establishes her as the central core of her owner's household. Without her, the home would not function. Furthermore, Jacobs establishes that Marthy's predominant authority stems from her "nice crackers." Cooking, then, not only establishes Marthy as the driving force of domesticity within the house, but places Marthy's greatest power within the kitchen.

Marthy's culinary ability undermines the authority of her owners. As her culinary reputation spreads, her owners, in order to "take care of such a valuable piece of property," grant her the ability to establish independence.[36] Working evenings, Marthy continues to produce her baked goods, but the long hours she keeps serve to establish her as something of a mystery. Already fully employed during the day, this substantial woman is able to produce an even greater abundance of culinary goods in the dead of night. These baked delights might come from the kitchen of Marthy's owners, but there is no doubt that the process of their creation is entirely a mystery. The proximity of the white mistress to the kitchen only highlights her own ignorance of Marthy's cooking methods. There is no way to emulate her final product, thus she is, literally, indispensable, for without her the white home would lose its great esteem from the community. Furthermore, latent in Jacobs's evaluation of her grandmother's practice is the notion that this power can be passed on through generations. While her white owners will never discover the method to her goods, future generations of kitchen slaves might. As a slave, Marthy is demonstrating an amazing amount of agency, which, by all accounts, will be passed on through her two children who assist her in her baking.

Marthy's fantastic crackers and preserves ultimately serve to undermine the Flints' efforts to exert their power as slave owners, and the crackers establish her as a woman of strength and independence. Ultimately, Jacobs's depiction of her grandmother demonstrates the individual power that can be acquired through the mastery of the kitchen. This poses a threat to the way in which the master can dispense with his slave. Mr. Flint, faced with financial distress, determines to sell off his property. Yet the notoriety around town that Marthy has gained through her culinary items becomes an impediment in Dr. Flint's plans to sell her. As she stands on the auction block, the townspeople cry out her name and ask who would sell such a slave: "Many voices called out, 'Shame! Shame! Who is going to sell *you* Aunt Marthy? Don't stand there. This is no place for *you*.'"[37] The cries of the townspeople serve to further the contradictory power at play in this scene. By aligning themselves with "aunt" Marthy, the townspeople move Marthy from the kitchen of her owners into their own families. Aunt, as an affectionate and familiar title commonly thrust upon black women by their white counterparts, also creates a new community, one that safely allows Marthy to participate in alongside the white townspeople within the confines of their homes and kitchens.

The townspeople do not ask why the Flints would sell their slaves; they question why they would sell a slave so valuable to the community as Marthy. The cry that "this is no place for *you*" serves to separate Marthy from the other slave populations. She, unlike the rest of the enslaved up for sale, is unique, different, and needed. As such, this scene demonstrates the dual result of such affiliations. As the town allocates Marthy to the status of "aunt," they effectively relegate her to the comfort and familiarity of their own homes and families. As aunt, she, like Jemima, can exist safely squared away in the domestic quadrant. What this method of comfort directly overlooks, however, is the way in which it undermines white authority. Mrs. Flint demonstrates an anxiety over her kitchen in a way Marthy's original owners did not. As a result, the white townspeople who have come to depend on her product to grace their own tables undermine the authority of ownership and control the Flints are able to exercise.

Ultimately, because of Marthy's skill, she is purchased and freed by a woman who continues to visit Marthy's table for "hot muffins, tea rusks, and delicious sweetmeats."[38] After gaining her freedom, Marthy's relationship with the white township continues to be established upon her culinary grace. Effectively, Jacobs's text serves to demonstrate the subversive possibilities that abound in inscribing the slave cook with mythic status. Her narrative, while filled with anecdotes of torture, oppression, and suffering, offers a surprising examination of the possibilities for recalcitrance within the plantation kitchen. Food then becomes an icon of power, and the cook its master. While in the kitchen, the slave cook holds the capabilities for becoming at once most intimate with the big house and most unknown by the slave owners.

Like the characterizations of Aunt Jemima in the late nineteenth century, Aunt Marthy demonstrates the fluidity of the power relationship within the slave kitchen. While Marthy's "grand big oven" always "baked bread and nice things for the town," Jacobs was always aware that the "choice bit" was in store for her.[39] Through maintaining the brand name of her product, Marthy is able to access an individual agency unknown to the white authority that is excluded from her domestic sphere. Ultimately, Marthy's ability to roam between the realms of slave and free and Aunt Jemima's ubiquity in middle-income American homes both affirm the unique power that culinary prowess affords, for if one has mastery over the dinner table, one has power over one's master. This, however, threatens the perceived status quo in the white imaginary, as it potentially upends the master-slave or superior-subordinate positions. It is for this reason Aunt Marthy must be transformed over time to Aunt Jemima, the emblem of happy servitude. While she exists outside of the time of slavery, as she is purchased off the shelves of the local grocer, one might imagine that she regrets those days are gone. She smiles, she offers her breakfast delights to nourish her owner's family, and she never seems to consider her own desires. She has no family of her own (at least not that her owners are aware of). She, seemingly, embraces her position at the helm of the kitchen and smiles out at her "masters" from the box on the shelf. Slaves like Marthy must eventually be transformed to mammies like Jemima, else the entire feeling of white safety is revealed for a fiction. Marthy's experiences, much as other slaves' experiences, must be sublimated to an explainable moniker of her humanity. Ironically, by situating the mammy type in the kitchen, attention is drawn to the power and function of food in establishing relational dynamics. By examining the duality of the kitchen slave, we recognize the incredible significance that control over foodstuffs imbues within the home and without.

PART 3 ▪ Consuming Popular Culture

Food Identity Defined in Television and Movies

CHAPTER 7

Scenes from the Dialogic Kitchen

"Thinking Culture Dialogically" in Italian American Narratives

JAMES CIANCIOLA

Introduction: Choosing the Ingredients

In *Were You Always an Italian? Ancestors and Other Icons of Italian America*, Maria Laurino observes that there is a discourse on Italian American culture that is undeveloped and limiting: "I have come to hate the books and documentaries about the 'Italian-American experience,' full of treacly discussions of food and family, describing 'the beautiful song' of our heritage, those snapshots of golden days forever gone."[1] Moreover, "the myth of the '*Italiano*,'" Laurino notes, is supported by what she calls "pasta/pizza/*paesano* tales" that trivialize the Italian American experience by "reshaping disparate character traits into a singular folkloric image, rendering us indistinguishable from each other, playing the Muzak of ethnicity."[2] One such image of Italian American culture involves a reductionistic narrative about the relationship between Italian Americans, food, cooking, and hospitality. For example, Davide Girardelli asserts that chain restaurants such as Fazoli's create, through their marketing and advertising, "constructed representations of Italians and Italian food" that "contribute to an overall (and often false) American understanding of what it means to be Italian."[3]

Such "constructed representations" also occur in popular American television programs. In *Happy Days* (1974–1984), for example, the Italian American character Al Delvecchio is assigned the role of cook and restaurant owner. However, cooking—or, more specifically, the importance of cooking to Italian American culture—is not a significant part of his character's identity. Instead, Delvecchio is reduced to a storytelling buffoon who outwardly possesses stereotypical Italian American traits such as dark black hair, a large nose, and, of course, an Italian last name. Similarly, in *Laverne and Shirley* (1976–1983), Frank DeFazio is the owner of a pizza restaurant. Yet the love of food and cooking, or the idea of the restaurant as an extension of Italian American hospitality, is not demonstrated by his character. Instead he is often represented as a loud, overly passionate man with more heart than brains.

A more recent reduction of Italian and Italian American narratives, one that seems to satirize the complex relationship between food, cooking, hospitality, and Italian American culture, is found in the children's television cartoon *Curious George* (2006–present). Chef Pisghetti is both a cook and a restaurant owner. Short and plump, he has dark hair and a thin mustache. He wears a chef uniform and speaks in broken English. Above his restaurant's red, white, and green awning is an image of a pizza, an image of him laughing, and a bowl of spaghetti and meatballs. Inside his restaurant, each table has a red-and-white-checkered tablecloth and a melted candle in an empty Chianti bottle. This stereotypical representation of the Italian American dining experience is spoon-fed to our children.

In these programs, Delvecchio, DeFazio, and Chef Pisghetti are recognizable characters, but at a cost. Their function as symbols of Italian American food, cooking, and hospitality—not to mention Italian American culture—perpetuates a particular kind of narrative: to borrow Laurino's term, a "treacly" monologue that shadows a richer story of the Italian American experience. To encourage a greater understanding of and receptiveness to this richer story, I offer an analytical concept drawn from the theory of Mikhail Bakhtin: the dialogic kitchen, which explores select Italian American characters in American films and short stories. This dialogism counters what

Bakhtin argues is a problematic monologism in some narratives, a restricted voice or perspective that "fails to capture the exigencies of heterodox discursive practices in the social world as well as the inherently dialogic orientation of all signifying practices."[4]

As Michael Gardiner explains, Bakhtin argues in *Problems of Dostoevsky's Poetics* that narrative monologism presents an ethical problem because it "objectifies and quantifies human subjectivity and robs individual creativity of any real significance."[5] Specifically, it does so because

> subjects continually strive to resist the constraints placed upon them by "externalizing secondhand definitions," which seek to curtail and "deaden" their thoughts and actions. Bakhtin passionately argues that there is something within a concrete individual that can only be revealed in a "free act of self-consciousness and discourse," an act of self-revelation which cannot be known or predicted beforehand.[6]

By analyzing representative examples of two genres—film and short fiction—using concepts from Bakhtin's theory and Walter Fisher's rhetorical perspective on symbols, I argue that the narratives in these genres suggest an overlap of sociocultural symbols, or shared spaces, of Italian Americanness via food, family, and hospitality. Such an approach that privileges the role of dialogue as a fundamental means of contemplating symbols in narrative contexts engages a well-established tradition of employing Bakhtinian theory to culture: "Since the early 1980s, 'thinking culture dialogically' has been synonymous with thinking about culture in a way inspired by the works of Bakhtin."[7]

Specifically, the iconic mafia movies *The Godfather, Part I* (1972), *Goodfellas* (1990), and *Donnie Brasco* (1997) and three short stories within *The Milk of Almonds: Italian American Women Writers on Food and Culture*—"Dizzy Spells" (1991) by Dorothy Bryant, "Go to Hell" (1999) by Nancy Caronia, and "Baked Ziti" (2002) by Kym Ragusa—represent a complex network of stories told in the dialogic kitchen. This study will focus on four symbols of this kitchen: cooking as social, cooking as a return to the ordinary, cooking as spectacle, and cooking as teaching.

Dialogue: Conversations Inside and Outside of the Kitchen

As a theoretical concept, the dialogic kitchen aims to explore the complexity of the human experience, and Mikhail Bakhtin uses a "dialogic orientation" to address that experience.[8] Bakhtin assumes "the dialogic nature of consciousness, the dialogic nature of human life itself. The single adequate form for *verbally expressing* authentic human existence is the *open-ended dialogue*," which is the kind that typically occurs in the dialogic kitchen.[9]

A dialogic orientation presupposes that language should not be understood as a means by which individuals and groups create a single, static reality in the world around them without taking into account the past, present, and future simultaneously:

> There is neither a first nor a last word and there are no limits to the dialogic context (it extends into the boundless past and boundless future). Even *past* meanings, that is those born in the dialogue of past centuries, can never be stable (finalized, ended once and for all)—they will always change (be renewed) in the process of subsequent, future development of the dialogue.[10]

Bakhtin's stress upon the unpredictable nature of language—and thus the dynamic subjectivity and creativity of humans—is a defining feature of the dialogic kitchen. In that kitchen, countless, ongoing, unending, intergenerational conversations may be carried on between the living and the dead, both literally and metaphorically.

In the stories and films explored in this study, the Italian American kitchen is dialogic in the sense that it is a place where writers have encouraged meaning to develop via open-ended dialogues in a paradoxically extraordinary yet ordinary setting. Thus these writers have allowed what Bakhtin sees as inherent qualities of language to emerge, rather than focusing restrictively on a single voice:

> Indeed, any concrete discourse (utterance) finds the object at which it was directed already as it were overlain with qualifications, open to dispute, charged with value, already enveloped in an obscuring mist—or, on the contrary, by the "light" of alien words that have already been spoken about it. . . . The dialogic orientation of discourse is a phenomenon that is, of course, a

property of *any* discourse. It is the natural orientation of any living discourse. On all its various routes toward the object, in all its directions, the word encounters an alien word and cannot help encountering it in a living, tension-filled interaction. [11]

For most early twentieth-century Italian immigrants, the "alien word" was not merely the English language itself, but words and phrases that did not translate in the context of Italian culture. Alien words, such as spaghetti and meatballs, emerged from the socioeconomic demands of their new culture, where the need for quick, cheap, and plentiful dishes trumped their Old Country tradition of a relaxed, gradual approach to dinner. Italians knew the words "spaghetti" and "meatballs" individually, but the words together were alien. Traditionally, the main meal of the day in Italy is *pranzo*, or lunch, which consists of two courses, the *primo* (pasta, rice, or soup) and the *secondo* (meat, fish, or vegetables with a side dish). The *primo* is served in a bowl. The *secondo* is served on a plate. In America the *primo* and *secondo* are conflated in spaghetti and meatballs.

Ironically, this popular Italian American invention is regularly employed as a signifier of Italian American dinner experience at home or in a restaurant (e.g., Chef Pisghetti's sign)—or of Italian Americans in general. When human experience is presented as an open-ended dialogue in Italian American narratives, this alien word works in tension with other linguistic signifiers that counter its limitations: these are dialogic narratives. In stories like Chef Pisghetti's that present a single, static perspective, that tension is absent because no open-ended dialogue is permitted to occur. The result is what Bakhtin calls "monologism," which has serious ethical implications. [12]

Monologic Discourse: A Rotten Ingredient

My four-year-old son, who is half Italian American, is exposed to monologic discourse that enforces stereotypes about Italian Americans in animated shows that aim to educate as well as entertain. In the episode "Marcello's Meatballs" of *Justin Time*, the moral of the story is respectable: try new foods even if they initially look or smell strange. [13] However, the means to achieve this moral is monologic.

In the episode, crooning gondoliers signify Venice, but this stereotype may be the closest the cartoon comes to cultural accuracy. It is Princess Sophia's birthday, and her favorite dish is spaghetti and meatballs. Of course, ordering spaghetti and meatballs in Venice— together or as the *primo* and *secondo*—would be like ordering grits in the Northeast or fresh oceanic fish in the Midwest, but the Venetian princess wants it. The cooks, Justin and pals, have spaghetti but no meatballs. Fortunately, a travelling purveyor of meatballs calls attention to his cart by singing, "Meatballs! I gotta meatballs!" in broken English. Our cooks are saved—until the meatballs drop into a canal, and they bravely substitute broccoli. While all of the children think the broccoli smells like "dirty socks" (imagine their reaction to *asiago* cheese or *baccalà* [dried cod], a mainstay in Venetian cuisine), Princess Sophia devours the spaghetti and broccoli, declaring, "That is delicioso."[14] As such, "Marcello's Meatballs" employs monologic discourse that replaces open-ended and complex notions of identity with simple stereotypes—spaghetti and meatballs, the meatball seller—that are essential to the story's plot and moral.

While *Justin Time*'s seemingly innocent example of monologic discourse is not as blatant as the 1939 *Life* interview with Joe DiMaggio, it encourages the same harmful stereotypes. In his homage to Joe DiMaggio, Joseph Durso details the athlete's success and his challenges as a recent Italian immigrant:

> He also had to endure the casual bigotry that existed when he first came up. Many of his teammates called him the Big Dago, and *Life* magazine, in a 1939 article intending to compliment him, said: "Although he learned Italian first, Joe, now 24, speaks English without an accent, and is otherwise well adapted to most U.S. mores. Instead of olive oil or smelly bear grease he keeps his hair slick with water. He never reeks of garlic and prefers chicken chow mein to spaghetti."[15]

Life magazine's description of the Big Dago is monologic because it does not inspire via open-ended dialogue a rich understanding of the authentic human experiences of DiMaggio's cultural identity. It voices a perspective without any expectation of another perspective's presence or response. As Bakhtin explains,

> Monologism, at its extreme, denies the existence outside itself of another consciousness with equal rights and equal respon-

sibilities . . . [and] *another person* remains wholly and merely an *object* of consciousness, and not another consciousness. No response is expected from it that could change everything in the world of my consciousness. . . . Monologue pretends to be the *ultimate word*. It closes down the represented world and represented persons.[16]

Once the shallow narrative of the *Life* article denies DiMaggio such a consciousness, DiMaggio has little agency to defy or correct it.[17] The "ultimate word" on DiMaggio sold, both literally and figuratively. Did Durso's story of DiMaggio's turning away from Italian roots make him easier to accept for fans who looked at baseball as the *American* pastime? Was the Big Dago a "story" of a successfully Americanized Italian? Do Chef Pisghetti and *Justin Time* shape what my son thinks an Italian American should be?

On Narrative: An Approach to Conversations in the Dialogic Kitchen

In contrast to the monologism of *Happy Days*, *Laverne and Shirley*, *Curious George*, *Justin Time*, and Durso's portrayal of DiMaggio, the dialogic kitchen is rooted in a freer, more complex narrative. Stories with such complexity are a means by which intergenerational conversations persist and co-create meaning because the language of storytelling is unstable and unpredictable, whether it appears in actual dialogues between characters or in the implied "conversation" created by the presence of the story itself or by the multiple meanings of words in various parts of the story (e.g., narration of plot or description of setting). Thus, dialogic narratives challenge an understanding of others as monologic, self-serving "object[s] of consciousness" rather than as authentic beings with a broad range of lived experiences.[18] And sometimes, such dialogue lives in otherwise dark stories, such as mafia movies.

In a chapter from *Teaching Italian American Literature, Film, and Popular Culture* entitled "Palookas, Romeos, and Wise Guys: Italian Americans in Hollywood," Peter Bondanella asks teachers and writers to get beyond "the fact that Americans of Italian descent virtually dominate the pantheon of gangsters in the cinema."[19] He also asserts that "any close examination of even the most stereotyped image can lead to interesting cultural and historical questions, and the problem of ethnic stereotyping requires that some films be screened that may, indeed, embody such a perspective."[20] The three films analyzed in this essay offer violent narratives of Italian American *mafiosi*. However, within these films are complex narratives that feature open-ended dialogue that represents human experience more authentically, thus exhibiting aspects of the dialogic kitchen.

Furthermore, these films and the short stories by Caronia, Bryant, and Ragusa are worthy of scholarly attention that explores how narratives embody dynamic, deeply held beliefs and values, reveal authentic aspects of cultural identity, and persuade audiences to think in certain ways about Italian American experiences. As Thomas B. Farrell asserts in *Norms of Rhetorical Culture*, "there is in the practice of rhetoric an invitation to struggle over the provisional meaning of appearance."[21] By seeking out stories that persuade us to engage in this struggle, we can better understand dialogic narratives and better challenge monologic representations of any culture.

While my analysis in this study relies on Bakhtin's dialogism as a theoretical framework, there is another interpretive layer to consider: how symbols of Italian American experience emerge in the dialogic kitchen. Once we view a kitchen as dialogic in an Italian American narrative, what symbols can we survey to better understand the nuances of language and meaning that emerge in this dialogic space? For this, we can turn to Walter Fisher's perspective on the role of narrative in the communication of ideas: here, symbols have a unique and central importance. Recognizing specific symbols that participate in the construction of a narrative allows us access to the rhetorical structure of the narrative; and by identifying symbols, we may uncover how we are persuaded to understand a particular narrative and its characters. As Fisher explains,

> symbols are created and communicated ultimately as stories meant to give order to human experience and to induce others to dwell in them in order to establish ways of living in common, in intellectual and spiritual communities in which there is confirmation for the story that constitutes one's life.[22]

In this way, Fisher asks the critic to "look at rhetorical communications as stories rather than as an [*sic*] 'arguments' in the traditional sense."[23] To view rhetorical acts as stories and, in turn, narratives as rhetorical allows us to focus upon what symbols are present, why they are present, and how they are utilized. As a result, we are encouraged to consider how symbols participate in the arguments contained within a narrative.

Symbols in Film and Short Fiction: Four Kinds of Cooking in the Dialogic Kitchen

The mafia is a symbol of power, raw violence, hierarchy, and, perhaps most importantly, of *family*. However, while the concept of family seems like an inviting symbol of the unyielding bond between men, one who steps out of line in this family could experience a public dressing down, a smack across the face, or even a bullet in the back of the head. In "Eating with the Mafia: Belonging and Violence," Martin Parker notes the irony of the desire to be in the mafia for its familial bonds: "Indeed, family is an odd metaphor to use to describe the sort of homosocial bonding that seems to characterize the day-to-day life of a wiseguy."[24] Parker points out that in this family, "there is violence continually lurking below the surface."[25] Yet, the lure of the mafia and its family ties has been sensationalized since its inception in America.

Mafia films are attractive, especially to men, because being in *the* family means honor, trust, and loyalty. And, of course, an assumption implied in these films is that if you (the viewer) were part of this opulent family, you wouldn't be the *stugots* who steps out of line—you would follow the family rules. So, one major reason mafia films make money is because they represent a dark, powerful world of family relationships that hold within them an exciting sense of mystery. It is precisely this sense of mystery that first initiated the stereotype of Italian American men as *mafiosi*. Put simply, early in the twentieth century, the word "mafia" sold newspapers:

> The term had such drawing power that to newspaper editors, who placed circulation above all other considerations, it seemed like good business to let the public go on thinking that the Mafia

was a gigantic network that enveloped nearly everyone with an Italian name.[26]

Of course, evidence of non-*mafiosi* Italians in America challenged these prejudiced conclusions. In "On Being a Sicilian in America," Jerre Mangione explains,

> In the early years of the [twentieth] century when the American press's vilification program was at its height, a number of fair-minded Americans (especially teachers and social workers) felt compelled to protest that the great majority of Italians were honest and law-abiding persons. They cited studies which indicated that crimes by Italian immigrants were of a lower percentage than crimes committed by native-born Americans. But the press, pandering to the bigotry of their readers, ignored all such protests.[27]

Consequently, instead of telling stories about their ancestors' countless contributions to Western civilization, or about the sacrifice it took to come to America, the media sold embellished stories of a violent minority within a peaceful majority. Such stories continue to sell in mafia films. However, the films that perpetuate the *mafioso* stereotype also suggest more dynamic themes, which may be comforting for the audience who are yearning for some sort of connection, some sort of family.

Drawing from Max Weber, Martin Parker points out that "the image of being part of a family is generally seen to be preferable to being a 'single cog in an ever moving mechanism.'"[28] Take the violence and corruption out of *The Godfather*, *Donnie Brasco*, and *Goodfellas*, and a sense of family still resides—especially in the dialogic kitchen. "An authentic companionship around simple hearty pleasures" develops in this kitchen—a place where Italian Americans do far more than cook and eat.[29] This authenticity can develop because the writers do not present their narratives from single-voiced perspectives. Instead, multiple voices develop a conversation of ideas about cooking in these stories in which utterances are "overlain with qualifications, open to dispute, charged with value" because of their nature as utterances and because of the symbolic context in which they are uttered.[30] Moreover, the particular facet of that context helps us explore the ways in which those utterances do not "[pretend] to be the *ultimate word*," but rather function as ongoing, open-ended dialogues.[31]

The first symbol to consider is cooking as a social activity, because the Italian American kitchen is often the heart of a family's socialization. The dialogic kitchen in the narratives discussed in this study represents the social space of many Italian American households, real and fictitious. Families and friends want to stay close to the action: here they smell fresh basil as it is chopped and see the fork technique for making beautifully textured gnocchi, but they also participate in conversations that come and go as pots simmer, sauces are stirred, and families and friends wait to eat. Conversation participants share the stories of the day and pass on (sometimes push) lessons, values, and traditions. But many voices are speaking.

Goodfellas, in particular, exhibits a tension between traditions in the conversations that we are invited to hear. In one slow pan across a prison scene that makes us rethink the notion that "crime doesn't pay," we first see Paul Cicero's thick fingers delicately slicing garlic with a razor blade while we hear Henry Hill's overdubbed narration: "In prison, dinner was always a big thing. We had a pasta course and then a meat or a fish. Paulie did the prep work. He was doing a year for contempt, and he had this wonderful system for doing the garlic. He used a razor and he cut it so thin that it used to liquefy in the pan with just a little oil."[32] While this could seem like a monologic moment—Paulie presented from Henry's perspective—Paulie is not merely a prep cook. He is also a critic, and Hill's narration introduces the cooks/*mafiosi* and their respective cooking responsibilities. We meet the elderly mobster, Vinny, who makes the sauce with—as Hill and Paulie note—"too many onions."[33] Paulie's criticism spreads to an off-scene character, who is concerned about the tomato-onion ratio: "Three onions! How many cans of tomatoes you put in there?"[34] Through the symbol of cooking as a social interaction, *Goodfellas* reveals the dialogic nature of this particular kitchen.

Cooking as Spectacle, Cooking as Teaching

This scene also suggests cooking as spectacle, a symbol that often develops in two ways: first, the cooking itself involves an appreciation of the knife techniques, the angle of the spoon as the sauce is stirred, the combinations of meats and herbs, the vibrant colors of yellow and red peppers, or even the size of the pots. The second aspect of cooking as spectacle recognizes the fact that some Italian American cooks in the films and stories I explore put on a theatrical display of their culinary skill for their kitchen audience, even if it is merely an audience of one. Both aspects of spectacle reveal the dialogic nature of the kitchen because they employ language or imply a conversation of ideas about how cooking is performed: even with no dialogue present, the camera reveals the multiplicity of culinary techniques and experiences; and the theatrical displays rely upon an audience's presence and response.

In addition, in most cases discussed here, the cooks also suggest the notion of cooking as teaching. Cooking as teaching occurs in *The Godfather* after Peter Clemenza answers nature's call on the side of the road, during which time he orders Rocco Lampone to shoot young Paulie Gatto. In one of the most famous lines in the history of mafia films, Clemenza casually tells Lampone to "Leave the gun. Take the cannoli."[35] His flagrant disregard for human life reveals the heart of a stone-cold killer, one aspect of the stereotype of Italian Americans as *mafiosi*. However, this stereotype works in tension with a theatrical and educational display of cooking in the scene after the hit.

The kitchen scene in the Corleone home, when juxtaposed with the cannoli scene, seems to suggest an authentic representation of the Italian American notion of family. Parker explains, "In the foreground Clemenza is lecturing Michael Corleone on how to make a good meat sauce, whilst in the background his men are sitting, eating, drinking, laughing."[36] The symbol of cooking as social emerges here, and it works in a complex way to humanize Clemenza, who, though cooking for killers and other criminals, cooks for his "subordinates," nonetheless.[37]

However, Clemenza also displays both cooking as spectacle and cooking as teaching, though the latter is the dominant theme. In a passage quoted by Parker, Clemenza shares his method for making sauce:

> Come over here kid. Learn somethin'. You never know, you might have to cook for twenty guys someday. You see, you start up with a little water, then you fry some garlic. Then you throw in some tomatoes, tomato paste. You fry it. You make sure it doesn't

stick. You get it to a boil. You shove in all your sausage and your meatballs. Add a little bit of wine, a little bit of sugar. And that's my trick.[38]

Clemenza isn't flashy in his engagement of cooking as spectacle, but he is sure to point out his "trick" to Michael Corleone.[39] Clemenza does not write down a recipe, he performs it. Yet this performance isn't merely aesthetic, nor is it simply about a damn good meat sauce. Clemenza is using cooking as teaching, both literally and symbolically.

The recipe for this meat sauce transfers a cooking tradition from one member of the family to the next, someone who will likely add his own trick. However, there is a more complex lesson that emerges in this scene: by teaching Michael how to make the meat sauce, Clemenza is also transferring a sense of power. He is indicating Michael's readiness to lead the family. This symbolic transference of power is also part of the Italian American experience, at least in my family, though it did not result in my becoming a Don. In my mother's kitchen, for instance, I had to be ready for the transference of kitchen "power" by watching, studying, tasting, practicing, and finally standing at the helm (or rather, the sauce pot) by myself. My age also prepared me for this sacred responsibility of feeding the family. And so too, when my son is old enough, has studied, tasted, and practiced our family's recipes, he will be worthy of the power to feed and to entertain.

Training to be the cook in an Italian American kitchen also requires patience and respect, which is evidenced in "The Exegesis of Cooking."

> I spent much of my childhood in my grandmother's kitchen. As I watched her cook, she would give me something from her preparations to assuage my hunger—a carrot, a piece of celery. Most of the foods she prepared took time. They needed first to be "cleaned," trimmed of fat or organs or bones in the case of chicken or meat or fish, or of stems and seeds in the case of vegetables. Then basted in egg and bread crumbs, for cutlets or zucchini flowers, or stuffed, for mushrooms. String beans had to be snapped at both ends, and after they were cooked, each one had to be carefully sliced along its length; for artichokes, every leaf had to be trimmed, then stuffed with chopped garlic and bread crumbs.[40]

By watching her grandmother cook—by willingly engaging in the act of cooking as spectacle—this young girl is showing the patience required of doing something properly. Likewise, by watching Clemenza cook, Michael is showing respect for his position in the family. He is ready for this final lesson of cooking as spectacle and as teaching, which enables us as viewers to see this dialogic kitchen take shape.

Cooking as a Return to the Ordinary

The Corleone kitchen scene also reveals another symbol of the dialogic kitchen: cooking as a return to the ordinary. Although he has just ordered a murder, Clemenza seems to be able to use the routine of cooking to refocus his attention on the quotidian. In this way, cooking may translate to a symbol of normalcy—it proves that everything is going to be all right (which, of course, it is not).

By contrast, "Go to Hell," a short story by Nancy Caronia, demonstrates that cooking as a return to the ordinary can be a means of enforcing monologic discourse that makes a dialogic kitchen seemingly impossible. In the narrative, the perverse and abusive Grandpa is a striking contrast to his wife, a devoted *nonna* who shares Old World sociocultural traditions with her young granddaughters. "We shopped all day," explains the narrator, "walking up and down Coney Island Avenue, the deli men giving us slices of salami and the bakers handing us cookies."[41] Once home, the Old World traditions continue when cooking as teaching takes place. The girls question why Grandma's meatballs "taste so different" than their "Irish American mother's."[42] These touching activities, conveyed through stereotypical imagery, seem to enact the type of discourse criticized by Laurino.

After this cooking-as-teaching scene, Grandma puts her granddaughters to bed, saying, "Be good and go ta sleep."[43] Here, her familiar bedtime expression is also a warning. True to their childish exuberance, they chat instead of going quietly to bed. Soon, Grandpa enters the bedroom, but not to scold:

> He came over to us, and since I was on the outside of the bed—I was older and less likely to fall out of bed—he grabbed my arm and said, 'ya wanna play?' I told him it was too late, but he didn't hear me or he didn't care, I don't know which, and next

he unbuckled his belt and opened his trousers.... and no matter how hard I kicked him with my legs he held my arms above my head with one hand and pushed my head into his crotch with the other.[44]

Fortunately, Grandma discovers this horrid act. After yelling between Grandma and Grandpa occurs "in dialect," Grandma and her granddaughters go into the kitchen, which—like the Corleone kitchen—is a safe place where good things happen.[45] The kitchen signals a return to tradition and comfort, where families converse freely and grandmothers cook for their grandchildren.

However, this kitchen is dominated by a single voice: Grandma responds to her traumatized granddaughter by saying, "What's wrong, you wan' something to eat maybe? Yeah, that'sa good, I'll make you somethin' ta eat."[46] Though her granddaughter agrees, she cannot eat Grandma's *farina*. She is sick to her stomach, but Grandma does not acknowledge why. Instead, Grandma maintains control of the narrative by speaking only of food, cooking, and eating. She seems to deny her granddaughter's trauma and thus the girl's right to be more than an object of consciousness.

However, Grandma shifts her monologic focus into a dialogic one when she asks, "Wha'sa matta' wid you? I made this fa you and now you don' want it? You kids. What am I gonna do?"[47] Like the common-phrase-as-warning she utters at bedtime, Grandma's question "Wha'sa matta wid you?" is more than a typical, guilt-inspiring demand.[48] This question serves as an effort to find normalcy in the midst of trauma, an effort that troublingly ignores that trauma. However, Grandma's next question makes the rhetorical and narrative qualities of the scene more complex. "What am I gonna do?" is a question that invites dialogue, though no response is recorded; also, it may be a question she is asking of herself as a woman married to someone who molests children.[49] Foregrounding of food and cooking is Grandma's way of controlling a narrative; but Caronia's story itself brings to life a part of the human condition that is so painful, so awful, so distressing that we try to forget it, to silence it. Her fiction gives it a voice and a presence, and thus Grandma's kitchen demonstrates not only monologic but also dialogic discourse, as it shows that the effort of cooking as a to return to the ordinary is not a panacea to heal all wounds.

Darker Realities in the Dialogic Kitchen

Thus, while the dialogic kitchen contains enjoyable stories, it also contains stories of pain, suffering, loneliness, and hopelessness. Here we are reminded of Fisher's discussion of the relationship between narrative and symbolism: "by 'narration,' I mean symbolic actions—words and/or deeds—that have sequence and meaning for those who live, create, or interpret them."[50] While the "pasta/pizza/*paesano*" tales perpetuated by the media are warm and inviting, they lack the dark realities that Italian Americans face as human beings.[51] Such stories fail to recognize the complexity of the symbolic actions within a narrative.[52]

Take, for instance, a scene of cooking as spectacle and as teaching in *Donnie Brasco*, when Lefty instructs Brasco. As in the scene from *The Godfather*, aspects of the dialogic kitchen are present here: it is sociable, there is a recipe being performed, and an older mobster is passing on his culinary skill to a younger mobster. Through his symbolic actions, Clemenza in *The Godfather* exudes a sense of control: the kitchen is tidy and orderly; it is evident that Clemenza is an experienced, authoritative cook and teacher; and the sauce is an obvious success. However, in *Donnie Brasco*, Lefty emerges as a pathetic loser when one juxtaposes the symbolic actions of his cooking scene with those of Clemenza.

Lefty's kitchen is a mess, and his cooking is chaotic and hard to follow as he attempts to teach Brasco not an Italian but a French recipe, *coq au vin*. He walks through the recipe—"can of tomatoes, punch of salt"—and his student replies inquisitively, "Punch?" Lefty repeats himself, "Punch, *punch* of salt."[53] Now Brasco questions his teacher outright, a dialogic act that surely would not occur in the Corleone kitchen scene: "Punch or pinch?" Brasco inquires.[54] Lefty repeats himself again, "Punch, punch, not pinch."[55] This odd word choice leaves Brasco and the audience asking, "What the hell is a punch?" Lefty is not in control of his kitchen or of his life.

Furthermore, Lefty loses control and credibility as a cook, as a teacher, and as a leader when he pours too much brandy into his frying pan. As the flames rise, he steps out of the way and insists that his wife put the fire out. Thus, the woman who moments before had said, "I can't cook special like Benny," takes control of the situation.[56] This scene employs symbols of the dialogic kitchen: it is a social place, where cooking is passed down from an older family member to a younger family member as a rite of passage to a new level of power and control. Yet this dialogic kitchen is not a positive expression of cooking as social, cooking as teaching, and cooking as spectacle. In Lefty's kitchen, these symbols are strained and meaningless.

This observation is consistent with aspects of what Fisher calls the narrative paradigm, which "can be considered a dialectical synthesis of two traditional strands that recur in the history of rhetoric: the argumentative, persuasive theme and the literary, aesthetic theme."[57] That is, through our reading of the authentic use and representation of symbols within the dialogic kitchen portrayed in *The Godfather*, Lefty and his kitchen in *Donnie Brasco* are wanting. In this narrative, we are persuaded to think of Lefty and his kitchen as disappointing, hollow representations of legitimate symbols.

In addition, the dialogic kitchen can also suggest an authentic representation of deep loss, not through meaningless symbols but through the apparent absence of symbols from the scene. A moving expression of this absence occurs in "Dizzy Spells," by Dorothy Bryant. The author describes a scene with her father, a lonely widower:

> I cut myself a piece of the dry, tasteless cheese, and I think of the cheese that hung over the wine barrels in our cellar, filling it with strong, musty smells. I remember my mother, Saturday noon, home from the shop alone, waving Flora and me off to the four-hour matinee at the local movie house. She sat at the kitchen table with a loaf of sourdough French, a thick red salami, a high-smelling gorgonzola, the newspaper, and a smile of blissful contentment as she anticipated an afternoon of solitude.[58]

Without the smell of "high-smelling gorgonzola" that contributes to the overall "musty smell" of the cellar, home itself is "dry" and "tasteless." These symbols are strikingly absent from the kitchen. The cheese her father typically eats alone is "dry" and "tasteless," surely the antithesis of the scent and taste of her mother's cooking. Yet the mother's kitchen scene is certainly not dialogic. Her kitchen is intentionally quiet and empty except for herself. Her mother's *intentional* act of solitude underscores her father's involuntary solitude. His solitude is most definitely unintentional. His wife has died, and his children have grown up and left home.

Surely her mother enjoyed typical activities of cooking and social-izing, but this Saturday afternoon is hers, an intentional break from the bustling kitchen. However, she is not the stereotypical Italian American mother whose work in the kitchen is present solely as a labor of love. When trying to recollect pleasant memories of her mother, the daugh-ter recalls that at mealtimes, her mother was "exhausted after a week of preparation," and she "waited apprehensively, almost resentfully, for the favorable verdict on her always superb cooking."[59] This antithesis of the joy of cooking as a welcome social activity within the dialogic kitchen challenges stereotypes of the ever-happy Italian American in the happy kitchen with a happy family.

Perhaps people do not want to be forced into cooking as a social act. Perhaps people do not want to return to the ordinary. Perhaps when many men cook, they perform cooking as an extraordinary spectacle of attention, whereas many women may be compelled to cook as a byproduct of living within a patriarchy. Yes, many Italian American women may enjoy cooking, but surely it does not offset the expectation that they cook and clean while men socialize; nor does it mean that they are always happy to perform the often overlooked and immeasurable work required before the "festive family dinners," which leave them "exhausted after a week of preparation."[60] Yet some-times, we do not ourselves wish to remember the darkness that often accompanies the light. Perhaps, we desire something not unlike pleas-ing "pizza, paesono tales" to deal with the pains of the past.[61]

Like "Dizzy Spells," "Baked Ziti" by Kym Ragusa tells the story of death, dying, struggle, failure, and loss, set against the story of a beloved Italian American tradition. This tradition—cooking baked ziti—cannot save anyone. It cannot inspire a return to a functional family within scenes of the dialogic kitchen: "Baked ziti is a specialty in my family, and my father is the master of the dish. . . . I have always wanted to record this recipe in some special way, as it's one of the only traditions my family has left."[62] Instead of resplendent scenes from the dialogic kitchen her family once enjoyed, the protagonist's life is filled with scenes of ghosts.

While re-watching an unfinished video she made as a child of her father baking ziti, she is aware of the fact that she was filming ghosts:

Ghosts: my grandmother, who will soon die of cancer, and Susan, who will go two weeks after her, lost to AIDS. And my father, who is a ghost of himself, of what he might have been. He too hovering between life and death, or perhaps between two deaths, AIDS and heroin. Three people becoming ghosts, my family.[63]

Perhaps this realization brings to mind that she continues to live with these ghosts. She can settle on a new reality, shaped by symbols of the dialogic kitchen, but this would mean pretending—like the grandmother in "Go to Hell"—that scenes from the dialogic kitchen can heal.

It would also mean a return to the false sense of innocence that was constructed and supported by the dialogic kitchen and its related symbols, cooking as social, cooking as a return to the ordinary, cooking as spectacle, and cooking as teaching:

My father still relates to me as if I were a little girl. He even speaks to me in a slight singsong voice that one might use with a child. 'Don't forget, always use flat-leaf parsley—that American parsley has no flavor,' he tells me again and again, each time as if for the first time, as if it were a revelation, a gift for being a good girl. . . . Maybe it's more comfortable for me to play that role with him. To pretend that I don't know what I know. To simply watch him cook, with innocence and awe, ignoring the rage that has settled inside me like a too-heavy meal that I can't digest.[64]

What makes the dialogic kitchen particularly interesting in this story is that the cook is not isolated from the conversations; instead, the cook is an active participant. In the dialogic kitchen, cooking is the backdrop to the multiple dramas that unfold through ceaseless conversations.

Conclusion: The Dialogic Kitchen and Italian American Experience

The dialogic kitchen challenges discourse about Italian Americans that has the effect of "reshaping disparate character traits into a singular folkloric image, rendering us indistinguishable from each other, playing the Muzak of ethnicity."[65] Using Bakhtin's dialogic orientation and Fisher's perspectives on narrative, I have sought to engage a range of stories set in the dialogic kitchen, ones that include Italians and Italian Americans whose songs of experience are as diverse as the characters themselves.

By examining Italian American culture through the lens of the dialogic kitchen and its complementary concepts, I aim to move beyond stereotypes and shallow narratives that trivialize the relationship between food, cooking, hospitality, and Italian American culture. As the television shows, mafia films, and short stories analyzed here demonstrate, we Italian Americans are more than families of emotional cooks who have a penchant for certain foods and traditions. Nor do we just hear "'the beautiful song' of our heritage" or see "those snapshots of golden days forever gone."[66] Rather, we also hear songs of darkness and brokenness; and we see portraits of Italian Americans' lived experiences.

CHAPTER 8

Consuming Pleasures

Nineteenth-Century Cookery as Narrative Structure in *Downton Abbey*

LINDSY LAWRENCE

Meals, their preparation and consumption, govern the narrative structure of *Downton Abbey*. It is at breakfast in the first episode that the news of the sinking of the *Titanic* and the death of James and Patrick Crawley as a result is delivered. The end of the first season comes as news of the outbreak of the First World War is announced at an afternoon picnic. In between, numerous dinners, teas, and breakfasts work to structure a heritage series about the intersections of an aristocratic family, their domestic servants, and the chaotic events of the first part of the twentieth century.

Given the ubiquity of meals and the symbolic functions they serve in nineteenth-century fiction and periodical columns, it is unsurprising that Julian Fellowes and the production team behind *Downton Abbey* would pay so close attention to food. This focus on food as a structuring device inserts *Downton Abbey* into the aspirational discourse of nineteenth-century and early twentieth-century cookbooks and domestic manuals. These manuals, etiquette guides, periodical essays, and cookbooks all focused on the management of the home. For example, Isabella Beeton's *Book of Household Management*, serialized in twenty-four monthly parts from 1859 to 1861 in association with her husband's *Englishwoman's Domestic Magazine* (1851–90), was one of several texts dispensing advice to the middle-class family.[1] Many of these guides adapted rulebooks for the aristocracy, providing readers with a glimpse of aristocratic habits alongside practical

cookery advice. Beeton's meal plans suggest how carefully she system-
ized the work of the household, effortlessly combining the glamorous
with the everyday. Menus for lavish, eighty-person dinners sit quite
comfortably next to menus for simple, seasonal family meals. In cen-
tering *Downton Abbey* on the work of the household, series creator
Julian Fellowes playfully blends issues of class and consumption.

Indeed, the consumption of serial narratives—be it a serial novel
or television series—has long been compared to eating too many
sweets. In other words, serial narratives, because they offer up fare
dependent on cliffhanger endings, complicated plot twists, and large
casts of characters, provide consumers with the narrative equivalent
of dessert. These narratives often delve into the near past, mining the
peccadillos of the aristocracy for their content. One of the most ardent
critics of *Downton Abbey*, Simon Schama, calls the series "a servile
soap opera," serving up to American audiences a form of "cultural
necrophilia."[2] Airing on commercial ITV in the United Kingdom
and on public television in the United States, *Downton Abbey* revels
in combining the highbrow appeal of a costume drama with soap
opera storytelling practices. It is this piquant blend of high and low
that makes *Downton Abbey* such a middlebrow pleasure for viewers,
but making this mixture work depends on the careful use of the discursive practices of conduct manuals and cookbooks from the long
nineteenth century.

Cookery and Heritage Film

All cookbooks and cooking advice manuals are, to a certain extent,
about lifestyle. As Lucy Scholes argues, there is an "idea of cookery
as entertainment, not sustenance."[3] Although Scholes is focused on
the contemporary celebrity chef, her points about how "TV celebrity chefs illustrate [the] tension between the public and the private
as they straddle that ever harder-to-distinguish boundary between
the domestic and the institutional" is apt for exploring how lifestyle
shows—both of the reality TV variety and heritage dramas—function
like conduct manuals.[4] Celebrity chefs like Jamie Oliver, Nigella
Lawson, and Giada De Laurentiis use their status to champion pet
causes, such as teaching kids to cook and consuming non-processed

foods. Other celebrities, such as Gwyneth Paltrow and Jessica Alba, use their star status to sell lifestyle cookbooks that tout clean eating or "honest" living. Paltrow's "goop" newsletter for June 4, 2014, includes advice on removing sugar from readers' diets, along with recipes using better sugar alternatives and arguments for a lifestyle change away from processed foods, as well as other recipes for readers.[5] All of these cooks and the cookery books, television series, blogs, and newsletters they produce are ultimately advising readers on lifestyle as much as they are about cooking. Even the stars of *Downton Abbey* have become purveyors of cookery entertainment. For instance, Laura Carmichael, who plays Lady Edith, and Joanne Froggatt, who plays lady's maid Anna, both gave interviews to American lifestyle food blog *The New Potato*, where they detailed their "ideal food day" and how they use diet "to practice beauty from the inside out."[6] The accompanying photo shoots depict both actors in contemporary dress, deliberately inverting the class dynamics of the show by placing Carmichael in a more downstairs environment and Froggatt in a more upscale space.

Like these contemporary cooks and cookery books, the discourse of food production in the nineteenth century navigates between the practical, the aspirational, and the condemnatory. Jean Ingelow, in an 1888 article in *Good Words* entitled "Taste," condemns many British food habits, including the consumption of desserts: "The quantity of sweet jam and sweet cakes eaten in Great Britain is out of all proportion to what other nations consume, excepting indeed the United States, where, in the name of sauce ('sass'), they eat jam at all meals and in large quantities."[7] Isabella Beeton steers the *Book of Household Management* (*BOHM*) away from such sweeping criticisms of consumption, preferring to advise her readers on how to construct a proper home, no matter the class level, rather than overtly discourage specific consumption habits. In so doing, Beeton crafts a kind of domestic discourse that sees upper-class and middle-class life on the same continuum.

In focusing on the use of nineteenth-century cookery discourse in *Downton Abbey*, I am not suggesting that the show merely uses recipes from cookbooks like the *BOHM* to enhance its historical accuracy, although the show uses many such conduct books, which often focused on meal production since it took up such a large portion of household management, and servants' memoirs in order to represent Edwardian country-house life as accurately as possible.[8] Rather, I am interested in the ways that *Downton Abbey* deploys a middlebrow discourse that combines a look at the practicalities of running a home with the entertainment of a glimpse into upper-class lifestyles that cookbooks and domestic manuals offered to readers in the nineteenth century. Many of the recipes in the *BOHM* require space or ingredients that the average, urban, middle-class household in the nineteenth century would find difficult to obtain.[9] Yet the advice portions of the *BOHM* move seamlessly between discussions of the role of the mistress of a middle-class home, details of the cost and number of servants for a country estate, directives on the relationship between the cook, housekeeper, and mistress, manners and discourse for a modest dinner party, and delineations of the roles of all the servants in a large establishment. The middle-class housewife would not necessarily need to know that the butler of a country estate was paid up to £50 per year, but the knowledge would give her a look into the world of the aristocracy. In highlighting the *BOHM*'s discussion of the mistress and servants, I am arguing that the discourse that permeates cookery books and conduct manuals also informs a heritage text like *Downton Abbey*, which is invested in recreating lived existence.

According to film scholar Andrew Higson, "The turn to the past has been a prominent feature of contemporary British cinema, as well, especially at the quality end of the market, in what has come to be known as the heritage film."[10] Heritage film consists of historical dramas, typically literary adaptations, which create for modern audiences a glimpse into Britain's past. These productions, such as *Remains of the Day* (1993), tend to be tipped with nostalgia for a less-complicated time. In *Film England: Culturally English Film Making since the 1990s*, Higson argues, "A certain category of middlebrow filmmaking endeavours to engage with audiences attached to a more traditional literary culture . . . by making films that appear 'literate' by comparison with most action-led-blockbusters—that is, films that draw on some of the same values as so-called quality literature."[11] As Higson notes, these are "films [and television series] that deal in various ways with the English past, heritage and tradition."[12] These films and television series "also in various ways expand and renew ideas of Englishness (and its constituent elements), challenge certain traditions and reimagine certain national myths."[13]

While Higson's work is predominantly on film, heritage television series and mini-series do much of the same cultural work in presenting to audiences a version of Englishness couched in "literate" appeals: "the dominant version of Englishness on offer tends to draw on upper-class English traditions of aristocratic wealth, Establishment politics and private school education."[14] Heritage productions are about reproducing the culture of the past for a contemporary audience, and more often than not, they are invested in offering up the lifestyles of the aristocracy for contemporary consumption. For instance, one of the pleasures of season four of *Downton Abbey* is watching the draconian but lovable cook, Mrs. Patmore, learn how to use an electric mixer, which is a period accurate machine, and the storyline represents the changes technology made to the country house. In reimagining certain myths about England in the early twentieth-century, *Downton Abbey* is focused on the "complex world of the country house and every detail that a servant would be expected to know."[15] The downstairs world of *Downton Abbey* is loosely drawn from a couple of different servants' memoirs, including Margaret Powell's delightful *Below Stairs: The Classic Kitchen Maid's Memoir*, and the series takes great pains to accurately recreate early twentieth-century fashions, foods, and technologies. The attention to historical detail in set dressing and costuming includes the food onscreen even resembling some of the sketches from Beeton's *BOHM*, particularly, the plates of towering jellies Mrs. Patmore makes for the luncheon after James and Patrick Crawleys' memorial service. This nostalgic look back at nineteenth- and early twentieth-century cooking practices, practices out of sync with most middle-class homes of the period as they emphasized fresh ingredients available to a country house but not necessarily an urban home, is steeped in the domestic discourse of cookery books like the *BOHM*.

Cooking with the *Book of Household Management*: Isabella Beeton's Domestic Discourse

The *BOHM* was by no means the only source of cooking or domestic advice in the nineteenth century. Sara Stickney Ellis's *The Women of*

England (1839) and *Daughters of England* (1842) and Annie Cobbett's *The English Housekeeper* were just a few of the numerous guides available. Such advice could also be found in periodicals such as the *Englishwoman's Domestic Magazine* (1857–59) and other magazines aimed at women. Even the *London Journal* (1845–1906), a weekly magazine marketed to the lower-middle and working classes, ran a feature from May 2 to September 12, 1857, called "The Science of Etiquette and Deportment and Dress." This series couches the "study of etiquette" as a scientific endeavor worthy of "sensible men" as it details the need for introductory letters and the etiquette of dining, habits that the lower-middle-class audience of the magazine would not necessarily need to know much less have the opportunity to put into practice.[16] In a later "Ladies Supplement," the *London Journal* interspersed cooking advice on puff pastries with a discussion of national habits. *Bow Bells* ran a series called "Popular Papers on Cookery and Domestic Economy" by Miss Kelman, a lecturer on cookery, in the 1880s.[17] The series focused on different cooking techniques, such as broiling or frying, and recipes for different dishes, such as croquettes of potatoes.

Mixing instruction and commentary on British cultural habits and morals was a common feature of these articles and manuals. Earlier in the nineteenth century, many domestic manuals connected morality and proper etiquette and household management, and many of these manuals focused on the behaviors and character of the ideal middle-class woman. Sarah Stickney Ellis's 1839 conduct book, *The Women of England,* complains that the "cultivation of the mental faculties ha[s] so far advanced as to take precedence of the moral, . . . leaving no time for domestic usefulness."[18] This situation has caused the "character of the women of England" to degrade into "the sickly sensibilities, the feeble frames, and the useless habits of the rising generation.[19] Much of Ellis's commentary focuses on middle-class women, and she avers that the problem facing the character of the majority of these women is the mimicking of upper-class behaviors.[20] Yet her condemnation of upper-class or aristocratic morals and habits is muted by mid-century as domestic guides turned from a focus on the moral or religious to the more practical skills necessary for an upwardly mobile society. Indeed, Isabella Beeton's *Book of Household Management*, which came to dominate the cookery and domestic manual market after its serialization from 1859–61 and publication in volume form in 1861, employs a discourse that combines a focus on the social aspects of dining with an emphasis on the pleasures of the well-run home, no matter the social level of the household. Margaret Beetham claims that Beeton's emphasis on the practicalities of household management "redefined the task of managing the domestic so that attention to the minutiae of daily life" was a means of "mobilising a series of far-ranging social shifts."[21] Moreover, the initial serialization of the *BOHM* allowed Beeton to concentrate on the details of everyday life in ways that previous domestic manuals could not because of the importance they laid on morality. Designed to appeal to the thrifty, urban mistress, the separate parts of the *BOHM* addressed the various issues that any well-run home would face. These include the mundane to the extreme, such as how to make starch, how to clean silk ribbons, and game dinners for thirty people.

Thus, while it is predominantly a cookbook, the *BOHM* operates within a complex teleology of class aspiration and practical advice. The *BOHM* traverses a wide range of information, but at its core, Beeton's vision of the well-run home depends on an attention to the details of everyday life, details that stretch beyond the meals and recipes that bind the *BOHM* together. The *BOHM* and its later editions and offshoots are invested in aiding the middle-class housewife in maintaining her family's social standing through proper household management, particularly helping her negotiate the changing urban landscape she was most likely to inhabit.[22] The *BOHM* does deploy class-consciousness in its advice, recognizing that the average reader does not have a large household with a cavalcade of servants. The reader of the *BOHM* would not have been the Lady Cora Granthams of her day. The *BOHM* is careful to recognize, however, that the role of the middle-class domestic manager is to run her home with the same precision and attention to detail as Lady Cora, the Dowager Countess, and Mrs. Hughes. Margaret Beetham argues, "In [Beeton's] text what keeps madness and the threat of the primitive at bay is not a moral or even a religious spirit, but the will and above all 'the skill' of the domestic woman. That will and skill in Beeton's text are essentially to do with order, with making sure that objects, people, and practices are all kept in their appropriate place."[23] Hence, Beeton offers a range of advice to the mistress of the house, including an emphasis on early rising, cleanliness, and discipline in dress and friendships, all intended to systemize the work of the home. To a certain extent, Beeton's domestic manager exists in the same sphere as Ellis's, where "the moral was enacted" through the practicalities of household management.[24] Yet Beeton's concept of domestic management is predicated on systemization. Her domestic manager is a "COMMANDER OF AN ARMY" whose "spirit will be seen in the whole establishment."[25]

This view of domestic management allows Beeton to avoid condemning aristocratic life in order to elevate the middle classes. Rather, Beeton sees a continuum between the frugalities of the well-ordered middle-class family dinner and the sixty–person menu for a supper at a ball:

> For both mistress and servants, as well in large as small households, it will be found, by far, the better plan, to cook, and serve the dinner, and to lay the tablecloth and the sideboard, with the same cleanliness, neatness, and scrupulous exactness, whether it be for the mistress herself alone, a small family, or for 'company.' If this rule be strictly adhered to, all will find themselves increase in managing skills.[26]

In constructing household management as a skill set applicable for every household, Beeton provides information that seems at first glance unnecessary for running an urban middle-class home with one to three servants. Some of her advice, such as the section on the household accounts, is tipped for the middle-class reader, but interspersed between these sections on frugality are other sections that are decidedly more aspirational, such as the section on the housekeeper and the one detailing the costs of servants for a country house like Downton Abbey, including the salaries for the butler (between £25 to £50 per year), footman (£15 to £25 per year, if in livery), the housekeeper (£20 to £45, per year, without a tea, sugar, and beer allowance), the lady's maid (£12 to £25 per year), the cook (£14 to £30 per year), the upper housemaid (£12 to £20 per year), and the scullery maid (£5 to £9 per year).[27] The annual cost of the full list of servants Beeton gives would be roughly £700 per year. As she notes, "all the domestics mentioned in the above table would enter into the establishment of a wealthy nobleman."[28] The average middle-class home taking in £500 could employ a cook, a maid of all work, and a nurse for the children when necessary, not a full establishment of servants.

Beeton provides the full range, however, because the *BOHM*, like the *Englishwoman's Domestic Magazine*, from which it was an off shoot, and later *The Queen*, all of which were published by Beeton's husband, Samuel Beeton, blended high culture with practical advice. A reader of *EDM* could learn about the latest fashions from Paris, along with practical sewing advice. This subtle shift in domestic discourse pivots domestic management and cookery away from the moral and toward aspirational living. Beeton recognized that the home visually symbolized a family's class position, and she presents the reader with a range of discourses, enabling the middle-class reader to aspire to upper-class habits while also attending to the realities of middle-class life. Yet, by disseminating the lifestyle of the upper classes through meal plans for sixty-person ball suppers or a seventy- or eighty-person bill of fare for a wedding or christening breakfast, Beeton suggested that the lifestyle of the country house was the one to emulate and that such a lifestyle can be emulated. Texts like the *BOHM* posit that the class behaviors imbued by etiquette—what fork to use at dinner and who enters a room first based on rank—are learned, not innate, suggesting a fluidity of class boundaries. Thus, lower- and middle-class families, unfamiliar with rigid codes of upper-class life, could ostensibly learn this discursive system, although in reality, the glimpse into upper-class lifestyles served more to entertain readers than to instruct them. Helen Day suggests, "Table manners, along with other social etiquettes, allowed the bourgeoisie to maintain the boundaries between themselves and the other classes as well as police the distinctions between individuals. Etiquette was a manifestation of both collective values and hierarchical differentiation."[29] As such, domestic discourse operated on multiple levels. It educated all classes of readers in proper behavior, but only the upper classes could perform all the various facets of such manners because only they had the resources to do so.

Taking Meals at Downton Abbey: Relationships between Mistress, Master, and Servants

The first two episodes of *Downton Abbey*, in particular, revolve around household functions, as Fellowes uses meals to establish the rhythms of this country house in the pilot episode—Miss O'Brien and Thomas's duplicitousness, the cook, Mrs. Patmore's cantankerous temper, and Carson's sense of refinement—and to establish Matthew Crawley's middle-class background in the second episode. Later episodes focus more narrowly on different servants' roles; for instance, episodes five and six address the issue of Mrs. Patmore's failing eyesight and its effect on household management. Indeed, the relationships in the Crawley family are not fully developed until episodes three and four, when Mary takes a lover with disastrous results, and Edith uses the information gleaned from Daisy to impugn Mary's reputation.

The servants in *Downton Abbey* illuminate work life below stairs and explain many of the upper-class habits and situations that would be unintelligible to a twenty-first-century audience. The presence of the servants during meals, for example, means that they overhear everything the family discusses, which they then relay back to the other servants in a variety of ways. Some of this information, particularly in the first episode, functions to inform viewers of important social and economic factors that affect the whole series. Miss O'Brien, Lady Grantham's lady's maid, is present when Lord Grantham delivers the news to Cora about the deaths of James and Patrick Crawley. Patrick was the heir to the estate and title. In relaying this information to Anna and Gwen, she also explains the "complication" their deaths pose for the family. Like many great houses from the time period, the estate is entailed, in this case meaning that only the next male heir can inherit both the title and the estate. Since Lord Grantham has only daughters, none of his children can inherit, and the family has neatly situated the eldest daughter, Mary, as the bride-apparent to Patrick, meaning that the estate will at least pass, presumably, to her children. Modern viewers unfamiliar with the concept of primogeniture and the complex legal systems of the Edwardian period need this servants' gossip primer so that they can grasp the later complex maneuverings of the Dowager Countess as she tries to decouple Cora's money from the entail.

Since meals are where the servants and the family have the most visible of their interactions, Fellowes uses meals to highlight class dynamics. As the pilot episode opens, the camera moves swiftly, at first following the scullery maid, Daisy, and then following the footmen dressed in full livery, cleaning up the previous night's drinks and laying out the tablecloth, setting the table for the family breakfast. The prevailing ideology of the period was that the work of keeping the house should be invisible to the family. No matter the class position of the establishment, servants would rise early in order to straighten rooms, clear from the evening before, blacken grates, lay fires, and set out breakfast. All of this work would occur before the family rose, meaning that the family of a country estate would never witness their servants actually working to maintain the home in spotless order. This emphasis on the invisibility of home management can also be found in texts like the *BOHM*, even though the middle-class domestic manager would find hiding the work of the home much more difficult with only one or two servants versus the large staff it took to run a country estate.

In the pilot episode of *Downton Abbey*, the need for the invisibility of the servants in the household's running creates a sense of bustle and urgency among the servants, who do not even finish their own breakfast before having to take tea trays up to the ladies. Mrs. Hughes, the housekeeper, is particularly hard on Daisy, the scullery maid, ordering her to be faster in laying the fires so that no one from the family will inadvertently see her. In contrast, the family moves more leisurely, taking their time getting dressed for breakfast. The contrast is emphasized by the newspapers, which are late as editors held the presses to include the reports of the *Titanic* sinking. The butler, Carson, finds their lateness annoying as it delays the ironing of the papers process, done so that family will not get news ink on their fingers. Despite the bustle of getting the papers, Lord and Lady Grantham read the papers leisurely, and the full confirmation of the *Titanic* sinking happens at breakfast, with Carson standing at attention next to the breakfast buffet. Breakfast is the only meal where the family serve themselves, although serve is perhaps a misnomer here as they merely plate their own food. It is all brought upstairs for them, and one of the duties of the butler is "to bring in the eatables at breakfast, and wait upon the family at table, assisted by the footman, and see to the cleanliness of everything at table."[30]

The odd class dimensions of the show are established here as Carson reassures Lord Grantham that at least the ladies were rescued from the *Titanic*, to which Lord Grantham replies, "You mean the ladies in first class? God help the poor devils below decks. On their way to a better life. What a tragedy."[31] Lord Grantham does not evade the question of class that so marked the tragedy of the *Titanic*. Carson, who as the butler, has invested his entire career in the maintenance of hierarchal lines, demurs, but this exchange situates the Crawley family uneasily within the world of privilege depicted in the series. Later in the episode, Carson informs the new valet, Mr. Bates, "Downton is a great house, Mr. Bates, and the Crawleys are a great family. We live by certain standards, and those standards can at first seem daunting."[32] Yet Lord Grantham overturns the rigidity of Carson's edict by coming downstairs to the kitchens and welcoming Bates, who was his batman in the Second Boer War. Later in the episode, Carson remonstrates with Lord Grantham about the unsuitability of Bates, who has a lame leg from shrapnel.

Carson is invested in the concept of Downton's greatness, and as the butler, it is his responsibility to ensure the house continues to live up to a certain standard of elegant efficiency. In episode two, he chastises William, the second footman, for a tiny tear in his livery: "William, are you aware that the seam at your shoulder is coming apart.... You will mend it now and never appear in public in a similar state of undress. .... To progress in your chosen career, William, you must remember that a good servant at all times retains a sense of pride and dignity; he reflects the pride and dignity of the family he serves. And never make me remind you of it again."[33] His ultimate rationale for why Bates is not working out is because he cannot serve at larger dinner parties when an extra pair of masculine hands is required, thereby lowering the dignity of the entire household. He tells Lord Grantham: "As it is, my lord, we may have to have a maid in the dining room."[34] Again, Lord Grantham takes a lighter view of the importance of rigid household management, saying: "Cheer up, Carson, there are worse things happening in the world."[35] Incredulous, Carson replies, "Not worse than a maid serving a duke."[36] At issue here is Carson's own sense of pride. Carson's professional identity is tied to Downton's projected status through proper household management.

As Beeton details, the serving of meals in a large establishment is the purview of the male servants: butler, footman, and valet. All three have separate roles within meal serving, with the butler overseeing meals and having control over the cellars, and the valet helping when necessary. The footman bears the bulk of the work of serving the meal, from laying the cloth and plate to waiting at table. Beeton precisely details just how the footman should serve: "While attentive to all, the footman should be obtrusive to none; he should give nothing but on a waiter, and always hand it with the left hand and on the left side of the person he serves, and hold it so that the guest may take it with ease."[37] Cutlery is to be removed as soon as it is finished being used between courses, and the footman is never to correct a diner, a transgression that Thomas makes in episode two with the new heir Matthew Crawley. Thomas assumes that Matthew does not know even the basics of table etiquette, even though dinner *a la française*, with a footman holding the platter as each individual diner helps themselves, would have been the common method of dining by the early twentieth century. Mary also assumes that Matthew does not know anything about proper behavior. She snidely reassures him after the exchange with Thomas, "You'll soon get used to the way things are done here."[38] He responds, "If you mean that I am accustomed to a very different life than this, then that is true."[39]

Admittedly, most of Matthew's social mistakes occur over meals and with dressing for dinner. At his first family dinner, he shocks Lord Grantham with the announcement that he has taken a job in Ripon, even though Robert wants Matthew to begin to learn how to manage the estate. He tells Lord Grantham that he will have plenty of time at the weekend for such work, prompting Lady Violet to query, "What is a weekend?"[40] He refuses to let Mosley, the butler-valet hired by Lord Grantham for him, do most of his job, which results in Mosley's humiliation over tea with the Dowager Countess, Lady Cora, and Mrs. Crawley. Matthew's insistence on dressing himself also causes friction, as Mosley feels useless in his chosen profession, a fact that Matthew cannot see at first. For Matthew, a middle-class lawyer, work is done outside the confines of the home. He does not see domestic service as a profession, even though after the First World War "nationally more than 1.4 million people were still employed in domestic service."[41] Eventually, Matthew begins to adopt the right behaviors, even impressing Mary at dinner with his ability to follow her belabored Greek myth analogy. With Matthew's transformation, the relationship between he and Mosley improves, as Matthew allows Mosley to do his job—for example, dress him.

At the center of the domestic issues addressed by the *BOHM* is the tension between the aspirations of the master and mistress of the house and the servants. Much of the *BOHM* is devoted to this relationship. The cookery section, for instance, is meant to be instructive to both the mistress and the cook. As Beetham notes, domestic service was "the biggest single occupation in the second half of the century."[42] "Beeton gave the cook an absolutely crucial place in the creation of a civilised and happy home, yet the cook was working class," suggesting that Beeton's focus on the relationship between the mistress and the servants, particularly the cook, is one that elucidates the tensions of nineteenth-century and early twentieth-century class dynamics.[43] Even a modest middle-class household only functioned well with servants since so many of the household tasks that are today done by an electronic device had to be done by hand, in often time-consuming and laborious ways.

One way to view the narrative structures of *Downton Abbey* is through this workplace relationship. Proper household management depended on servants such as the housekeeper seeing "herself as the immediate representative of her mistress, and bring[ing], to the management of the household, all those qualities of honesty, industry, and vigilance, in the same degree as if she were at the head of her *own* family."[44] The butler also was an essential component of any well-regulated country house. In her discussion of domestic servants, Beeton emphasizes the symbiotic relationship between the master and mistress and the servants, arguing,

> The sensible master and the kind mistress know, that if servants depend on them for their means of living, in their turn they are dependent on their servants for very many of the comforts of life; and that, with a proper amount of care in choosing servants, and treating them like reasonable beings, and making slight excuses for the shortcoming of human nature, they will save in some exceptional cases, be tolerably well served, and in most instances, surround themselves with attached domestics.[45]

Admittedly, the phrasing here is awkward as it suggests that domestic servants need to be trained. Yet this paragraph comes after a discussion of how masters and mistresses mistreat servants while still expecting perfect service, which Beeton argues is unrealistic. The master-servant relationship is a working one, and, as such, proper conduct must govern it. In *Downton Abbey*, this relationship is seen in how Lord Grantham keeps Bates on as his valet, despite the complaints of the other servants. It is also seen in how Carson and Mrs. Hughes interact with most of the family. There is a regard and respect in the interactions, and when Mrs. Hughes has the opportunity to marry, which means leaving the career she has established for herself, she ultimately chooses to stay at Downton, valuing the life of independence that domestic service has given her. Even the Dowager Countess takes enough interest in the servants to know that Mosley has returned to the village and that his father would be pleased to have him back.

The importance of the cook to proper household management is emphasized in episode five of season one when Mrs. Patmore begins to lose her eyesight. At the beginning of the episode, she argues with Lady Cora, refusing to change the dessert for a dinner party because the food had already been ordered based on the menu Lady Cora and Mrs. Patmore had agreed upon previously. When Daisy offers to read the recipe aloud, Mrs. Patmore snaps at her in desperation. Later in the episode, she cannot see the kitchen table well enough to put down a chicken from the oven. She drops the chicken, and Anna and Gwen have to rescue it from the stable cat, plate it, and give it to Thomas and William to take up. This small disaster leads to Mrs. Patmore dusting the raspberry meringue with salt instead of sugar. When Lady Cora discovers the mistake, she orders Carson to "bring fruit, bring cheese, bring anything to take this taste away."[46] While Matthew and Mary laugh over the mistake, Sybil and Lord Grantham worry about what punishment Mrs. Patmore might dish out to Daisy. Yet Cora and Lord Grantham do not reprimand or even consider firing Mrs. Patmore for the mistake. Rather, they uncover the issue and send Mrs. Patmore to a specialist in London for cataract surgery, keeping her position open for her until her return. Indeed, the Granthams might have many faults, but treating their servants poorly is not one of them.

By depicting the relationships between the servants and the family at Downton Abbey in this light—only Miss O'Brien and Thomas see it as adversarial—Fellowes builds into the series a means of exploring class issues in a more organic manner. In an interview about *Gosford Park*, Fellowes claims, "What I was trying to express was that in these great houses there were two different worlds all operating within feet of each other."[47] Fellowes's interest in the way class shapes culture and experience does not mean that he merely recreates Edwardian class positions without any critique. In a *Fresh Air* interview, Fellowes states, "From that [experience of seeing the downstairs world] grew a kind of interest, in a way, of the unfairness of class, the fact that it is so arbitrary in its selection . . . and yet it shapes a life and creates entitlement."[48] Fellowes, however, is not interested in using *Downton Abbey* to comment on contemporary culture in the way that critiques such as Gail Dines and Simon Schama assume that highbrow heritage film and serial productions must do. Instead, he uses the medium of heritage film to explore the various facets of early twentieth-century life. Fellowes reminisces,

> I was staying in a house and I got lost and I went through the wrong door, and I was standing at the top of the staircase that led down into the kitchens and everything. And there was a tremendous row going on between what sounded like four or five, six people shouting. . . . And I suddenly had such a powerful sense of the lives that were being lived by the people who worked there. Not, you know, only the family who lived there, but people who worked there were also, you know, enjoying life or hating each other or loving each other or whatever.[49]

It is this tension between the classes combined with Fellowes's focus on the fabric of every day that allows *Downton Abbey* to comment on the social changes of the early twentieth century without adopting a pedantic model.

Middlebrow Consumption: *Downton Abbey* as Too Many Sweets

Yet such a model is what television critics desire from the series. Despite *Downton Abbey*'s popularity, television critics and public historians like Schama take issue with the show on a variety of levels. Most of these critics pursue one of two arguments against the show.

They critique the show on the basis of historical accuracy, or they dismiss the series as being a soap opera, and, therefore, unworthy of the critical attention it has garnered. The title of John Heilpern's article on the series, "Escapist Kitsch Posing as 'Masterpiece Theatre,'" implies that PBS's *Masterpiece*'s typical programming is more elite or highbrow than *Downton Abbey*. In the article, he sneers that Americans "swoon over *Downton* as a *superior* soap opera—as any old *Masterpiece Theatre* import is invariably claimed to be a masterpiece."[50] In other words, Heilpern thinks even PBS has been duped by the show's literate packaging.

Indeed, there seems to be a whole genre of television criticism devoted to reminding audiences that *Downton Abbey* is a soap opera, that the British class system is not something to be nostalgic for, and that we "can do better than *Downton Abbey*" when it comes to television drama.[51] Martin Pengelly laments that the show is a "ludicrous melodrama" that cannot move beyond "flogging the hoary old country-house potboiler of upstairs, downstairs."[52] Gail Dines finds the series more insidious in its replication of Edwardian class dynamics. She complains,

> In record numbers, we tune in to watch the soap-opera lives of the idle rich and the overworked poor, no doubt identifying with the former rather than the latter.... The politics of the show are excruciating for anyone with a progressive bent. Each week the most pressing issue is whether the daughters of the family will find a suitable husband, or if the stately home will survive, given that it is being run by Lord Grantham, the moronic patriarch of the family who squandered his wife's fortune. Forget what was actually happening to real people in England at that time, what with mass poverty, the privations of war and rampant disease. What really matters is that a good maid is so hard to come by that the "ladies" of the house are forced to dress themselves for dinner.[53]

Schama, too, finds the historical inaccuracies of the show problematic, arguing that "history's meant to be a bummer, not a stroll down memory lane. Done right, it delivers the tonic of tragedy, not the bromide of romance."[54]

Dines and Schama both take issue with the historical accuracies of the show because they both want *Downton Abbey* to use its historical backdrop to address contemporary issues of economic and class disparities. Admittedly, Dines's and Schama's conflation is a simple one to make. After all, one of the studies written about the original *Upstairs, Downstairs*, another television drama investigating the tensions between an aristocratic family and their servants, intersperses the narrative of the show with a historical narrative of the late nineteenth and early twentieth century, situating actual history as a backdrop to the show's narrative.[55] Clearly, there is a tendency for scholars and critics to situate historical television dramas within a standard of historical accuracy these narratives are not striving for. Yet Dines's and Schama's remarks about *Downton Abbey*'s failures of historical accuracy are of a piece with a misconception about the role of heritage film and historical fiction in general.

The critics of *Downton Abbey* are also disturbed by the soap opera narrative at the core of the heritage packaging. Schama asserts that the American audience for *Downton Abbey* is so "desperate for something, anything, to take its mind off the perplexities of the present [that they seem] only too happy to down [the series] in great, grateful gulps."[56] In Schama's opinion, American viewers have been duped by the show's Masterpiece Classic marketing and by our own fascination with the "cultural necrophilia" of the British country house into believing that the sentimental pap *Downton* serves to us is an accurate reflection of early twentieth-century life.[57] Heritage production is the main fare of *Masterpiece Classic* and the BBC, which produces many of these shows. In the past decade, the BBC has produced adaptations of twentieth- and twenty-first-century novels set in the early part of the twentieth century, including Andrea Levy's *Small Island*, Sebastian Faulk's *Birdsong*, and Winifred Holtby's *South Riding*, to name a few. Nor is the BBC the only British television company to do this kind of middlebrow television production. Channel Four has adapted *Any Human Heart*, based on William Boyd's novel, as well as the *Red Riding* trilogy and *Boy A*. ITV, which produces *Downton Abbey*, has also produced *Brideshead Revisited* (1981), *Agatha Christie's Poirot*, and *Inspector Morse*, among other long-running adaptation staples.

All of these networks also produce the kind of middlebrow literate fare that is loosely associated with adaptations, including *Inspector*

Lewis (ITV), *Endeavour* (ITV), *Mr. Selfridge's* (ITV), *Call the Midwife* (BBC), and the two seasons of the rebooted *Upstairs, Downstairs*. American viewers have consumed most of these shows through the various Masterpiece series aired on PBS, divided into Masterpiece Classic, Masterpiece Mystery, and Masterpiece Contemporary in 2009, and Masterpiece's production arm has contributed funding to many of these series. Indeed, ITV Studios and Masterpiece for PBS have co-produced *Mr. Selfridge's* and *Endeavour* (an *Inspector Morse* spin-off chronicling Morse's early days as a detective constable in the 1960s). Carnival Films, a British production company now owned by NBC Universal, co-produces *Downton Abbey* with Masterpiece. Even *Sherlock* is co-produced by WGBH, a Boston-based PBS affiliate that also co-produces *Mr. Selfridge's*. Thus, Masterpiece is actively investing in middlebrow productions, television series and miniseries that draw on television serial conventions, including the soap opera.

In taking issue with the soap opera narrative employed by *Downton Abbey*, Schama also makes the classic comparison of such television fare to too much rich food.[58] American audiences are gulping down the show, ingesting it in large, uncontrolled quantities, Schama argues. William Thackerary makes the same argument in the first *Roundabout Paper* for the *Cornhill* in January 1860, when he avers, "Novels are sweets. All people with healthy literary appetites love them—almost all women;—a vast number of clever, hard-headed men."[59] He goes on to lament the affects of too many sweets or novels early on in life:

> But surely as the cadet drinks too much pale ale, it will dis-
> agree with him; and so surely, dear youth, will too much nov-
> els cloy on thee. . . . If you go into Gunter's, you don't see those
> charming young ladies (to whom I present my most respectful
> compliments) eating tarts and ices, but at the proper evening-tide
> they have good plain wholesome tea and bread-and-butter. . . .
> I make no doubt that the eminent parties above named all par-
> take of novels in moderations—eat jellies—but mainly nourish
> themselves upon wholesome roast and boiled.[60]

The proper diet would be more literate and nonfiction fare. Geraldine Jewsbury makes a similar argument in her review of Wilkie Collins's *The Moonstone* in 1868 when she claims, "When persons are in a state of ravenous hunger they are eager only for food, and utterly ignore all delicate distinctions of cookery; it is only when this savage state has been somewhat allayed that they are capable of discerning and appreciating the genius of the *chef*."[61] She goes on to explain that once readers have finished essentially binge reading the end of *The Moonstone*, they will appreciate Collins's skill in ending the mystery.

The criticisms of Jewsbury and Thackeray are echoed in television criticisms, except, for television critics, at stake is the notion of good or quality television. Such television, as Pengelly asserts, consists of shows like *The Sopranos* or *Mad Men*. American cable television networks produce all of these shows, which are aimed at a more highbrow audience. They also lend themselves to back-to-back viewing or binge watching, a habit Pengelly admits to even as he makes distinctions about what fare viewers should be watching in such a gluttonous fashion. *Downton Abbey* irritates because as middlebrow fare it appears to have all the hallmarks of the more elite cultural artifacts that Pengelly and others prefer.

As many serial and television scholars have asserted, however, such a conception of the serial readers and viewers as "simply a captive audience passively lured to a form suited to a society that 'perpetually defers desire in order to promote continued consumption'" overlooks the ways the audiences are active consumers of the pleasures offered by serial narratives.[62] Participatory or fan culture, enabled by the ubiquity of the World Wide Web in the first world, demonstrates how viewers of mass media artifacts like *Downton Abbey* interpret, predict, rewrite, and engage with these texts. As Jennifer Hayward explains, all serial narratives have "distinctive (and much derided) narrative tropes: sudden returns from the dead, doubles, long-lost relatives, marginal or grotesque characters, fatal illness, dramatic accidents, romantic triangles, grim secrets, dramatic character transformations."[63] As a carefully scripted, highly serialized television series, *Downton Abbey* uses all of these narrative tropes as it also deploys the highbrow trappings of heritage film, including a focus on the daily life of the early twentieth-century. In focusing on the inner workings of a country house with a new middle-class heir, *Downton Abbey* is able to explore the changes in class and gender roles that effected England in the early twentieth century in such a way as to illuminate

CONSUMING POPULAR CULTURE

how gradual many of these changes were. The sweeping revolution version of history championed by Schama and Dines fits neither the story-telling structures of serialized television nor the everyday focus of middlebrow domestic serials.

What these critics also miss is the way that this show uses late nineteenth-century and early twentieth-century food culture, particularly the discursive practices of middle-class cookery, as a way to relate the early twentieth-century to contemporary audiences. *Downton Abbey* may feature a country house run by a veritable army of servants and it may chronicle the problems of a wealthy family, but its use of nineteenth-century cookery situates the show within a discursive space focused not on replicating the mores and values of the Edwardian aristocracy, but on depicting the ways domestic management, particularly of dining, could effect social change in the time period of the narrative. The servants are not depicted as servile dupes of the class system, but as active participants in running the estate. In portraying the servants as employees working alongside the Granthams, Fellowes presents a more complicated view of class.

CHAPTER 9

Pie as Nostalgia

What One Food Symbolizes for Every Generation of Americans

RACHEL S. HAWLEY

"Maybe when he said 'your mother's pie' he didn't mean my *mother, he meant everyone's mother. The iconic all-American mother created by advertisers and politicians as a short-hand for family values and a longing for baked goods."*

—Warner Brothers, *Pushing Daisies*

Over the last decade, film and television screens have seen a resurgence of productions that are designed specifically to elicit nostalgia for the past. The last few years have brought us films that stimulate an older generation's childhood memories by revisiting the things they loved as children, including *Transformers, Star Trek, The Wizard of Oz,* and a new film version of the 1980s animated television series *Jem and the Holograms,* just to name a few. Though, strictly speaking, none of these films would fall under Fredric Jameson's definition of the "nostalgia film," by which he means films such as *American Graffiti* and *The Way We Were* that paint ideal pictures of unrealistic pasts, nevertheless these films all do market themselves to appeal to a generation's sense of nostalgia.[1]

In television, however, there are a few recent shows that fall in line with Jameson's definition, including the critically acclaimed *Mad*

Men (AMC), *The Americans* (TNT), and *Boardwalk Empire* (HBO). Alongside these very pointedly generationally aimed productions are the 2007 Sundance darling film *Waitress* and the critically acclaimed television series *Pushing Daisies* that, while not specifically aimed at a particular era or generation, nonetheless strive to elicit nostalgia for all generations in their style, plot, and, most particularly, their use of one object: pie. And while they take place in the present with all the technological, financial, and social availabilities in the present, the nostalgia factor influences the characters—and through them the audience.

This chapter will explore how pie is a nostalgic object, specifically as used in American culture, which elicits a general nostalgia for all generations of Americans. It will look at the use of pie in this way through several of America's cultural texts, but particularly how it is used in *Waitress* and *Pushing Daisies*. It will also look at how gender differences in the perception of nostalgia complicate the issue, made particularly poignant by pie's association with women.[2]

America and Pie

American as apple pie. Pie in the sky. A finger in every pie. Pie is so much a part of American culture that it has come to be thought of as a uniquely American thing, though it is not. Pie has been around for centuries in one form or another and can be found in many varieties in many nations. The British favor meat pies, especially a hand-held version that is popular at football matches. The French have tarts and quiche. The Greek have spanakopita. Indians have samosas. Americans have them all, though the strongest associations are with sweet over savory, with the exception of potpies. Even sweet pies come in different compositions from fruit-filled double-crust pies to meringue, custard, and even the uniquely American Boston Cream pie, which is really more of a cake. The common images associated with pie are small rural houses with white picket fences and pies cooling on the windowsill: images straight out of a Norman Rockwell painting. Individuals long for the days when they tugged at their mother's apron strings, watching her sweat over the perfect piecrust in the ultimate act of love for her family.

When my friend and I went to see *Waitress* in the theater, we began to fidget with cravings that seemed insatiable. We left the theater and went in search of good pie, and for months, every time we encountered a restaurant with pie on the menu we felt the need to order a piece and share it. They were all quite tasty, not a bad pie in the bunch, but there was always something missing in the experience. The *idea* of a good pie completely overshadowed the experience of it. Our situation was not unique, for seldom does that pie satisfy the longing for it. As M.F.K. Fisher writes in her essay "Apple Pie," published by *Esquire* magazine, "A lot of people have never really had the chance to eat a decent apple pie, but after a minute's sensual reflection will know positively what they would expect if they did. They can taste it on their mind's tongue: thin flaky pastry and hunks of sweet apples bathed in syrup; rich but sturdy dough filled with finely sliced tart apples seasoned with cinnamon."[3] There is something about the idea of home-baked pie that makes people yearn with longing for something ethereal and nameless that can never be recaptured because that moment is gone. Pie is an American object of nostalgia.

Defining Nostalgia

From the Greek *nostos* (return home) and *algia* (painful condition), the term nostalgia was first used to describe homesickness in Swiss mercenaries by psychologist Johannes Hofer in 1688. It has since taken on many different meanings, culminating in Jameson's definition of the nostalgic memory, which he defines as one that is misleadingly false in that it causes a person to idealize a time in his or her life where things *seemed* simpler.[4] Sociologist Fred Davis declares that time to be adolescence—the time between being a child and an adult, rife with all the turmoil such a transition makes in our lives. This simplistic idealization comes about by virtue of the fact that childhood was a time of relative ease when responsibilities were lighter and the world appeared to work the way it was supposed to—the only way the childhood self knows the world to work. In Davis's words, "nostalgia . . . retains the capacity to impart charm and goodness to what at the time may have been experienced as ordinary and uneventful."[5]

For Americans, then, the time period that pie brings to mind is the time of our youth. This idea is complicated by what Davis calls "collective nostalgia," which he explains as "what was new, different, and fashionable—or, better still, slightly outrageous and unconventional—during this cohort's adolescence . . . 'all other things being equal' emerge[s] as the symbolic objects of the next mass nostalgia wave."[6] Even though most people individually probably would reflect poorly on their adolescence as a miserable time, "at the level of culture—that is, a people's orienting beliefs and imagery concerning the nature of human experience—adolescence would probably retain its centrality as the main repository for nostalgic materials."[7] Pie can be seen as a source of nostalgia for all living generations for a time from as early as the 1940s to the 1980s.

Nostalgia and Food

Food is one of the most prominent elicitors of nostalgic sensations and is particularly unique in this regard both because of all of the senses that combine to create nostalgic emotions (smell, taste, touch, and even sound) and its presence as both an ethereal and concrete object. While food is present and can be eaten, digested, and cease to exist, it is also a tradition. Food is, of course, primarily associated with the domestic sphere and therefore with oppressive traditions toward women. The phrase "barefoot, pregnant, and in the kitchen" comes to mind. Family recipes are passed down from generation to generation, usually from mother to daughter, and are always present unless irrevocably lost to the world. Food is therefore both temporary and timeless. In her essay "Culinary Nostalgia," Anita Mannur argues that food is the major source of nostalgia for diasporic people, especially Indians. She explains,

> The desire to remember home by fondly recreating culinary memories cannot be understood merely as reflectively nostalgic gestures; rather such nostalgically-framed narratives must also be read as meta-critiques of what it means to route memory and nostalgic longing for homeland through one's relationship to seemingly intractable culinary practices which yoke national identity with culinary taste and practices.[8]

Mannur goes on to explain how Indian cookbooks that are circulated in America for the benefit of experiencing a more authentic Indian food gloss over class and regional differences to create an inauthentic nostalgia. As in most nations, in India every region and social class has its own unique palates and recipes that get labeled "Indian," and diasporic Indians ignore those conflicts or consider them less significant than the idea of sharing food from their homeland as a way of connecting to their collective past. Americans rely on food for their sense of identity as well. And there is one very important food that, as a nation, we cling to for our cultural identity.

Pie Transcends Race and Social Class

In America, there is no American cuisine *per se*. That is, while many associate cheeseburgers, pizza, and French fries as America's culinary contributions to the world, like pie, none of these foods originate in America. If America has a style of food, it is that of potpourri—many ethnic foods encompass the American palate. But there is only one food that people *claim* to be so American that other American things are measured by its likeness. In fact, pie is so American that it is an example of one food that transcends region, race, and class in its ability to create nostalgia. While it may elicit images of a white, middle-class, small suburban town, pie, in and of itself, transcends those boundaries. For instance, one of the earliest examples of the use of pie in performance is in American vaudeville and film as the product thrown in the face of the butt of a joke. This "low" humor has a class relegation of its own. "Pie in the sky" dreams are often associated with a lower-class desire to move up in the world. And pie-eating contests are often staples of farming communities and state fairs.

Meanwhile, Mark Twain, at the height of his career and wealth, loved pie so much that his housekeeper, Katy Leary, concerned when he refused to eat lunch, settled on an unusual method of enticing his appetite. She claims,

> I made arrangements with a bakery in the neighborhood to make a nice fresh huckleberry pie every forenoon, and bring it to the house. Then I'd get a quart of milk and put it on the ice, and

have it all ready—the huckleberry pie and the cold milk—about one o'clock.

He'd eat half the huckleberry pie, anyway, and drink all the milk. "Oh, that was delicious, Katy," he'd say, because he just loved huckleberry pie.[9]

Such a measure was the ultimate in decadence that only the truly wealthy could afford to indulge.

Pie as an object of both nostalgia and American national identity transcends race barriers with one very specific type of pie: sweet potato pie. Sweet potato pie is associated with African Americans in that it is considered one of the main staples of a southern "soul food" diet. As Tracy N. Poe explains in her essay "The Origins of Soul Food in Black Urban Identity: Chicago, 1915–1947," many African Americans who moved north during the Great Migration established cafes, grocery stores, butcher shops, and bakeries that reminded them of their southern roots. She writes, "Southern food . . . was a way of preserving something that reminded them of home and family when they moved into the unfamiliar urban environment. . . . Migration strengthened their desire to preserve their traditions."[10] She goes on to explain that these southern foods were actually created and prepared by African American slaves who were employed in the plantation kitchens and, therefore, also had a lot of similarities to African cuisine. She mentions the sweet potato, in particular, because of its resemblance to the African staple food, the yam.

Eugenia Collier, in her often anthologized story "Sweet Potato Pie," uses sweet potato pie as a symbol of the lost childhood of the African American narrator who has outgrown his roots, having moved on to a better life, but who still longs for the feeling of safety and home that the pie represents. In this story the narrator, Buddy, begins his narrative by reminiscing about his childhood in the bosom of his loving family, starting off on a very nostalgic note. In the present time of the story he is a professor visiting New York for a conference. He goes to visit his brother in Harlem, and though he has never lived there himself, he remarks, "Whenever I come to Harlem I feel somehow as if I were coming home—to some mythic ancestral home."[11] Clearly, his nostalgia relates to Harlem because it has become home to his family and, more importantly, his race. His sister-in-law, Bea, feeds him a dinner of "fish fried golden, ham hocks, and collard greens, corn bread" and, for dessert, "homemade sweet potato pie," all foods that he relishes as part of his homecoming, a cure for his homesickness.[12]

When the meal is over and Buddy announces that he needs to return to the hotel, Bea packs up the rest of the pie for him to take in a brown paper bag. When they arrive outside the hotel, he and Charley get into an argument because Charley refuses to let Buddy take the pie-filled brown paper bag into the big fancy hotel. He explains, "Folks in that hotel don't go through the lobby carrying no brown paper bags. That's *country*. And you can't neither. You somebody, Buddy. You got to be right."[13] The pie, then, and the bag that it comes in, is the representation of his poor past life that he has been revisiting for the evening. Buddy keeps insisting that he wants the pie and that he doesn't care for appearances but eventually gives in.

As he walks through the lobby he notices that Charley is right about the lack of paper bags and thinks, "To Charley a brown paper bag symbolizes the humble life he thought I had left."[14] For Buddy, however, the contents of that bag, the sweet potato pie, symbolized the past that he by no means wants to leave behind. And when he gets up to his room, he begins the reminiscence that opens the story. The pie is inextricably linked to positive emotions about a childhood filled with poverty and despair. But it is also a childhood filled with love and intimacy.

In a similar turn, African American president Barack Obama sees pie as a common ground upon which to talk to his supporters. In a campaign speech on the status of the economy in West Philadelphia on October 11, 2008, he told the story of when he stopped at a diner for some pie in Ohio and tried to order sweet potato pie. They didn't have any, so he ordered coconut cream, and the Ohio governor ordered lemon meringue. Then he and the governor posed for photos with the wait staff. Obama was telling a story in which he reached out to a state and its governor by reaching out to its working class, and he was telling that story to a mixed-race crowd who all cheered every time he said the word "pie" (fifteen times).

Of course, President Obama is well known for having been raised in a modest home, but he was raised primarily by his white grandmother, so while pie, for him, may be a source of nostalgia, his love of sweet potato pie comes from a very different source, Michelle Obama's family. He claims that he would like to have a sweet potato pie contest so he could "put it up against my mother-in-law's sweet potato pie."[15] He uses the different kinds of pies and the location, a rural Ohio diner, to unite his multi-racial crowd around a shared American tradition. Though Obama doesn't make any direct allusion to pie as it relates to his childhood, adolescence, or young adulthood, it clearly has a sentimental meaning for him and especially his audience, which is made up of people of all ages who seem to have very similar attachments. Therefore, it is an example of a truly collective nostalgic object.

Pie as Adolescent Angst

As discussed, Davis theorizes nostalgia, particularly the collective type, as being intrinsically linked to adolescence. Therefore, it is no surprise that pie plays a significant role in one of the greatest American coming-of-age novels. Mark Twain uses pie in three major ways in his novel *The Adventures of Huckleberry Finn*. The first is the most obvious. As mentioned earlier, Twain himself has a great love of pie, particularly huckleberry pie, for which he named his title character. He also expressed his great love for pie in his travelogue, *A Tramp Abroad*, where he complains quite a lot about the terrible food in Europe and, as soon as he gets a chance, explains that he has ordered a special meal, "a modest, private affair, all to myself."[16] For this meal he orders a long list of foods including "Apple pie. Apple fritters. Apple puffs, Southern style. Peach cobbler, Southern style. Peach pie. American mince pie. Pumpkin pie. Squash pie. All sorts of American pastry."[17]

He loved pie so much, in fact, that according to the *Oxford English Dictionary*, Twain actually coined its usage as a term meaning "something very pleasant or pleasurable to deal with; something to be eagerly appropriated; a prize, a treat" when he first used it in *The Adventures of Huckleberry Finn*.[18] The term "easy as pie" continued to be used in such a way through the first decade of the twentieth century, though its use has faded in recent years.

These first two usages, alone, are significant because of their appearance in a novel about a young boy's coming-of-age adventures. While Huckleberry Finn makes his first appearance in Twain's *The*

Adventures of Tom Sawyer, a book more associated with children's literature than his other works, it is significant that Huck gets his own adventures in a novel with much more adult themes: a nostalgic story in and of itself. That is, Twain is writing about his own adolescent era. And as Huck moves through adolescence and struggles to achieve manhood by freeing Jim, a family slave, and escaping with him to the North, he achieves a greater understanding of the world. This greater understanding of the world was something Twain himself experienced in young adulthood as he traveled and moved north, eventually marrying into a family of northern abolitionists.

The third use of pie in the novel is significant because the two boys, Huck and Tom, use pie ostensibly to help Jim escape from slavery and into freedom. One of the many elaborate plans that the boys conceive in order to free Jim involves baking a rope ladder made out of an old sheet into what they call "witch pie." This creation is part of a plan to free a man from his child-like condition of servitude as a slave and release him into the world as a free agent, a fully-grown man. And while the escape plan Huck and Tom conceive for Jim's freedom affords them a good deal of space for some last childish pranks of adolescence and looming entrance to the adult world, it unfortunately stunts Jim's free access to his own manhood, forcing him to comply in their coming-of-age games.

Pie, particularly a pie-eating contest, plays a significant role in another popular male bildungsroman, "The Body," written by Stephen King and best known by the film adaptation, *Stand by Me*. "The Body" is yet another work that is by definition nostalgic because it takes place in the decade of the author's adolescence; as the narrator tells us, "it happened in 1960, a long time ago . . . although sometimes it doesn't seem that long to me."[19] It is the story of four boys who are twelve, going on thirteen, whose adventure takes place on a long trek to see the dead body of a boy their age whose location they learn of when one of them overhears his older brother and his friends discussing it. The four younger boys then take off in search of the body and in the process experience their "fall from innocence," as King labels the story's theme.[20]

The narrator, Gordie, tells the story as a memory through his adult eyes, reflecting on his adolescence as a time where he first becomes a man. As they make their way to the body, the narrator begins to tell the other boys the story of a pie-eating contest during a small town's "Pioneer Days," which, based on the description, must be some sort of small town fair. The naming of the fair sets the stage for a community's collective nostalgia for the past.

On the last night of Pioneer Days there are three contests, "an egg-roll for the little kids and a sack-race for the kids that are like eight or nine, and then there's the pie-eating contest,"[21] which, based on its differentiation from the other two and the list of participants, is for adults. The story is about a boy named Dave Hogan who is apparently recently of age to participate in the contest, and everyone expects him to enter because "he's fat. He weighs like one-eighty and he's always getting beat up and ranked out. And all the kids, instead of calling him Davie, they call him Lard Ass Hogan."[22] Hogan, then, is still a "kid" like his peers, but is suddenly able to enter the "adult" contest at the fair, a moment that marks his growth from a boy into a man.

In Gordie's story, Hogan enters the pie-eating contest, as expected, not with the goal of winning the five dollar prize, but with the goal of getting revenge on all of the people of the town who have made his adolescence so unbearable. In preparation for the contest he drinks a bottle of castor oil. Then, on about his third pie he begins to "deliberately torture himself with grisly fantasies," imagining the pies as "cow-flops" or "greasy-grimey gopher guts."[23] These techniques combine to make him projectile vomit over the entire table of pies and into the second row of the audience. This moment sets off a chain of vomiting that overtakes the entire crowd, and he declares the contest a draw and returns home to his own bed. With this event, we are meant to believe that Hogan has finally stood up for himself; he has become a man, not by winning the adult contest, but by succeeding at his own agenda: getting revenge on the cruel town. That Gordie is telling this story on a trip to see a dead body and achieve his ultimate loss of innocence points to the adolescent angst he feels. And the adult narrator's use of the story within the story compounds his sense of nostalgia for that time.

The way in which the adult Gordon presents the internal story is striking as well. Young Gordie starts to tell the story the way he told it on their adventure, full of interruptions from the other boys. But as the story starts to take shape, the fitful narrative is replaced

CONSUMING POPULAR CULTURE

by the streamlined text the adult Gordon published. It is introduced with these words: "From *The Revenge of Lard Ass Hogan*, by Gordon Lachance. Originally published in *Cavalier* magazine, March, 1975. Used by permission."[24] This juxtaposition shows the story as a pivotal point in Gordie's life in that he is composing a story as a child that would mark the profession of his adult life. As the revenge is complete, Gordon reverts back to young Gordie's telling of the story to his friends. All told, the scene shows the fluidity with which past and present can move and interact in the mind, all revolving around the great nostalgic item that is pie.

Pie in *Waitress* and *Pushing Daisies*

The film *Waitress* also shows a moment of nostalgia for adolescence, though most of the nostalgia of the plot revolves around a longing for childhood. The film is about three women who work in a diner, probably for minimum wage plus tips. They are working-class women whose manners occasionally border on the vulgar and who have simple dreams and, especially in the case of the lead character, are very unhappy. Jenna (Keri Russell) is a woman trapped in an abusive marriage and menial job whose only outlet for pleasure is in the creation of pies. Her friends and fellow waitresses Becky (Cheryl Hines) and Dawn (Adrienne Shelly) are so jealous of her talent for making pies that they profess to her that though they would not want to be her for anything in the world, they wish they could make a pie like she can. The owner of the diner she works in, Old Joe (Andy Griffith), even declares her the best pie maker in the world. Through the course of the film she embarks on a romance with the new doctor in town, Dr. Pomatter (Nathan Fillion), and her navigation of life, through pie, is expressed in this relationship.

She determines to use this one talent to her advantage by saving up, hording away money from her husband, so that she can enter a pie-baking contest and win the money she needs to escape her abusive marriage. Her unplanned pregnancy, however, puts a crimp in her plans, and she dreads the birth of the child she can only see as the chains that will bind her forever to her husband, Earl (Jeremy Sisto), and her unsatisfying present life. In a dangerous act of rebellion she embarks on an extra-marital affair with her new, married obstetrician, Dr. Pomatter.

When they first meet, Jenna, who is expecting to see her regular obstetrician, brings a special pie that she created when she was a child and was a favorite of her regular doctor. She ends up giving the pie to Dr. Pomatter, reluctantly, and when they meet later he expresses just how impressed he was with her creation.

> **Dr. P:** Did you make that marshmallow pie that you brought me?
>
> **Jenna:** Yes, I did. Marshmallow Mermaid Pie. I invented it when I was nine years old, in my mermaid phase.
>
> **Dr. P:** That was probably the best pie I've ever tasted in my life. That pie was . . . was biblically good, that's how good that pie was. That pie could win pie contests and ribbons and things.[25]

He goes on to tell her about a pie diner he frequented as a kid and the waitress he was madly in love with. He reflects, "When I saw you sitting here, alone, in your uniform, I had a flashback. You made me think of her. You kind of remind me of her."[26] The pie, a creation from her childhood, and its creator elicit nostalgia in Dr. Pomatter for an adolescent crush. It is also with this discussion of pie that their flirtation begins and Jenna embarks on a new phase in her life of guilty pleasure and "naughty pie."

Though Jenna uses pie to express a variety of emotions and names them accordingly ("Bad Baby Pie," "I Hate My Husband Pie," and "Falling in Love Chocolate Mousse Pie"), as the story unfolds it reveals that her expertise in pie baking comes from her mother. She treasures the times she spent as a kid at her mother's feet in the kitchen, enjoying the love her mother baked up for her family in the form of pies. In fact, when asked what pie she plans to make for the pie-baking contest she explains, "I was thinkin' I would make one of my real unusual ones like my mom used to make. One where you wouldn't think the ingredients would go together, but they do."[27] The most powerful emotion, then, behind her pie baking is nostalgia for her mother.

In the pivotal scene of the film, Dr. Pomatter shows up at Jenna's house and asks her to teach him how to make a pie. As she does so, she explains about her mother's pie baking and sings him the song her mother used to sing to her—a lullaby about baking a pie for a child so she won't be sad. The refrain, "Gonna make a pie with a heart in the middle," tightly intertwines pie with the figurative heart that represents a strong bond of love. The pie made by a mother is "filled with strawberry love," a heart, and allows the mother to pass on her love to her daughter eternally.[28] The love is literally baked into the pie and consumed by the pie eater. Later, when the unwanted child is born, Jenna instantly falls in love with her and begins to plan her future for her daughter, kicking her husband out of her life and ending her affair with Dr. Pomatter. In celebration of her happy day, Old Joe gives Jenna a check big enough for her to open up her own pie shop and names it after her daughter, Lulu. Therefore, the entrance of the next generation is the catalyst for starting her new, happier life, which she constructs according to the model of her childhood. The final images of the film are of mother and daughter, reenacting the past, baking pie together and singing the song above and creating memories for Lulu that will become a source of her later nostalgia for a mother's love.

The plot of *Pushing Daisies* has its nostalgic appeal as well. In the pilot episode, "Pie-Lette," the opening exposition explains that Ned (Lee Pace) has the ability to touch dead things and bring them back to life, but once he touches them a second time they die again irrevocably. If he doesn't touch them the second time within one minute, someone else near him will die. He discovers this gift when he's nine and in love with his neighbor Charlotte 'Chuck' Charles. One day his mother dies and he brings her back to life and only learns about the time limit on his gift when Chuck's father dies one minute later. That same night he learns about the second-touch rule, as his mother kisses him goodnight. "First touch life. Second touch dead forever."[29] In the same episode, though in the present day, he uses this power to bring the adult Chuck (Anna Friel) back to life, permanently, after she is murdered on a cruise.

In both the pilot and a later episode, "Smell of Success," the audience finds out that Ned grew up at a boarding school where his father abandoned him. He became obsessed with pies and started secretly baking them in the middle of the night and curling up in bed with his creations at nine years of age. This obsession no doubt arises from the fact that the first time his mother died, she was baking pie. He uses his gift for bringing things back to life to bring old, rotten fruit back to its fullest freshness to bake into his pies. Pie, then, is used as a way of connecting him and his gift to his mother, whom he couldn't permanently save the way he eventually saves Chuck. In "Dim Sum Lose Some" it is revealed that his parents actually met over pie, which introduces the idea of pie as romantic love. Pie is not just a symbol of the love a parent and child share, but can equally bring about the love between two adults, as we also saw in *Waitress* in the relationship of Jenna and Dr. Pomatter.

Chuck is also the recipient of Ned's "living touch," though her Aunts Vivian (Ellen Greene) and Lily (Swoosie Kurtz) still believe her to be dead. They are inconsolably depressed and never leave their home. In order to help them along, then, Chuck starts sending them anonymous pies laced with homeopathic mood enhancers to help them get over their grief. The anti-depressants work so well that the aunts actually revert back to their youthful attitudes. They begin gradually by bringing laughter and singing back into their home and taking on new projects. Eventually, with the encouragement of Chuck's friend Olive (Kristen Chenowith), they return to their earlier love and career as synchronized swimmers, The Darling Mermaids, and take to the pool again and enjoy the happiness they experienced before the tragic death of their niece. Pie, here, is used as a vehicle for the anti-depressants that restore the aunts' youth, their niece's precious act of love.

The nostalgic element of the show is enhanced even more by the fact that every episode begins with a flashback to Ned's childhood. In fact, Ned spends a lot of time mulling over his past and reconciling it with his present.

Nostalgic Art

In both *Waitress* and *Pushing Daisies* pie is presented as a nostalgic element for the characters, and through them their audience, and the cinematic style and setting of each are designed to create a sense of nostalgia in their respective audiences, as well. As Svetlana Boym points out, "the past is not supposed to reveal any signs of decay; it has to be freshly painted in its 'original image' and remain eternally young."[30] While she is referring particularly to our memories of the past, the same could be said of nostalgic art or, in this case, the artistry of the film or television show. By this term I mean art that is designed to represent and romanticize an earlier time period for all of the nostalgic reasons discussed so far in this chapter. While such art attempts to capture the sentiments of the previous time period, such attempts are based on what the artist can only imagine the past to have looked like.

The nostalgic image, on the one hand, tries to recapture the popular aesthetic of culturally produced texts of the era that it is trying to interpret, but through its interpretation it also creates an unreal nostalgic aesthetic text of its current era, which involves itself into a never-ending cyclical loop of production and representation. Paul Grainge discusses the nostalgic mode, as opposed to the nostalgic mood that is created by the object, which is explored in Jameson's theory of the "nostalgia film." Grainge further explains, "The nostalgia mode does not find utopian meaning in the past, but indiscriminately plunders it for style, refracting the past through fashion and glossy images of 'pastness.'"[31] Moreover, since the sky didn't look any bluer in the 1950s or duller in the 1970s than it does now, as viewing the films of those eras might suggest, the artistic renderings of nostalgic images obviously don't offer real depictions of the time period but a view tinted by memory and the cultural productions of that time period.

It only seems natural, then, that the grounding of the aesthetic in a past era can be removed from the formula, leaving only the nostalgic aesthetic and a representation of the present through a nostalgic lens. In other words, a text can be set in the present, complete with modern dress, props, and automobiles, but still elicit the *feeling* of nostalgia for a hypothetical "simpler, better time." Both *Waitress* and *Pushing Daisies* achieve this level of nostalgia, in different but complementary ways, and predominantly by using images of pie.

In both the film and the series, the pie diner and shop are stylized in such a way as to elicit nostalgia. In *Waitress*, the diner is very old-fashioned with tan booths and a rustic dining counter. The outside is an old-fashioned roadside diner with a large piece of pie on the oversized sign declaring, "Joe's Pie Diner." The waitresses wear light blue uniforms in the style of the mid-1970s television series *Alice*. Meanwhile The Pie Hole of *Pushing Daisies* has a similar, though brighter, interior décor. The floors and tablecloths are checkered and the dining counter is in the style of Edward Hopper's 1942 *Nighthawks*. The outside of the diner is shaped like a pie and inserted into the first-floor corner of a big city office building, the contrast of which makes the pie-shaped diner look even more rustic next to the looming symbol of modern architecture. Both films use a wide-angle lens, especially from the top, frequently, and most often to focus in on the pies themselves. *Pushing* is full of bright, energetic colors that seem so extreme they give the show a Technicolor feel. Whereas, in contrast, the colors of *Waitress* are so muted and the lighting so dull that they create a look reminiscent of the grainy films of the 1970s. Though these styles are vastly different from each other, they are equally different from the non-nostalgic film, which either attempts to portray life in its truest, unexaggerated light or strives to emphasize the psychological, usually by incorporating a very dark and disturbing tone.

The Gender of Pie

The idea of nostalgia in itself is problematic from a feminist perspective, given a history of misogynistic patriarchy. The idea of pie as a nostalgic object, then, is complicated by its relationship to women and, specifically, mothers. In his monograph, Davis cites a study performed in 1959 that shows that men experience nostalgia more often than women, and he attributes that to the fact that, at that time, men had had more changes in their lifetime to be nostalgic about, whereas women had lived their lives in the same sphere (the home/domestic space) and therefore had less to regret. He ignores, of course, the fact that nostalgia for the past elicits a strong desire to *return* to that past, something many such men would desire because it involves returning to a time when their careers were not threatened by women entering the workforce and when the responsibilities of the domestic could be left to their wives. Jonathan Steinwand explains, "Girls and boys of any nation are taught about gender identities by having their attention directed to selected masculine and feminine role models. Such models are produced, selected, and publicized by enthusiasts, emulated out of nostalgia, and usually oriented toward a future by some underlying political motive."[32] Women, therefore, are hardly likely to be nostalgic for a past that reflects their decrease in agency and their lack of available choices, landing most of them squarely in the realm of "motherhood."

In fact, Janice Doane and Devon Hodges, in their book *Nostalgia and Sexual Difference,* define nostalgia a bit differently than the male authors' definitions offered above. They claim nostalgia "is a retreat to the past in the face of what a number of writers—most of them male—perceive to be the degeneracy of American culture brought about by the rise of feminist authority."[33] This is a vastly different definition of nostalgia because while it does not remove the sense of "bittersweet" pleasure in the feeling of nostalgia, it locates that feeling in men as a longing to return to the patriarchal power structure that gave them security and freedom from guilt or obligation. Ellen G. Friedman goes so far as to suggest that women's ideals lie in the future. In her essay on modernism, postmodernism, and the canon, she writes that, whereas men write about their longing for the past and with "the profoundly nostalgic conviction that the past has explanatory or redemptive powers," the same does not hold true for the canonical works of women.[34] Friedman explains, "Women's works of modernity . . . show little nostalgia for the old paternal order, little regret for the no longer presentable. . . . Although all the texts of modernity express a yearning for the unpresentable, female texts often evoke this unpresentable as the not yet presented."[35]

In effect, all of these explanations of the cause of male nostalgia are true and even work together. Whereas men long for the days before their lives were disrupted by major changes, one of the biggest societal changes that has affected the male gender has been feminism, a movement that released women from the role of housewife and mother and asked men to take on more domestic responsibility. Therefore, even if each man, individually, has more to be nostalgic for, men as a group have a common cause for a "collective nostalgia" for a "simpler" time when society was unequally divided and everyone had his or her appropriate place in it.

This complication is no less true today than when Davis wrote about it, as is clear by the nostalgic series mentioned earlier: *Mad Men, The Americans,* and *Boardwalk Empire.* Each takes place in an era when women had less agency, and each highlights the gender differences of the time period as "realistically" as possible. While all may create characters that are critical of their own time period, the nostalgic tone of the shows invites people to interpret the various injustices as somehow innocent and unintentional. In the pilot of *Mad Men*, for example, when Pete (Vincent Kartheiser) sexually harasses Don's new secretary, Peggy (Elizabeth Moss), Don (Jon Hamm) lectures him on the evils of damaging a woman's reputation on her first day.[36] This exchange initially suggests Don as an enlightened man of his time and a friend to feminism. Then, later that same day, he walks out of a meeting with a female client because he refuses to answer to a woman who doesn't know her place. Meanwhile, in the very last scene of the episode, Pete shows up at Peggy's door after his bachelor party with the boys, and she invites him in, thus proving herself deserving of the reputation he earlier implied with his sexual overtures to her at work. It is with scenes like this in mind that we must acknowledge that nostalgia is still a highly conservative emotion that does not mesh well with feminism.

If the major memory that pie elicits is that of mothers baking pies for their children, then pie is strongly linked to the image of domestic motherhood. In *Waitress* pie is even more intrinsically linked to the domestic role of the female in several ways. Pie is used in courtship, not just for Jenna and Dr. Pomatter, but also for Dawn, who asks Jenna to make her a special pie to take on a first date. Jenna's husband, Earl, also alludes to this domestic ideal when he asks her to quit her job because he wants her making pie only for him. And although Jenna is the inventor of the pies served at Joe's Pie Diner, "27 varieties and a new one I invent every day," she is neither the owner nor the manager, but hired labor.[37] As the film title informs us, she is a waitress and nothing more.

Of course, Jenna is not happy in her current state. She has by no means reached a place of domestic felicity. In fact, it seems contrary to feminist ideals that the act of her becoming a mother would be the moment when she finally gets her life in order. But she does so by taking back her power in several ways. She tells Dr. Pomatter shortly before she comes to term, "I don't want to be rescued."[38] By the end of the film, she rescues herself. She decides to leave her abusive husband the second she holds her baby for the first time. She then breaks off her relationship with a married man because she can see that his wife really loves him, an act that expresses her solidarity with her sex. Ultimately, she takes Old Joe's gift and opens her own pie diner, where she is owner, pie baker, and boss. Writer, director, and co-star Adrienne Shelly called the film "a love letter to my daughter."[39] Considering the lengths that Jenna goes to because of the birth of her own daughter, that love letter would seem to be a lesson in the evils of letting the world define you and encouragement to be the agent of your own happiness.

This newfound independence, unfortunately, doesn't come from her talent as a pie baker in a pie-baking contest or her extreme drive to work hard and earn her way in the world. She owes her ability to make good for her daughter and escape her abusive husband to a man, Old Joe. The fact that he is an *old* man, of a bygone era, and played by Andy Griffith, who could be said to be a nostalgic icon of a conservative era in his own right, complicates the celebratory nature of this analysis thus far. It is one of the few things about the film that is problematic, but it also seems to be the exception that proves the rule. That is, though this essay is an attempt to show how nostalgia can be used as a feminist tool, that Shelly felt it necessary to have Old Joe rescue Jenna makes it clear that the film hasn't introduced a feminist nostalgia just yet. But it is certainly a step forward.

Meanwhile, *Pushing Daisies* presents a male pie baker who, while also influenced by his mother in his love for pie, is already, at the outset, owner of his own business. However, pie's association with the domestic still holds. In the episode "Frescorts," Emerson's mother comes to visit and suspects him of having a girlfriend.[40] When he denies this, she says, "Well somebody's been feeding you. What's her name?" "Pie maker," he responds, sarcastically, putting an end to her hopes. To his mother, pie is still a domestic product utilized for court-ship. But Emerson dispels that myth and offers a new interpretation— the independent man who can buy his pie for himself, instead of rely-ing on a woman to make it for him. In fact, the whole premise of the series calls into question the idea of domestic felicity in that the lovers can't touch because, if they did, Chuck would die again.

The central ingredient of pie, however, doesn't change, and that is love. Through most associations with pie, love consistently serves as an ingredient and product of this national icon. Katy Leary is concerned for her master's health, so she feeds Mark Twain pies. Adrienne Shelly wrote *Waitress* as a love letter to her daughter. In *Pushing Daisies*, Chuck raises the bees that make the honey that she bakes into her piecrusts with great love. And even the complicated *deus ex machina* move of Old Joe's generous gift to Jenna comes from a genuine feeling of love for her and her baby. Therefore, it is clear that the sense of nostalgia elicited by pie is directly related to a sense of comfort for love that we, as a society, long for and associate with our youth and, in most cases, particularly with an idealized maternal love.

Conclusion

My mother has never liked pie. At every holiday I can recall, my grandmother or one of my aunts would dish up generous helpings of delicious fruit, pumpkin, or chocolate pie, and my mother would abstain, though she never missed an opportunity to seize someone's unwanted (and oftentimes wanted) crust. In preparing for this chapter, I asked her if pie ever inspired more than distaste in her mind, and she confessed that it did hold some charms for her. While she never felt even a passing desire to eat a proffered piece of pie, she always enjoyed the look and smell of it because it reminded her of her childhood. Like Jenna and many other Americans, she associates pie with her mother's relentless slaving over the perfect homemade piecrust. It was such a laborious act that it was only taken up on very special occasions. And while my grandmother never liked to discuss her cooking techniques with anyone, something that has been an endless source of frustration for myself as the self-appointed heir to her culinary talents, when making pies, she always made an exception, explaining her process in the minutest of details in a picture-perfect moment with her daughters. "It was such a labor of love," my mother exclaimed, "that even though I didn't like pie, I always ate it because it was so rare and so special."

CHAPTER 10

The Last Twinkie in the Universe

Culinary Hedonism and Nostalgia in Zombie Films

CAMMIE M. SUBLETTE

Seize the moment. Think of all those women on the Titanic *who waved off the dessert cart.*

> —ERMA BOMBECK, "Seize the Moment—June 25, 1991"

It seems to me that our three basic needs, for food and security and love, are so mixed and mingled and entwined that we cannot straightly think of one without the others.

> —M.F.K. FISHER, *The Art of Eating*

But if you're gonna dine with them cannibals, sooner or later, darling, you're gonna get eaten.

> —NICK CAVE, "Cannibal's Hymn"

Zombie films are first and foremost about consumption, and not just the consumption of brains. As Michael Newbury notes, "no genre is more routinely, even structurally, and disturbingly obsessed with food supply, food chains, and the question of who eats what or whom than the apocalyptic zombie movie."[1] In the imagined filmscapes of zombie apocalypse, humans often struggle for basic subsistence. Food competition, scarcity, and uncertainty force survivors to reimagine food sources, often with the terrible and ironic twist that, like the zombies they flee, some human survivors end up subsisting on the flesh of other humans. However, beyond the horizon of subsistence is the fantasy or ideal meal, the one talked about, sought after, debated, and, occasionally, consumed. This perfect meal varies from survivor to survivor, film to film, but certain themes reiterate in zombie-film culinary fantasy. Generally, this meal is about culinary pleasure, not survival. Further, this fantasy meal hinges on the consumption of whatever is most glaringly absent in the new culinary experience of subsistence. If processed foods abound in the apocalyptic landscape, the sought-after meal is often a meal of organic produce and farm-fresh eggs and milk. Alternatively, if one or more processed foods become scarce, those foods—such as the Twinkies in *Zombieland*—become the Holy Grail. Most importantly, the pleasure derived from this ideal meal is almost always saturated in cultural longing and marinated in memory, exhibiting deep nostalgia for a pre-apocalyptic past.

That zombie films act as extended critical metaphors of capitalist consumption gone awry has been effectively argued by a number of scholars. In her 2006 book, *Pretend We're Dead: Capitalist Monsters in American Pop Culture*, Annalee Newitz writes,

> One type of story that has haunted America since the late nineteenth century focuses on humans turned into monsters by capitalism. Mutated by backbreaking labor, driven insane by corporate conformity, or gorged on too many products of a money-hungry media industry, capitalism's monsters cannot tell the difference between commodities and people.[2]

The rest of the story, in the zombie film at least, is that because these monsters cannot tell the difference between commodities and people, they consume the people. As Newbury frames the issue, "the zombie is a reshaping of the individual subject by forces larger than the self into something purely, brutally, and rapidly consuming."[3] And while some zombie films are rather subtle in this consumer-gone-feral symbolism, critic Philip Horne recalls that in George A. Romero's 1978 *Dawn of the Dead*, the metaphor of capitalist consumption is literalized, as our survivors are holed up in a shopping mall, and zombies chomp at the doors of consumerism.[4] Kyle Bishop likewise effectively argues that Romero's *Dawn of the Dead* was the first zombie film to focus directly on the metaphor of consumption, staging the zombie apocalypse in the heart of middle-class material excess and allowing the survivors to enact various capitalist fantasies of unbridled consumption.[5] Bishop writes of *Dawn*'s extended metaphor of capitalism, "The metaphor is simple: Americans in the 1970s have become a kind of zombie already, slaves to the master of consumerism, and mindlessly migrating to the malls for the almost instinctual consumption of goods."[6] Gareth Schott notes that a number of film critics were quick to perceive Romero's "scathing commentary on American consumer culture."[7]

Critics aside, a good many viewers of the film apparently were caught up in the utopian fantasy of free-for-all consumption afforded by the film, for as Romero reported, "'I've seen audiences get off on the idea of having possession of the mall. That's a dangerous fantasy.'"[8] The danger resides in the mall's ability to transform a happy retreat into an isolating prison. What first seems a utopian dream of safety and comfort ultimately turns into a wasteland of materials, affording survivors absolute lethargy and purposelessness in the zombie apocalypse. Bishop explains what (besides the zombies) has gone wrong for these survivors:

> Romero's zombies are not merely a metaphor; they are the catalyst that reveals the true problem infecting humanity: pervasive consumerism. The surviving humans are inescapably consumers, and because the mall provides them with all the supplies they could want, they no longer have the need (or, perhaps more importantly, the ability) to produce goods themselves. Thus in the new social paradigm of *Dawn*, surviving humans lose what Marx calls their identity as "species beings" and are reduced to the level of "life-activity" alone; any labor they do expend is for sheer survival. . . . [B]y losing their productive labor, the feckless individuals living in Romero's mall ultimately lose that which makes them essentially "human," and they regress to a more primitive, animal state.[9]

In Bishop's view, then, the danger of the fantasy is found in its dedication to consumption devoid of labor, dreams, satiated desire, artistic creation, or philosophical contemplation. The consumers lose all other pursuits and become mindless consumers or, as Bishop puts them, "idle proletarians," workers without work or even the promise of progressive purpose on the horizon.

Although critics have firmly established a connection between capitalist consumption and the zombie film, few have focused on food consumption within these films, an oversight that I find unfortunate. Food, the assumption seems to be, is just an aspect of survival. As such, food is significantly different from other capitalist consumptions—unless it reeks of excess or extravagance. But as Mary Douglas and Baron Isherwood argued in 1979, "'Goods that minister to physical needs—food or drink—are no less carriers of meaning than ballet or poetry. Let us put an end to the widespread and misleading distinction between goods that sustain life and others that service the mind and heart—spiritual goods.'"[10] Although there seems to be the need for a third category here—the purely material, the goods that nourish neither the body nor the soul but simply act as hyper-temporary symbols of successful and conspicuous capitalist consumption—Douglas and Isherwood nevertheless remind us that to ignore the symbolic import of edible goods is to ignore much of the reason we consume them in the first place. Food studies scholar Warren Belasco writes, "Food indicates who we are, where we came from, and what we want to be."[11] A study of the food consumed in zombie films, therefore, potentially tells us more about both the characters' and viewers' collective traumas and longings and the cultural moment than does any other aspect of these films.

The one critic who has focused on the human food consumed in zombie films, Newbury, finds the portrayal of food supplies wanting and the lack of efforts to establish sustainable food sources abysmal. He writes, "The contemporary zombie movie extinguishes with brutal enthusiasm all aspirations to retrieving the pastoral, the natural, or alternatives to the industrial food chain."[12] Thus, as he notes, many post-1990 zombie films are littered with references to corporate junk food, with Coke, Pepsi, McDonald's, and Starbucks (or a generic stand-in clearly invoking these corporations and their products) often featured prominently. Indeed, Newbury argues,

Seen as one part of the discussion about the cataclysmic problems of the industrial food chain, the fast and rabid zombies of very recent years embody quite literally the unrestrained, manic, hyperaccelerated, and mindless appetite of the contemporary food consumer: an eater, according to apocalyptic journalists, produced by food marketing, fast-food chains, manufacturers of junk food, and corporate slaughterhouses.[13]

Newbury's point here is a good one—our contemporary corporate foodscape spirals out of control in its imbalanced and mindless push to force food and food substitutes on the affluent, even as the impoverished struggle for subsistence. Newbury sees the zombie film as an apt metaphorical vehicle for our out-of-control food chain. Further, as more than one of those apocalyptic journalists and food writers whom he mentions would report, given our global expansion, lack of sustainable foods, and increased dependence on processed and corporate foods, zombies are the least likely cause of our global demise.[14] Thus, zombies most certainly function on some level as symbolic representations of the many real disasters looming on the horizon.

What Newbury's argument does not address, however, is the way that food choices in zombie films speak to something other than a food apocalypse. Although he notes that these films often feature survivors enjoying candlelight dinners and the occasional exotic foods antithetical to corporate junk, Newbury does not linger over what these scenes may tell us about why these characters are driven to these food choices and rituals, save that "alternatives to the industrial food chain . . . are persistently imagined as a means of temporary release or escape from the apocalyptic present in recent zombie movies."[15] Thus, he reads these moments of food enjoyment and ritual as escapism, and I agree. But *why* these foods serve as vehicles for psychological escape from the zombie apocalypse is something that deserves significantly more investigation, for an understanding of food and cultural trauma, regardless of what kind of danger lurks on the other side of the dining room, provides important keys to reading our contemporary food choices, whether guided by psychological desires, physical needs, or material limitations.

The overwhelming abundance of corporate junk food in many zombie films, as Newbury notes, points to the reality of our contemporary foodscape: loaded with processed chemicals and preservatives, the foods most likely to endure in an apocalyptic scenario do not even qualify as food in locavore food journalist Michael Pollan's view.[16] Over and over again, survivors in zombie films subsist on junk food, and often this is simply representative of the new reality: junk food has a long shelf life and seems ubiquitous, and survivors in the zombie apocalypse have much humbler expectations for their own longevity than they did before the apocalypse and thus tend not to ponder the long-term health implications of subsisting exclusively on Twinkies and Pepsi. However, availability and nutrition aside, sometimes this junk-food subsistence is about more than eating to live. Sometimes, the consumption of junk food is also about hedonistic pleasure and nostalgia.

In the case of consuming junk food for subsistence because no other food is available, Danny Boyle's 28 Days Later (2002) may provide the best example.[17] Newbury details the much-discussed opening of the film, wherein Jim (Cillian Murphy) awakens from a coma in a deserted hospital, detaches himself from an IV, presumably what has been sustaining him during the month-long zombie outbreak, and goes in search of nourishment and other people.[18] For Newbury, the significance of this scene is that it unfolds in a landscape littered with corporate junk food: sodas, chocolate bars, and chips are scattered about, and Jim enacts the increasingly obligatory moment of zombie-apocalypse Pepsi (or Coke) consumption.[19] However, what Newbury mentions but then overlooks is that after draining a can of Pepsi, Jim hardly pays attention to the food surrounding him. Newbury writes, "Jim combs London looking for food while stumbling over brightly colored bags of it," but the truth is that Jim is looking only for other people. He continuously yells "Hello?" in his search for survivors among the wreckage. Thus, he ignores the bodega, loaded with food, albeit no doubt of the processed variety, in favor of a church, where he hopes to find other people seeking sanctuary. He seems remarkably unconcerned with food, despite his emaciated frame and apparent lack of sustenance.

Until later in the film, soda and chocolate bars will provide the only food for Jim's subsistence. Initially, he takes no pleasure in the consumption of the available junk food, even suffering from a terrible headache, which, as Newbury remarks, Jim's survivalist companion,

Selena (Naomie Harris), declares is caused by consuming too much sugar.[20] Food psychologist Elizabeth D. Capaldi offers a scientific explanation for why Jim may be less than keen on the available junk foods; researchers have found that sweet foods fail to attract starving mice as much as other, more protein-rich and fatty foods. Capaldi writes, "Apparently there is something aversive or unpleasant about sweetness when food deprivation is high."[21] Perhaps a better explanation for Jim's headache and food avoidance, though, is that he has just awakened from one trauma, a month-long coma, into an arguably worse trauma—his discovery that London has been decimated by some unknown cause.

For Newbury, the implication in Boyle's film is that corporate junk food may act as temporary nourishment in the worst of situations, but it is hardly the rich and sustainable foodscape needed for continued longevity of the species. Newbury claims, "In [recent zombie films,] models of Western modernity necessarily become scavengers, hunters, and gatherers, locavores on the landscape of a devastated consumerism emblematized crucially by the flotsam and jetsam of corporate junk and fast food."[22] However, in *28 Days Later*, as in most zombie films, the pursuit of idealized meals is driven by nostalgia, not by an imagined slow-food alternative. Indeed, in a scene not described by Newbury, Jim and three other survivors go on a supermarket "shopping" spree, delighting in the acquisition of many canned, processed, and sugary junk foods as well as the only produce still edible, irradiated apples. The only comestibles given any deep consideration in terms of top-shelf quality are the bottles of sixteen-year-old single-malt liquor selected by one of the survivors. The group later consumes their food outdoors, in what can only be described as a quaintly pastoral space, one complete with wild horses playfully galloping across a field. In this case, the people with whom they consume the food and the setting in which they consume the food trump the actual food; and, importantly, as soon as they have shared their feast, the survivors grow nostalgic, reflecting on the past and all that they have lost.

Simon Pegg and Edgar Wright's *Shaun of the Dead* (2004) takes a different approach to the role and meaning of junk food in the zombie apocalypse.[23] This film is, after all, part 1 of Pegg and Wright's playfully dark "Blood and Ice Cream Trilogy."[24] Before the zombie apocalypse, Shaun (Simon Pegg) and his best friend, Ed (Nick Frost), drink beer and soda and consume junk food exclusively; their hedonism is propped up with sugar and other carbohydrates. As Newbury notes, in an early scene, we see Shaun walking to the corner deli, then pondering whether to select the diet soda or the regular, the implication being that this represents the extent of Shaun's consideration of healthy eating.[25] When he and his girlfriend Liz (Kate Ashfield) celebrate their anniversary, Shaun neglects to make the reservation at a nice restaurant—"the place that does all the fish," as he promises—so they end up dining at Shaun's favorite bar, the Winchester Tavern, on a meal of beer and bar nuts. Later, he and Ed gleefully select the Winchester Tavern when seeking a place to hide out from the zombies, for it is fortified with the only foods they seem to consume, beer and junk food. As Liz's jealous friend David points out, Shaun's "idea of a romantic nightspot and an impenetrable fortress are the same thing."[26]

Shaun perhaps lacks imagination, unaware how much his life revolves around the youthful frivolities and pleasures of a much younger man, which is demonstrated, at least in part, by his food choices. However, that he behaves with childish hedonism when selecting nourishment hardly distinguishes him from his fellow humans. As food psychologist Leon Rappoport finds in a study that he and colleagues conducted on food selection, "while pleasurable (good-tasting) foods were generally thought to be unhealthy, pleasure was, nevertheless, the most important criterion in most people's food choices; health was secondary."[27] Thus, the majority of us are likely making our food choices in much the same way that Shaun and Ed do: we eat what tastes good to us, what gives us pleasure. Hedonism is thus our guiding principle. And depending on our food aversions, as well as tastes to which we have grown accustomed or have fond associations, what we find pleasurable in food selection varies. However, this variation does not mean that Shaun's pleasure in eating ice cream is any less fulfilling or meaningful—at least psychologically—than the pleasure experienced by a fine diner enjoying caviar. In fact, that Shaun takes his friends to the Winchester—which is stocked with the food provisions Shaun and Ed most enjoy—to weather the zombie apocalypse reflects the same search for safety, food and resource abundance, and normalcy that other zombie film survivors find in malls, churches, pastoral farms, or their childhood homes.

After the apocalypse, Shaun consumes precisely the same foods as before and during the apocalypse, only now pizza seems to have made it into the rotation of ice cream, chocolate bars, bar snacks, beer, and soda. Having stared into the abyss of zombie apocalypse, Shaun has fully adopted his once tenuously held philosophy of *carpe diem* existence. Ed has been transformed into a zombie, whom Shaun keeps locked in the garden shed and visits regularly so they can continue to play video games together. Presumably, Ed now consumes more meat than previously, but we don't get many of the details. Regardless, the two are still the best of chums, particularly since they already behaved like zombies prior to Ed's actually becoming one. Newbury claims, "Shaun himself, in the dead-end routines of his modern life, is repeatedly represented as a close relative of the living dead."[28] True, but in Pegg and Wright's comic treatment of the theme, Shaun's zombie-like lifestyle appears more enjoyable than threatening. Having survived the zombie apocalypse, he seems entitled to hedonistic consumption *sans* guilt.

Like Shaun, Columbus (Jesse Eisenberg), the unlikely hero of Ruben Fleischer's *Zombieland* (2009), is more dead than alive when the zombie apocalypse begins.[29] His state, though, looks more tragic than comic, for he is paralyzed by his fear of—as he puts it—"well, everything."[30] Although we are told that he is a college student, by all appearances he lives practically as a shut-in, his life consumed by the online world of video games and chat rooms. As a paranoid recluse, Columbus eats takeout (mostly pizza) and corporate junk food common to gamers who stay up late and snack to stay alert. Thin, haggard, and suffering from serious gastrointestinal disorders, Columbus takes very little pleasure in food, though he does stand by his food choices early in the film, when his "hot neighbor," known only as 406 (Amber Heard), seeks refuge in his apartment. Offering her Mountain Dew Code Red and Teddy Grahams, the only food he has available, Columbus seems both proud of his food stock and vaguely aware that these are not exactly the comfort foods one reaches for when in distress. Because his whole life has been a long and drawn-out series of distressing moments of fear, isolation, rejection, and illness, however, Columbus would be hard-pressed to name a food that may represent comfort for anyone else.

Despite his limited knowledge of other people and what they

might eat, Columbus does enact one of the most basic rituals of human companionship: upon 406's arrival, he offers his guest food and drink. As Rappoport asserts, "it is through the sharing of food that people demonstrate their support and acceptance of communal ties."[31] This basic gesture is repeated time and again in zombie films, notably also in *28 Days Later*, in a particularly touching scene in which Frank (Brendan Gleeson) and his daughter Hannah (Megan Burns) offer Jim and Selena some of "Mom's Crème de Menthe" to welcome them to their home.[32] Mom is obviously absent, a victim of the zombie apocalypse, her favorite drink preserved as a kind of memorial to her, and yet Frank and Hannah are willing to sacrifice this symbolic link to their lost loved one in order to enact one of the oldest and most honored of human rituals—the sharing of food upon the arrival of guests. As noted above, the ritual is even enacted in *Zombieland*, in the home of an incredibly backward, socially awkward, and culturally isolated character. Thus, food as cultural connection, as human to human introduction and symbol of acceptance, takes on new import in the zombie film, at least in part because humans are constantly trying to distinguish and isolate themselves and other humans from the zombies that would prey on them.

Eventually, socially awkward as he is, Columbus meets up with three other survivors, though in these meetings no food is shared or exchanged; only whiskey is shared (sort of) by way of introduction to Tallahassee (Woody Harrelson). Indeed, throughout the film, our four survivors consume so little food that it's difficult to fathom how they are, in fact, surviving. Wichita (Emma Stone) and Little Rock (Abigail Breslin), despite being surrounded by food in a grocery store and again in a souvenir shop, do not seem to eat anything, though Wichita drinks some wine and Little Rock requests "sugar-free gum, if you have any."[33]

Tallahassee drinks whiskey, eats something that resembles a charred marshmallow, and, finally, near the film's end, devours the elusive Twinkie with clear hedonistic delight. About that Twinkie: Columbus takes much of the mystery out of the reason Tallahassee hunts the Twinkie, noting, "Something about a Twinkie reminded him of a time not so long ago, when things were simple and not so fucking psychotic. It was like if he got a taste of that childhood treat, the world would become innocent again and everything would return to normal."[34]

Added to this rather detailed explanation of food nostalgia is Tallahassee's own sense of the urgency in consuming this last remnant of American culture, this Twinkie, before it's too late. When asked if he's willing to die and lead others into death for a Twinkie, he responds, "There's a box of Twinkies in that grocery store. Not just any box—the last box that anyone will enjoy in the whole universe. Twinkies have an expiration date. Someday very soon, life's little Twinkie gauge is gonna' go empty."[35]

Tallahassee fondly recalls his home life before the apocalypse, unlike the other survivors, and, not surprisingly, this recollection begins with a glorious moment at the breakfast table, where he serves his little boy pancakes covered in Hungry Jack syrup. A man who has given up living for anything except revenge against the mindless mass of zombies who robbed him of his son, Tallahassee alone of the survivors has a past worth remembering fondly, and thus he demonstrates the most uncomplicated food nostalgia in the film. His desire for Twinkies gives him a quest, something to transport him back in time. In her book-length study of nostalgia, Svetlana Boym writes, "Nostalgia (from *nostos*—return home, and *algia*—longing) is a longing for a home that no longer exists or has never existed."[36] In Tallahassee's case, this longed-for home once existed; viewers are given no indication that his relationship with his son was anything other than the bliss Columbus imagines as Tallahassee passes around a picture of his lost child. Thus, Tallahassee's longing for a Twinkie is deeply inflected with nostalgia for his pre-apocalypse life with his son. Tallahassee's own explanation, though, that there is a shelf-life on Twinkies and there is a "last box" out there somewhere that he needs to find and consume, suggests that even his seemingly straightforward nostalgia-driven hedonism may contain complications. In his quest for the Twinkie, Tallahassee seeks not just a return to the past, but also closure from its haunting horrors.

The food nostalgia in Francis Lawrence's *I Am Legend* (2007) shares a good deal in common with that demonstrated by Tallahassee in *Zombieland*.[37] Like Tallahassee, Dr. Robert Neville (Will Smith) has a past worth remembering. Flashbacks to his past include many scenes of domestic bliss, as well as the almost paralyzing horror of his wife and daughter dying in a helicopter explosion at the start of the zombie apocalypse. Thus, much of Neville's behavior has to do with re-creating his domestic utopia, something he accomplishes largely through food preparation and consumption. Neville has an extremely well-fortified pantry filled with canned goods and other nonperishables in his reinforced and barricaded home, and he seems to enjoy the rituals of cooking meals for himself and his dog, Sam, the only other survivor of his family. He serves Sam on the floor, but he serves her on a plate like his own, and he serves her the same foods that he eats. At one point, he chides her, "Eat your vegetables," an indication that Sam has become a surrogate child to Neville.[38] His longing for the past transforms into a longing for death once Sam is killed, but Neville is rescued from his suicidal assault on the zombie horde by Anna (Alice Braga) and her child, Ethan (Charlie Tahan), who then begin to establish the kind of return to normalcy the terribly lonely doctor should welcome. Neville, however, has as much trouble coping with their entrance into his life as he had coping with Sam's death. As much as his cooking and eating rituals have suggested he yearns for a return to domesticity, when Anna prepares breakfast and attempts to serve Neville at the kitchen table, Neville gets angry, smashes his plate of food, and storms out of the room. His justification is that he was "saving that bacon" Anna has prepared, but for what or whom he was saving it is unclear.[39] Perhaps it represents the same kind of closure for him that the Twinkie represents for Tallahassee, but unlike Tallahassee, Neville does not want closure from his haunted past. Thus, he saves the bacon indefinitely, awaiting a blissful reunion that will not and cannot happen in his new reality. As Boym writes, "the stronger the loss, the more it is overcompensated with commemorations, the starker the distance from the past, and the more it is prone to idealizations."[40] In fact, Neville wishes to alter the time and space in which he resides, seeking a complete return to an idealized past. Again, Boym is instructive, noting, "The nostalgic desires to obliterate history and turn it into private or collective mythology, to revisit time like space, refusing to surrender to the irreversibility of time that plagues the human condition."[41] Unlike Tallahassee, who uses food to find a degree of closure from the past, and unlike Frank and Hannah, who sacrifice their food memorial to a dead woman for the greater good of connecting to the living, Neville clings to the past, his reluctance to consume or share with others his small stock of perishable food representative of his trauma-ridden nostalgia.

In recording the history of nostalgia, Boym notes that when it first became a medical diagnosis in the seventeenth century, the Swiss doctors who diagnosed it believed that nostalgia could be cured.[42] These doctors—who found the condition most in soldiers living far from home—prescribed leeches, a trip to the Alps, and opium. Eventually, though, as Boym narrates, the medical profession gave up treating nostalgia, handing it over entirely to poets and philosophers such that "by the twenty-first century, the passing ailment turned into the incurable modern condition."[43] Accordingly, most of the survivors in zombie films demonstrate an exacerbated form of this incurable modern condition, for they desperately want to escape their current situation, and nostalgia is simply a yearning for another time or place. However, many of these survivors do not wish to return to an actual past or place, nor do they necessarily imagine an idealized future, and thus they exhibit a complicated form of "sideways nostalgia" described by Boym. This sideways nostalgia often appears as a deep yearning for change, sometimes via an idealized past that never existed, but often as a sort of ambiguous and difficult to articulate alteration of time and place: "Nostalgics from all over the world would find it difficult to say what exactly they yearn for—St. Elsewhere, another time, a better life. The alluring object of nostalgia is notoriously elusive."[44] And the food sought and consumed in the zombie film can be a telling indication of this elusive object of nostalgia.

Aside from Tallahassee, the other survivors in *Zombieland* all demonstrate a version of food nostalgia, albeit much more subtly than Tallahassee, whose quest for the Twinkie is downright psychotic at times. Columbus's nostalgia is the most sideways of the survivors, for he craves not a return to his miserable past, but rather a revision of that past. To some extent, thanks to a bottle of 1997 wine shared with Wichita, Columbus gets to rewrite his history. As Wichita and Columbus drink the wine and discuss the merits of the wine by contemplating whether or not 1997 was "a good year," Columbus describes a year filled with disappointments and rejections, culminating in his failure to be invited to the eighth-grade Sadie Hawkins dance. "Those bitches!" Wichita declares of Columbus's ex-classmates, and then she stands, extends her hand in an invitation to dance, and says, "On behalf of all the eighth-grade girls, I'd like to make it up to you."[45] Thus, thanks to the bottle of wine from the pre-apocalyptic past, Columbus gets to live out the sideways nostalgic's fantasy of rewriting the past with a better outcome, simultaneously escaping the nightmarish present, if only for a moment.

This kind of sideways nostalgia is demonstrated time and again in zombie films, most frighteningly in *28 Days Later*. After the tragic death of Frank, when Jim, Selena, and Hannah seek refuge in a make-shift military compound, Major Henry West (Christopher Ecceleston) and his band of scary men greet them with, among other things, a candlelight dinner. Jim witnesses some part of this dinner's prepa-ration in the kitchen, as Private Jones (Leo Bill), the cook, wears an aspect of maternal domesticity via an apron tied over his camo mil-itary fatigues. Jones hugs a mixing bowl to his side and whisks an omelet while he is taunted by two other soldiers who are raiding the kitchen's pantry. Jones defends his food supplies like a mother shooing away greedy children, in a pseudo-comic take on domesticity floun-dering in a hyper-masculine environment. Jones again appears in the apron at the dinner table, serving the candlelight meal this time. In addition to the standard fare of canned meats and vegetables, Jones has gone out of his way to procure and prepare an omelet "in honor of our guests."[46] Although comically happy and endlessly hounded by the other men, Jones nevertheless acts as a nostalgic stand-in for the glaringly absent hostess at the dinner party. The dish Jones has prepared, the omelet, acts as food nostalgia, a reminder of a time and place when fresh foods were in abundance and canned foods merely a convenient option as opposed to a survivalist necessity. However, when the omelet turns out to be inedible and Major West first shames Jones and then begins asking the Hannah if she can cook, seemingly oblivious to the fact that she is grief-stricken from the recent death of her father, it becomes apparent that this nostalgia is frighteningly sideways. One soldier attempts to mollify the others, saying, "We'll all have eggs again . . . once everything is back to normal," to which the others reply with cynicism and derision.[47]

Ultimately, these men do not seek a return to the past: they are living out a survivalist fantasy and intend to take any female survivors as sex slaves, ostensibly with the ultimate goal of repopulating humanity. Major West promises the men a new utopian (for them) future in which they have absolute dominion over all things, human and non-human. Boym writes, "Nostalgia is not always about the past; it can be retrospective but also prospective. Fantasies of the past determined by needs of the present have a direct impact on realities of the future."[48] The future imagined by these soldiers is more horrifying than even our hapless survivors' zombie-ridden present, for the soldiers' utopian vision includes absolute patriarchy under military rule and a violent rupture with most previously honored social contracts. Their vision for the future involves another form of cannibalism, that of metaphorically consuming other humans by holding them in slavery. So important to even this distorted vision of the future is food, however, that when asked what he has learned from the zombie kept on a leash, presumably to study, Major West says, "He's telling me that he will never bake bread, farm crops, raise livestock. He's telling me that he's futureless."[49] To give up on the production and preparation of food is to give up on the future.

Despite Major West's deranged focus on a misogynist new world, in general, zombie film survivors' food choices rarely suggest that they are either planning for or imagining much of a future. Mostly, they eat in order to survive in the present and to transport themselves into the past or an idealized past. Their food hedonism is nearly always linked to some variety of nostalgia, often with an idealized or revised past providing temporary psychological escape from the horrors of the zombie apocalypse. And if it seems that these survivors are gluttonous consumers of nostalgia food, this is because of the very elusive nature of the object of nostalgia. Boym writes, "Nostalgia tantalizes us with its fundamental ambivalence; it is about the repetition of the unrepeatable, materialization of the immaterial."[50] Thus, although *Zombieland* ends with a happy scene of Tallahassee's reunion with a Twinkie, because of the nature of nostalgia, should the movie continue, Tallahassee's bliss would soon be replaced by craving and desire. Nostalgia consumption is necessarily insatiable, never-ending, filled with moments of hedonistic bliss followed quickly by frustrated desire.

NOTES

Introduction: American Self-Fashioning and Culinary Consumption

1. Toni Morrison, *The Bluest Eye* (New York: Vintage International, 1970), 50.

2. Enoch Padolsky, "You Are Where You Eat: Ethnicity, Food and Cross-Cultural Spaces," *Canadian Ethnic Studies* 37, no. 2 (2005), accessed January 19, 2015, *EBSCOhost*.

3. Allison Carruth, *Global Appetites: American Power and the Literature of Food* (Cambridge: Cambridge University Press, 2013), 4.

4. Thorstein Veblen, *Theory of the Leisure Class* (New York: Dover, 1994), 46.

5. Jean Baudrillard, *For a Critique of the Political Economy of the Sign* (St. Louis: Telos Press, 1981), 31.

6. See also Pierre Bourdieu, *Distinction: A Social Critique of the Judgement of Taste* (Cambridge: Harvard University Press, 1984), 31. Bourdieu posits conspicuous consumption as a form of "naïve exhibitionism" that contrasts other (still ideologically underpinned) aesthetic judgments.

7. Daniel Miller, *Consumption and Its Consequences* (Cambridge: Polity Press, 2012), Kindle edition.

8. Ibid.

9. Carruth, *Global Appetites*, 4.

10. Raj Patel, *Stuffed and Starved: The Hidden Battle for the World Food System* (Brooklyn: Melville House, 2012), Kindle edition.

11. Isabelle de Solier, "Making the Self in a Material World," *Cultural Studies Review* 19, no. 1 (2013), accessed January 19, 2015, *EBSCOhost*.

12. Ibid., 11.

13. Bruce Pietrykowski, "You Are What You Eat: The Social Economy of the Slow Food Movement," *Review of Social Economy* 62, no. 3 (2004), accessed January 11, 2015, *EBSCOhost*.

14. Anita Mannur, "Culinary Nostalgia: Authenticity, Nationalism, and Diaspora," *MELUS* 32, no. 4 (2007): 12, accessed January 10, 2015, *MLA International Bibliograpy*.

15. Leon Rappoport, *How We Eat: Appetite, Culture, and the Psychology of Food* (Toronto: ECW Press, 2003), 21.

16. Fred L. Gardaphé and Wenying Xu, "Introduction: Food in Multi-Ethnic Literatures," *MELUS* 32, no. 4 (2007): 7, accessed January 10, 2015, *MLA International Bibliography*.

17. Laurier Turgeon and Madeleine Pastinelli, "'Eat the World': Postcolonial Encounters in Quebec City's Ethnic Restaurants," *Journal of American Folklore* 115 (2002): 250, accessed January 10, 2015, *JSTOR*.

18. Warren Belasco, "Food Matters: Perspectives on an Emerging Field," in

Food Nations: Selling Taste in Consumer Societies, ed. Warren Belasco and Philip Scranton (New York: Routledge, 2002), 4.

19. For more on cultural omnivorousness, see sociologists Oriel Sullivan and Tally Katz-Gerro's "The Omnivore Thesis Revisited: Voracious Cultural Consumers," *European Sociological Review* 23, no. 2 (2007), accessed January 10, 2015, *EBSCOhost*. One of the more interesting ways that the "omnivore thesis" challenges long-held understandings of consumption is via its revision of Pierre Bourdieu's theory of cultural stratification, as Sullivan and Katz-Gerro note.

20. Mannur, "Culinary Nostalgia: Authenticity, Nationalism, and Diaspora," 13.

21. Davide Girardelli, "Commodified Identities: The Myth of Italian Food in the United States," *Journal of Communication Inquiry* 28, no. 4 (2004): 309.

22. Carole Counihan, ed., *Food in the USA: A Reader* (New York: Routledge, 2002), 24. See also food historian Raymond Sokolov's *Fading Feast* (New York: Farrar Straus & Giroux, 1981) for another argument that America does not have a monolithic food identity. Sokolov argues that our multinational national diet, eclectic as it is, precludes the development of a national cuisine. However, his book was also an attempt to record and preserve many of the regional foodways that he and the contributors to the book in the 1980s were convinced would soon be refashioned to satisfy mainstream palates. His book, however, and others like it, were positioned on the cusp of a renewed interest and appreciation for regional dishes.

23. Chez, "Popular Ethnic Food Guides," 235.

24. Sherrie A. Inness, ed., *Kitchen Culture in America: Popular Representations of Food, Gender, and Race* (Philadelphia: University of Pennsylvania Press, 2001), 3.

25. Ibid.

Chapter 1. "Between Bolted Beef and Bolted Pudding": Boston's Eating Houses and Nineteenth-Century Social and Cultural Change

1. "Journeymen Ship Carpenters and Caulkers of Boston," *New England Artisan*, June 21, 1832, 1. Thanks to Christopher Sawula for alerting me to this.

2. For general overviews of the market revolution and the social changes it caused, see Charles Sellers, *The Market Revolution: Jacksonian America, 1815–1846* (New York: Oxford University Press, 1994); Sean Wilentz, "Society, Politics, and the Market Revolution, 1815–1848," in *The New American History*, ed. Eric Foner (Philadelphia: Temple University Press, 1997), 61–84; Bruce Laurie, *Artisans into Workers: Labor in Nineteenth-Century America* (Urbana: University of Illinois Press, 1997).

3. John R. Gillis, *A World of Their Own Making: Myth, Ritual, and the Quest for Family Values* (New York: Basic Books, 1996), 90–94.

4. "Why We Get Sick," *Harper's New Monthly Magazine* 13 (October 1856): 642.

5. I examine this dining landscape more fully in my forthcoming book, Kelly Erby, *Restaurant Republic: The Rise of Public Dining in Boston*, from the University of Minnesota Press.

6. Female eating-house proprietors in nineteenth-century Boston were rare, but they did exist. Unfortunately, their numbers are impossible to determine.

Census takers did not record occupational information for women until 1880. Likewise, city directories recorded occupational information only for heads of household, typically men. Meanwhile, business directories often listed only the initials of proprietors, making it impossible to determine whether the person was male or female. Nevertheless, seven female names do appear in the 1850 federal census as restaurant proprietors. What specific genre of restaurant venue these women operated is not known. Another clue about female proprietorship is provided by the *Married Women Doing Business Certificates,* a collection available at the Boston City Archives. Between 1862 and 1974, Chapter 209 of the Massachusetts General Laws required any married women doing business on her own account to record in the City Clerk's Office a certificate stating her name and the name of her husband, as well as the nature and location of her business. The surviving certificates show that between 1862 and 1891, there were thirteen married women who recorded their business as an "eating house." It is likely that many women married to eating-house proprietors also assisted in the business and thus would have been present in the venue. *Married Women Doing Business Certificates,* vols. 1–6, Boston City Archives, Boston, MA.

7. According to Daniel E. Sutherland, meals were an important part of a domestic servant's wages during this period. *Americans and Their Servants: Domestic Service in the United States from 1800 to 1920* (Baton Rouge: Louisiana State University Press, 1981), 113.

8. Jessica Ellen Sewell, *Women and the Everyday City: Public Space in San Francisco, 1890–1915* (Minneapolis: University of Minnesota Press, 2011), 77.

9. In the antebellum period, respectable women's dining options included ladies' hotel dining rooms and confectionaries. These venues made themselves suitable for their well-heeled female clientele by providing overtly feminine dining environments, considered virtuous and respectable enough for women to patronize even when unescorted. I examine women's expanding dining options in my forthcoming book *Restaurant Republic.*

10. Sewell, *Women and the Everyday City,* 77.

11. The *Boston Daily Globe* reminisced about the city's early eating-house trade in "Congress Street: Once a Place for Epicurean Enjoyment," June 2, 1889, 8.

12. In 1832, the mayor and city aldermen voted to extend liquor licensing to those businesses that sold food to be consumed on the premises. Prior to this, a business owner had to demonstrate he provided both board and rooms if he wanted a liquor license. Even after the relaxation of requirements, the liquor-licensing laws were widely violated throughout the century.

13. According to the *Boston Directories,* approximately 85 percent of restaurant keepers in 1830 had the same business address as their home address. This figure was 95 percent in 1840, 77 percent in 1850, and 71 percent in 1860. In making these calculations, I rather forwardly assumed that those residents who listed only a business address or only a home address in the directories instead of two different addresses lived and worked in the same building. This is not an outlandish assumption but it is unconfirmed. *The Boston Directory Containing Names of the Inhabitants, Occupations, Places of Business, and Dwelling Houses* (Boston: Charles Stimpson, 1830); *The Boston Directory Containing Names of the Inhabitants, Occupations, Places of Business, and Dwelling Houses* (Boston: Charles Stimpson,

1840); *The Boston Directory Containing Names of the Inhabitants, Occupations, Places of Business, and Dwelling Houses* (Boston: George Adams, 1850); *The Boston Directory: Embracing the City Record, a General Directory of the Citizens, and a Business Directory* (Boston: Adams, Sampson, & Co., 1860).

14. Richard Pillsbury, *From Boardinghouse to Bistro: The American Restaurant Then and Now* (Boston: Unwin Hyman, 1990), 28.

15. These common marketing techniques, which applied earlier in the century as well, are described in "All Around the Hub," *Boston Daily Globe,* February 24, 1878, 2; "Dinner for a Dime," *Boston Daily Globe,* December 24, 1885, 4.

16. "Congress Street," 8; "All Around the Hub," 2.

17. "Why We Get Sick," 642; "Congress Street," 8.

18. In their respective American travelogues, Englishmen Edward Abdy, Charles Dickens, and Basil Hall each commented on American eating-houses and the lack of conversation that went on inside them. Edward Abdy, *Journal of a Residence and Tour in the United States* (London: J. Murray, 1835); Charles Dickens, *American Notes* (1842; reprint, Gloucester, MA: P. Smith, 1968); Basil Hall, *Travels in North America in the Years 1827 and 1828* (New York: Arno Press, 1974). See also "Why We Get Sick," 645.

19. "Dinner for a Dime," 4.

20. Of course, some diet reformers urged Americans to stay away from meat. See Stephen Nissenbaum, *Sex, Diet, and Debility in Jacksonian America: Sylvester Graham and Health Reform* (Westport, CT: Greenwood Press, 1980).

21. Andrew Haley, *Turning the Tables: Restaurants and the Rise of the American Middle Class, 1880–1920* (Chapel Hill: University of North Carolina Press, 2011), 141–42.

22. "Congress Street," 8.

23. C. W. Gesner, "Concerning Restaurants," *Harper's New Monthly Magazine* 32 (April 1866): 592. See also *Boston Daily Globe,* February 24, 1878.

24. Dell Upton, *Another City: Urban Life and Urban Spaces in the New American Republic* (New Haven: Yale University Press, 2008).

25. Oscar Handlin, *Boston's Immigrants: 1790–1880* (Cambridge, MA: Belknap Press, 1991), 92–93.

26. John Eaton Whiting, *A Schedule of the Buildings and Their Occupancy, on the Principal Streets and Wharves in the City of Boston* (Boston: Press of W. L. Deland, 1877).

27. "Sayings and Doings in Boston," *Spirit of the Times: A Chronicle of the Turf, Agriculture, Field Sports, Literature, and the Stage* 13 (January 27, 1844): 576.

28. Ibid., 576.

29. In an article in 1887, the *Boston Daily Globe* looked back at restaurants in the 1830s. "Old Time Caterers," *Boston Daily Globe,* February 14, 1887, 2.

30. "Boston's Working Women—About the Women Who Work in Restaurants," *Boston Globe,* January 13, 1883, 1. This article compared the wages of men and women waiters in eating-houses. Female waiters, as I explain in *Public Appetite,* did not become prominent until after the Civil War.

31. "Dinner for a Dime," 4.

32. "Affairs about Home," *Boston Herald,* April 10, 1857, 4.

33. "Police Court," *Boston Daily Atlas,* October 13, 1854, 2. See also the *Boston Daily Atlas,* January 8, 1849, 2.

34. On the servility with which nineteenth-century Americans associated waitering, see Kelly Erby, "Worthy of Respect: Black Waiters in Boston before the Civil War," *Food and History* 5 (February 2008): 205–18.

35. "Seventh Census of the United States," 1850, Manuscript Population schedules, Boston City, Suffolk County, Massachusetts.

36. *Ballou's Dollar Monthly Magazine* 3 (May 1856): 416.

37. "Restaurant Calls," *Boston Daily Globe,* March 25, 1884, 9; "Restaurant Calls," *Boston Daily Globe*, July 10, 1887, 9; "Slang in Restaurants," *Boston Daily Globe,* February 24, 1889, 18.

38. "Hash house" became another name for a cheap eating establishment that catered to workingmen.

39. Menu quoted in Jan Whitaker, "Prices," Restauranting through History," accessed January 6, 2014, http://restaurant-ingthroughhistory.com/restaurant-prices/.

40. "What Food Costs," *Boston Daily Globe*, May 1, 1887, 20; "Restaurant Costs," *Boston Daily Globe*, June 26, 1887, 18.

41. "A Fifteen-Cent Dinner," *Boston Daily Globe*, December 11, 1883, 6; "Dinner for a Dime," 4.

42. "A Fifteen-Cent Dinner," 6.

43. "Eating House Remodeled," *Boston Daily Advertiser*, June 5, 1850, 2.

44. "All Around the Hub," 2.

45. As described in Albert Benedict Wolfe, *The Lodging House Problem in Boston (Cambridge: Harvard University Press, 1913)*, 50; "His Luncheon and Hers," *Boston Daily Globe*, January 7, 1894, 16. Whether the napkin rack existed earlier in the century is unclear but seems likely.

46. For example, the *Harper's New Monthly* magazine that explained the hierarchy of eating-houses noted differences in style and service between venues but not in fare. Gesner, "Concerning Restaurants," 592.

47. "Sayings and Doings in Boston," 576.

48. On the concept of cultural capital, see Pierre Bourdieu, *Distinction: A Social Critique of the Judgment of Taste* (Cambridge, MA: Cambridge University Press, 1984), 66.

49. On the general status anxiety and loss in economic security of nineteenth-century clerks, see Brian Luskey, *On the Make: Clerks and the Quest for Capital* (New York: New York University Press, 2010).

50. "Why We Get Sick," 645.

51. Hasia Diner discusses the wonder of the wide availability of meat to Irish, Italian, and Jewish immigrants in his *Hungering for America: Italian, Irish, and Jewish Foodways in the Age of Migration* (Cambridge: Harvard University Press, 2003).

52. Boston baked beans were distinctive because they were made with brown beans instead of white and baked with pork. In addition, they were left whole as opposed to other versions, in which the beans were mashed slightly.

53. On the reluctance of some white Bostonians to dine among blacks, see the *Liberator*, January 22, 1831.

54. The *Christian Recorder* reprinted Frederick Douglass's 1846 story on June 10, 1886, in "Anniversary Exercises," 1.

55. Clifton Joseph Furness, "Whitman Looks at Boston," *New England Quarterly* 1 (July 1928): 356.

56. John Daniels, *In Freedom's Birthplace: A Study of the Boston Negroes* (Boston: Arno Press, 1914), 94–95.

57. Sir John Acton, *Acton in America: The American Journal of Sir John Acton, 1853*, ed. Sydney Jackman (Shepherdstown, WV: Patmos Press, 1979), 48.

58. Elizabeth Hafkin Pleck, *Black Migration and Poverty, Boston, 1865–1900* (New York: Academy Press, 1979), 159; John Weiss, *Life and Correspondence of Theodore Parker* (New York: D. Appleton & Co., 1864), 2:95; Joseph Willard, *A Half a Century with Judges and Lawyers* (Boston: Houghton Mifflin, 1896), 239.

59. Oscar Handlin, *Boston's Immigrants: 1790–1880* (Cambridge: Belknap Press, 1991), table XIII; Carroll D. Wright, *The Census of Massachusetts, 1880* (Boston: Wright & Potter Printing Co., 1883), 424–25. Unfortunately, it is impossible to determine the specific genre of eatery these immigrants operated. Leonard P. Curry, *The Free Black in Urban America, 1800–1850: The Shadow of a Dream* (Chicago: University of Chicago Press, 1981), 19–20.

60. Edward Abdy, quoted in Curry, *The Free Black in Urban America, 1800–1850*, 19–20.

61. "Seventh Census of the United States," 1850, Manuscript Population schedules, Boston City, Suffolk County, Massachusetts.

62. *The Boston Directory, for the Year 1855: Embracing the City Record, a General Directory of the Citizens, and a Business Directory* (Boston: Geo Adams, 1855); John Weiss, *Life and Correspondence of Theodore Parker*, 2 vols. (New York: D. Appleton & Co., 1864), 2:95.

63. Rayford Whitingham Logan and Michael R. Winston, *Dictionary of American Negro Biography* (New York: W. W. Norton and Company, 1982), 565.

64. Lucius Robinson Paige, *History of Cambridge, Massachusetts, 1630–1877, with a Genealogical Register* (Boston: H. O. Houghton and Company, 1877); Rayford Logan and Michael R. Winston, eds., *Dictionary of American Negro Biography* (New York: W. W. Norton, 1982).

65. Shane White, "Freedoms' First Con: Changing Notes: African Americans and Changing Notes in Antebellum New York City," *Journal of the Early Republic* 34, no. 3 (Fall 2014): 385–409.

66. Stephen Mihm, *A Nation of Counterfeiters: Capitalists, Con Men, and the Making of the United States* (Cambridge: Harvard University Press, 2007), 1–7, 238.

67. White, "Freedoms' First Con."

68. *Boston Daily Globe*, November 12, 1880, 1.

69. See, for example, "Affairs in and about the City," *Boston Daily Atlas*, February 4, 1854, 2.

70. "He Berated the Cook," *Boston Daily Globe*, April 17, 1890, 8.

Chapter 2. Nervous Kitchens: Consuming Sentimentality Narratives and Black-White Intimacy at a Chicago Hot Dog Stand

I am grateful for the indispensable advice and input from both Psyche Williams-Forson and Sheri L. Parks. Thank you to my colleagues in Michelle V. Rowley's course, from which the original idea for this chapter was developed. Special thanks to Cristina Jo Pérez, Paul Nezaum Saiedi, Melissa Susan Rogers, Darius Bost, and Douglas S. Ishii for your constructive feedback and endless support.

1. Denis R. Byrne, "Nervous Landscapes: Race and Space in Australia." *Journal of Social Archaeology* 3, no. 2 (2003): 169–93.

2. *This American Life: Pandora's Box,* directed by Christopher Wilcha (New York: Showtime, 2007), digital file.

3. Chicago Public Radio, "This American Life TV Show Nominated for Five Emmys," *prnewswire.com*, 2008, http://www.prnewswire.com/news-releases/this-american-life-tv-show-nominated-for-five-emmys-64933537.html.

4. Virginia Heffernan, "This American Life—Ira Glass—Television—Review —NYTimes.com," *The New York Times—Breaking News, World News & Multimedia*, March 22, 2007, accessed December 19, 2011, http://www.nytimes.com/2007/03/22/arts/television/22heff.html.

5. Rebecca Ann Wanzo, *The Suffering Will Not Be Televised: African American Women and Sentimental Political Storytelling* (Albany: State University of New York Press, 2009), 10.

6. The narrative conventions through which African American women are forced to express their subjectivities for political power include notions of progress, the utilization of hierarchies of suffering subjects, the homogenization of suffering, and self-transformation as the best response to structural inequality; those with real pain are depicted as hysterical and abnormal.

7. Wanzo, *The Suffering Will Not Be Televised*, 24.

8. Ibid., 9.

9. Ibid., 11.

10. Ibid., 80.

11. Ibid., 59.

12. Sarumathi Jayaraman, *Behind the Kitchen Door* (Ithaca, NY: Cornell University Press, 2013), 131–35.

13. Frances Beale, "Double Jeopardy: To Be Black and Female," in *Words of Fire: An Anthology of African-American Feminist Thought*, ed. Beverly Guy-Sheftall (New York: New Press, 1995), 150–51.

14. According to hot dog historian Bruce Kraig's *Hot Dog: A Global History* (London: Reaktion Books, 2009), the Chicago hot dog stand became a defining characteristic of working class Chicago neighborhoods, where "intangibles of warm memory converge with the specific taste memory."

15. In "The Body Politic," in *Words of Fire*, ed. Guy-Sheftall, Paula Giddings notes how Saartjie Baartmann, a Khoikhoi woman displayed by British scientists in the early nineteenth century, stands as the "central image for the black female throughout the nineteenth century." Her case stands as an important antecedent for how displaying and gazing at sensationalized Black women's bodies served ideas of civility associated with white masculinity.

16. Barbara Thompson, ed., *Black Womanhood: Images, Icons, and Ideologies of the African Body* (Seattle: University of Washington Press, 2008).

17. Sheri L. Parks, *Fierce Angels: The Strong Black Woman in American Life and Culture* (New York: Ballantine Books, 2010), 36–37. "The myth grew so familiar that it left little room to see the lives that slave women actually lived. And to a large

extent, black people have bought that image, too, handing their own mothers over to the myth" (ibid.).

18. Patricia Hill Collins, *Black Sexual Politics: African Americans, Gender, and the New Racism* (New York: Routledge, 2004). For more on the construction and pervasiveness of the mammy trope in popular media and material culture, see Kimberly Wallace-Sanders, *Mammy: A Century of Race, Gender, and Southern Memory* (Ann Arbor: University of Michigan Press, 2008), 1–14; Trudier Harris, *From Mammies to Militants: Domestics in Black American Literature* (Philadelphia: Temple University Press, 1982), xi–xvi; Marylin Kern-Foxworth and Alex Haley, *Aunt Jemima, Uncle Ben, and Rastus: Blacks in Advertising, Yesterday, Today, and Tomorrow* (New York: Praeger, 1994); and Maurice Manring, *Slave in a Box: The Strange Career of Aunt Jemima* (Charlottesville: University of Virginia Press, 1998).

19. Psyche Williams-Forson, *Building Houses out of Chicken Legs: Black Women, Food, and Power* (Chapel Hill: University of North Carolina Press, 2006), 188. Williams-Forson importantly notes how the large black woman continues to resonate on television, film, and advertisements because of her comforting aesthetic appeal. There is a familiarity with which American visual culture utilizes the mammy trope.

20. Micki McElya, *Clinging to Mammy: The Faithful Slave in Twentieth-Century America* (Cambridge, MA: Harvard University Press, 2007), 41.

21. Ibid., 45. "Circulating through these justifications of segregation and violence is a profound nostalgia for sanctioned physicality between black women and both white women and men. They express a longing for access to black women's bodies, beds, and private lives, the last now concealed from them in segregated black neighborhoods and institutions. Denied here was the fact that whites continued to claim sexual access to black people within coercive as well as consensual frameworks, while often responding to even the suggestion of black men's cross-racial desire with violence and murder" (ibid.).

22. A recurring theme in mammy letters and other language of mammy nostalgia involves expressing longing for mammy's bosom.

23. M. Miller-Young, "Putting Hypersexuality to Work: Black Women and Illicit Eroticism in Pornography," *Sexualities* 13, no. 2 (2010): 219–35.

24. D. Hernandez, "Playing with Race: On the Edge of Edgy Sex, Racial BDSM Excites Some and Reviles Others," *Colorlines* 7, no. 4 (2004): 14–18.

25. Ada Demaj, "Touching Race through Play: Sadomasochism, Phenomenology, and the Intertwining of Race," *Annual Review of Critical Psychology* 11 (2014): 98. Demaj argues that historical racism necessarily informs current practices of racial BDSM that often become justified through expression of personal desire. The neoliberal focus on the individual rather than the structural belies the fact that race play "brings forth the ways in which institutionalized relations of domination and submission are always already imbued with eroticism, and that the erotic elements of contemporary sadomasochistic relations are inextricably linked to historical oppressive relations" (ibid.).

26. Wanzo, *The Suffering Will Not Be Televised*, 3.

27. Ibid., 148–49.

Chapter 3. A Pedagogy of Dining Out: Learning to Consume Culture

1. Theodore Levitt, "The Globalization of Markets," *Harvard Business Review* 61, no. 3 (1983): 92.

2. Ibid., 93.

3. Wimal Dissanayake, "Globalization and Experience of Culture: The Resilience of Nationhood," in *Globalization, Cultural Identities, and Media Representation*, ed. Natascha Kramer and Stefan Gentz (Albany: State University of New York Press, 2006), 26.

4. Roland Robertson, "Glocalization: Time-Space and Homogeneity-Heterogeneity," in *Global Modernities*, ed. Mike Featherstone, Scott Lash, and Roland Robertson (Thousand Oaks, CA: Sage, 1995), 26.

5. Anita Mannur, "Culinary Nostalgia: Authenticity, Nationalism, and Diaspora," *MELUS* 32, no. 4 (2007): 13, accessed January 10, 2015, *MLA International Bibliography*.

6. Ibid.

7. Craig J. Thompson and Zaynep Arsel, "The Starbucks Brandscape and Consumers' (Anticorporate) Experiences of Glocalization," *Journal of Consumer Research* 31 (2004): 632.

8. "Store Design," Starbucks, January 1, 2014, accessed September 27, 2014, http://www.starbucks.com/coffeehouse/store-design.

9. Ibid.

10. Blair Taylor, "2013 Year in Review," Global Responsibility Report Goals and Progress 2013, January 1, 2014, accessed September 27, 2014, http://www.starbucks.com/responsibility/global-report.

11. Thompson and Arsel, "The Starbucks Brandscape," 634.

12. Ibid., 638–39.

13. Edward W. Said, "Orientalism Reconsidered," *Cultural Critique* 1 (1985): 89.

Chapter 4. Hunger Pains: Appetite and Racial Longing in *Stealing Buddha's Dinner*

1. Mary Douglas, "Deciphering a Meal," in *Implicit Meanings: Essays in Anthropology* (London: Routledge and Kegan Paul, 1975), 249.

2. Linda Kay Brown and Kay Mussell, *Ethnic and Regional Foodways in the US: The Performance of Group Identity* (Knoxville: University of Tennessee Press, 1984), 3–4.

3. Ibid., 4.

4. Sau-Ling Cynthia Wong, *Reading Asian American Literature: From Necessity to Extravagance* (Princeton, NJ: Princeton University Press, 1993), 20.

5. Ibid., 44.

6. Bich Minh Nguyen, *Stealing Buddha's Dinner* (New York: Viking, 2007), 10.

7. Ibid.

8. Ibid., 11.

9. Douglas Biber and Edward Finegan, *Sociolinguistic Perspectives on Register* (New York: Oxford University Press, 1994), 4.

10. Roland Barthes, "Toward a Psychosociology of Contemporary Food Consumption," in *Food and Culture: A Reader,* 2nd ed., ed. Carole Counihan and Penny Van Esterik (New York: Routledge, 1997), 34.

11. Biber and Finegan, *Sociolinguistic Perspectives on Register*, 51.

12. Nguyen, *Stealing Buddha's Dinner*, 51.

13. Ibid., 53.

14. Anne Anlin Cheng, *The Melancholy of Race: Psychoanalysis, Assimilation, and Hidden Grief* (New York: Oxford University Press, 2001), 8–9.

15. Ibid., 10.

16. Nguyen, *Stealing Buddha's Dinner*, 125.

17. Ibid., 75.

18. Ibid., 50.

19. Timothy K. August, "The Contradictions in Culinary Collaboration: Vietnamese American Bodies in *Top Chef* and *Stealing Buddha's Dinner*," *MELUS* 37, no. 3 (2012): 109.

20. Nguyen, *Stealing Buddha's Dinner*, 56.

21. Deborah Kalb, "Q and A with Writer Bich Minh Nguyen," *Haunting Legacy,* August 1, 2012, http://www.hauntinglegacy.com/qas-with-experts/2012/8/1/qa-with-writer-bich-minh-nguyen.html.

22. Nguyen, *Stealing Buddha's Dinner*, 102.

23. Ibid.

24. Ibid., 57.

25. Ibid., 70 (emphasis in original).

26. Ibid., 71

27. Ibid., 128.

28. Ibid., 80.

29. Ibid., 81.

30. Ibid.

31. August, "The Contradictions in Culinary Collaboration," 108.

32. Nguyen, *Stealing Buddha's Dinner*, 235–36.

33. Bich Minh Nguyen, "How I Found My Mother," in *Requiem for a Paper Bag: Celebrities and Civilians Tell Stories of the Best Lost, Tossed, and Found Items from Around the World*, ed. Davy Rothbart (New York: Fireside, 2009), 52.

34. "A Conversation with Bich Minh Nguyen," Reading Group Guide, Penguin.com, accessed November 15, 2013, http://www.penguin.com/read/book-clubs/stealing-buddhas-dinner/9780143113034.

35. Nguyen, "How I Found My Mother," 53.

36. Nguyen, *Stealing Buddha's Dinner*, 244.

37. "A Conversation with Bich Minh Nguyen."

38. Julie Guthman, "Can't Stomach It: How Michael Pollan et al. Made me Want to Eat Cheetos," *Gastronomica: The Journal of Culture and Food* 7, no. 2 (2007): 76.

39. Bich Minh Nguyen, "Goodbye to My Twinkie Days," *New York Times,* November 16, 2012, http://www.nytimes.com/2012/11/17/opinion/goodbye-to-my-twinkie-days.html.

40. Susan Sontag, "Notes on 'Camp,'" in *Against Interpretation and Other Essays* (1961; repr., New York: Picador, 2001), 292 (emphasis in original).

41. Nguyen, "Goodbye to My Twinkie Days."

42. "A Conversation with Bich Minh Nguyen."

43. August, "The Contradictions in Culinary Collaboration," 108.

44. Nguyen, "Goodbye to My Twinkie Days."

45. "A Conversation with Bich Minh Nguyen."

46. Nguyen, "Goodbye to My Twinkie Days."

47. Ed Schiffer, "'Fable Number One': Some Myths about Consumption," in *Eating Culture*, ed. Ron Scapp and Brian Seitz (Albany: State University of New York Press, 1998), 290.

Chapter 5. Consuming American Consumerism in *The Road*

1. Cormac McCarthy, *The Road* (New York: Vintage International, 2006), 17.

2. Ibid., 52.

3. Ben De Bruyn, "Borrowed Time, Borrowed World, and Borrowed Eyes: Care, Ruin, and Vision in Cormac McCarthy's *The Road* and Harrison's *Ecocriticism*," *English Studies* 91, no. 7 (2010): 778, accessed April 26, 2012, EBSCOhost.

4. McCarthy, *Road*, 59.

5. Michael Pollan, *The Omnivore's Dilemma* (New York: Penguin Books, 2006), 7.

6. McCarthy, *Road*, 3.

7. Ibid., 6.

8. Ibid.

9. Ibid., 20.

10. Ibid., 53.

11. Ibid., 82.

12. Ibid.

13. Jonathan Safran Foer, *Eating Animals* (New York: Little, Brown and Company, 2009), 2.

14. McCarthy, *Road*, 83.

15. Ibid., 120.

16. Randal S. Wilhelm, "'Golden chalice, good to a house god': Still Life in *The Road*," *Cormac McCarthy Journal* 6 (2008): 129, accessed August 20, 2012, https://journals.tdl.org/cormacmccarthy/index.php/cormacmccarthy/issue/archive.

17. Brad Kessler, "One Reader's Digest: Toward a Gastronomic Theory of Literature," *Kenyon Review* 27, no. 2 (2005): 156, accessed April 26, 2012, *JSTOR*.

18. Ibid., 159.

19. McCarthy, *Road*, 110.

20. Ibid., 111.

21. Ibid., 127.

22. Paul Rozin, Maureen Markwith, and Caryn Stoess, "Moralization and Becoming a Vegetarian: The Transformation of Preferences into Values and the Recruitment of Disgust," *Psychological Science* 8, no. 2 (March 1997): 67, accessed January 23, 2015, *JSTOR*.

23. Erik J. Wielenberg, "God, Morality, and Meaning in Cormac McCarthy's

The Road." Cormac McCarthy Journal 8, no.1 (2010): 14, accessed August 20, 2012, https://journals.tdl.org/cormacmccarthy/index.php/cormacmccarthy/issue/archive.

24. McCarthy, *Road*, 172.

25. Ibid., 198.

26. Ibid.

27. Ibid.

28. Wielenberg, "God, Morality, and Meaning," 8.

29. McCarthy, *Road*, 284.

30. Ibid., 286.

31. Ibid.

32. Pollan, *Omnivore's Dilemma*, 6.

33. McCarthy, *Road*, 252.

34. Ibid., 22.

35. Ibid., 243.

36. Ibid., 91.

37. Ibid., 92.

38. Ibid., 56.

39. Don Colbert, *The Seven Pillars of Health* (Lake Mary, FL: Siloam, 2007), 65.

40. Ibid., 66.

41. Ibid., 67.

42. Ibid.

43. Michael Pollan, *In Defense of Food: An Eater's Manifesto* (New York: Penguin Press, 2008), 1–2.

44. Ibid., 7.

45. Maguelonne Toussaint-Samat, *A History of Food*, trans. Anthea Bell (Malden: Wiley-Blackwell, 2009), 690.

46. McCarthy, *Road*, 29.

47. Ibid., 35.

48. Ibid., 61.

49. De Bruyn, "Borrowed Time," 777.

50. McCarthy, *Road*, 141.

51. Ibid.

52. Ibid., 145.

53. Ibid., 153.

54. Pollan, *In Defense of Food*, 8.

55. Foer, *Eating Animals*, 55.

56. McCarthy, *Road*, 157.

57. Ibid., 169.

58. Ibid., 174.

59. Ibid., 5.

60. Kessler, "One Reader's Digest," 151.

61. Ibid., 164.

62. McCarthy, *Road*, 23.

63. Ibid.

64. Ibid., 24.

65. De Bruyn, "Borrowed Time," 782.

66. Wilhelm, "'Golden chalice, good to a house god,'" 133.

67. McCarthy, *Road*, 4.

68. Ibid.

69. Ibid., 287

70. Ibid.

71. Ibid.

Chapter 6. From Aunt Jemima to Aunt Marthy: Commodifying the Kitchen Cook and Undermining White Authority in *Incidents in the Life of a Slave Girl*

1. "About the Jim Crow Museum," Ferris State University, accessed March 17, 2014, http://www.ferris.edu/jimcrow/more.htm.

2. Jennie Rothenberg Gritz, "New Racism Museum Reveals the Ugly Truth behind Aunt Jemima," *The Atlantic*, April 23, 2012, accessed March 18, 2014, www.theatlantic.com/.

3. Ibid.

4. About these Aunt Jemima figurines, dolls, and knick-knacks, Micki McElya writes, "Items such as these infiltrated the intimate spaces of people's daily lives and reinforced ideas of white supremacy and black servility as much as they sold products." Micki McElya, *Clinging to Mammy: The Faithful Slave in Twentieth-Century America* (Cambridge: Harvard University Press, 2007), 27. For an extended study of mammy collectibles, see Patricia A. Turner, *Ceramic Uncles & Celluloid Mammies: Black Images & Their Influence on Culture* (Charlottesville: University of Virginia Press, 1994). For an extended study of Aunt Jemima, both regarding the trademark and the mythologized southern plantation slave narrative linked to the trademark, see M. M. Manring, *Slave in a Box: The Strange Career of Aunt Jemima* (Charlottesville: University of Virginia Press, 1998).

5. For more on the significance of the kitchen to Aunt Jemima, see Kimberly Wallace-Sanders, *Mammy: A Century of Race, Gender, and Southern Memory* (Ann Arbor: University of Michigan Press, 2008), 4. Commenting on the introduction of Aunt Jemima (portrayed by Nancy Green) at the 1893 Columbia Exposition in Chicago, Wallace-Sanders writes, "Aunt Jemima was introduced . . . as a Reconstructionist alter ego to the mammy; the mammy's domain is the nursery, while Aunt Jemima's is the kitchen" (ibid.).

6. Trudier Harris, *From Mammies to Militants: Domestics in Black American Literature* (Philadelphia: Temple University Press, 1982), 3–4.

7. Mary Titus, "The Dining Room Door Swings Both Ways: Food, Race, and Domestic Space in the Nineteenth-Century South," in *Haunted Bodies: Gender and Southern Texts*, ed. Anne Goodwyn Jones and Susan V. Donaldson (Charlottesville: University Press of Virginia, 1997), 249.

8. Alice A. Deck, "'Now Then—Who Said Biscuits?' The Black Woman Cook as Fetish in American Advertising, 1905–1953," in *Kitchen Culture in America*, ed. Sherrie A. Inness (Philadelphia: University of Pennsylvania Press, 2001), 70.

9. Arthur F. Marquette, *Brands, Trademarks, and Good Will: The Story of the Quaker Oats Company* (New York: Basic, 1966), 144. McElya (*Clinging to Mammy*) disputes some of the narratives regarding Aunt Jemima that Marquette repeated

in his study, but both agree about the general marketing of Nancy Green as Aunt Jemima, a physical incarnation of the R. T. Davis Milling Company's "Aunt Jemima" product brand.

10. Doris Witt, *Black Hunger* (New York: Oxford University Press, 1999), 27.

11. Ibid., 10.

12. Ibid.

13. Deck, "'Now Then—Who Said Biscuits,'" 72.

14. The anxiety underpinning this power dynamic is only exacerbated by the widespread fear and paranoia among white slave owners that their slaves might harm them. Some owners feared violent revolts or rebellions, while others were concerned that their slaves would take the more subtle action of poisoning their food.

15. Michel Foucault, "The Subject and Power," in *Michel Foucault: Beyond Structuralism and Hermeneutics*, 2nd ed., ed. Hubert L. Dreyfus and Paul Rabinow (Chicago: University of Chicago Press, 1982), 220.

16. Ibid. As a side note, the modes of defiance latent in Foucault's assessment of power are pivotal in assessing the power structure at all. Thus, "at the very heart of the power relationship . . . are the recalcitrance of the will and the intransigence of freedom" (ibid., 221–22). While, typically, Foucaultian power formations exclude the examination of foci such as slavery as they necessarily limit the intrinsic freedoms of the subjects, thus limiting the options for recalcitrance, the ability of the slave cook to captivate the imagination of the plantation owner establishes the kitchen as a space within the domestic sphere in which the slave had recourse to dominance.

17. Linda Naranjo-Huebl, "'Take, Eat': Food Imagery, the Nurturing Ethic, and Christian Identity in *The Wide, Wide World*, *Uncle Tom's Cabin*, and *Incidents in the Life of a Slave Girl*," *Christianity and Literature* 56, no. 4 (2007): 598.

18. Harriet Jacobs, *Incidents in the Life of a Slave Girl* (New York: Dover Publications, 2001), 12.

19. Ibid., 15.

20. Ibid., 41.

21. Ibid.

22. Anne Bradford Warner, "Harriet Jacobs's Modest Proposals: Revising Southern Hospitality," *Southern Quarterly* 30, no. 2–3 (1992): 25.

23. Jacobs, *Incidents in the Life*, 41.

24. Warner, "Harriet Jacobs's Modest Proposals," 24.

25. Jacobs, *Incidents in the Life*, 29.

26. Ibid.

27. Warner, "Harriet Jacobs's Modest Proposals," 24.

28. Jacobs, *Incidents in the Life*, 14.

29. Ibid.

30. Ibid.

31. Ibid.

32. Ibid.

33. Titus, "The Dining Room Door Swings Both Ways," 247.

34. Jacobs, *Incidents in the Life*, 12–13.

35. Ibid., 9.

36. Ibid.

37. Ibid., 13.

38. Ibid., 75.

39. Ibid., 14.

Chapter 7. Scenes from the Dialogic Kitchen: "Thinking Culture Dialogically" in Italian American Narratives

1. Maria Laurino, *Were You Always an Italian? Ancestors and Other Icons of Italian America* (New York: W. W. Norton & Company, 2000), 30.

2. Ibid., 31.

3. Davide Girardelli, "Commodified Identities: The Myth of Italian Food in the United States," *Journal of Communication Inquiry* 28, no. 4 (2004): 309.

4. Michael Gardiner, *Dialogics of Critique: M. M. Bakhtin and the Theory of Ideology* (London: Routledge, 1992), 23.

5. Ibid., 24.

6. Ibid., 26.

7. Finn Bostad et al., eds. *Bakhtinian Perspectives on Language and Culture: Meaning in Language, Art, and New Media* (Gordonsville, VA: Palgrave Macmillan, 2005), 4.

8. M. M. Bakhtin, "Discourse in the Novel," in *The Dialogic Imagination: Four Essays by M. M. Bakhtin*, ed. Michael Holquist, trans. Carl Emerson and Michael Holquist (Austin: University of Texas Press, 1981), 279.

9. M. M. Bakhtin, *Problems of Dostoevsky's Poetics*, ed. and trans. Caryl Emerson (Minneapolis: University of Minnesota Press, 1984), 293.

10. M. M. Bakhtin, *Speech Genres and Other Late Essays*, ed. Caryl Emerson and Michael Holquist, trans. Vern W. McGee (Austin, University of Texas Press, 1986), 170.

11. Bakhtin, "Discourse in the Novel," 276, 279.

12. Bakhtin, *Problems of Dostoevsky's Poetics*, 292–93.

13. Brandon James Scott, *Justin Time*, television episode, Guru Studio, 2011.

14. Ibid.

15. Joseph Durso, "Joe DiMaggio, the Yankee Clipper and an American Icon, Dies at 84," *The New York Times on the Web*, March 9, 1999, accessed August 12, 2014, http://www.nytimes.com/learning/teachers/featured_articles/19990309 tuesday.html.

16. Bakhtin, *Problems of Dostoevsky's Poetics*, 292–93.

17. Ibid., 292.

18. Ibid.

19. Peter Bondanella, "Palookas, Romeos, and Wise Guys: Italian Americans in Hollywood," in *Teaching Italian American Literature, Film, and Popular Culture*, ed. Edvige Giunta and Kathleen Zamboni McCormick (New York: The Modern Language Association of America, 2010), 222.

20. Ibid.

21. Thomas B. Farrell, *Norms of Rhetorical Culture* (Binghamton: Yale University Press, 1993), 47.

22. Walter Fisher, *Human Communication as Narration: Toward a Philosophy of Reason, Value, and Action* (Columbia: University of South Carolina Press, 1989), 63.

23. Ibid., 144.

24. Martin Parker, "Eating with the Mafia: Belonging and Violence," *Human Relations* 61, no. 7 (2008): 996.

25. Ibid.

26. Jerre Mangione, "On Being a Sicilian American," in *Studies in Italian American Social History,* ed. Francesco Cordasco (Totowa: Rowman and Littlefield, 1975), 41.

27. Ibid.

28. Parker, "Eating with the Mafia," 996.

29. Ibid.

30. Bakhtin, "Discourse in the Novel," 279.

31. Bakhtin, *Problems of Dostoevsky's Poetics*, 293.

32. *Goodfellas*, directed by Martin Scorsese, 1990; Burbank, CA: Warner Home Video, 1997, DVD.

33. Ibid.

34. Ibid.

35. *The Godfather*, directed by Francis Ford Coppola, 1972; Hollywood, CA: Paramount Pictures, 2001, DVD.

36. Parker, "Eating with the Mafia," 991.

37. Ibid.

38. Ibid.

39. Ibid.

40. Alane Salierno Mason, "The Exegesis of Eating," in *The Milk of Almonds: Italian American Women Writers on Food and Culture,* ed. Louise DeSalvo and Edvige Giunta (New York: Feminist Press at the City University of New York, 2002), 261–62.

41. Nancy Caronia, "Go to Hell," in *The Milk of Almonds,* ed. DeSalvo and Giunta, 97.

42. Ibid.

43. Ibid.

44. Ibid.

45. Ibid., 98.

46. Ibid.

47. Caronia, "Go to Hell," 98.

48. Ibid.

49. Ibid.

50. Fisher, *Human Communication as Narration*, 58.

51. Laurino, *Were You Always an Italian?*, 31.

52. Fisher, *Human Communication as Narration*, 58.

53. *Donnie Brasco*, directed by Mike Newell, 1997; Golden Valley, MN: Mill Creek Entertainment, 2000, DVD.

54. Ibid.

55. Ibid.

56. Ibid.

57. Fisher, *Human Communication as Narration*, 58.

58. Dorothy Bryant, "Dizzy Spells," in *The Milk of Almonds*, ed. DeSalvo and Giunta, 59.

59. Ibid.

60. Ibid.

61. Laurino, *Were You Always an Italian?*, 31.

62. Kym Ragusa, "Baked Ziti," in *The Milk of Almonds*, ed. DeSalvo and Giunta, 276.

63. Ibid., 277.

64. Ibid., 282.

65. Laurino, *Were You Always an Italian?*, 31–32.

66. Ibid., 31.

Chapter 8. Consuming Pleasures: Nineteenth-Century Cookery as Narrative Structure in *Downton Abbey*

1. Isabella Beeton, *Mrs. Beeton's Book of Household Management*, ed. Nicola Humble (London: Oxford University Press, 2000). The *Book of Household Management (BOHM)* was actually a separate publication from the *Englishwoman's Domestic Magazine (EDM)*. The two are easily conflated since the *EDM* heavily advertised the *BOHM* and several of the features found in the *BOHM* were first published in the *EDM*. See Kathryn Hughes, *The Short Life and Long Times of Mrs. Beeton: The First Domestic Goddess* (New York: Alfred A. Knopf, 2006), 187.

2. Simon Schama, "'Downton Abbey' Returns," *The Daily Beast*, January 16, 2012, accessed July 23, 2013, http://thedailybeast.com.

3. Lucy Scholes, "A Slave to the Stove? The TV Celebrity Chef Abandons the Kitchen: Lifestyle TV, Domesticity, and Gender," *Critical Quarterly* 53, no. 3 (2011): 45, accessed March 27, 2014, *Wiley Blackwell Online*.

4. Ibid., 46.

5. Gwyneth Paltrow, "Fed Up with Sugar: The Goop Guide to Alternative Sweeteners," goop, June 4, 2014, accessed June 5, 2014, http//:goop.com.

6. "*Downton Abbey's* Laura Carmichael: On Shoes, Wigs, & Why Mary and Edith Will Never Get Along," The New Potato, February 2, 2015, accessed February 11, 2015, http//:thenewpotato.com; "*Downton Abbey's* Joanne Froggatt: On Spray Tanning & Saying 'I Love You' to Mr. Bates," The New Potato, February 9, 2015, accessed February 11, 2015, http//:thenewpotato.com.

7. Jean Ingelow, "Taste," *Good Words*, 1888, 413, accessed July 1, 2015, http://babel.hathitrust.org/cgi/pt/search?q1=jean%20ingelow;id=ien.35556000746594;view=1up;seq=15;start=1;sz=10;page=search;orient=0.

8. Many of the recipes in the *BOHM* were taken directly from other cookbooks, many of them older sources. See Hughes, *The Short Life*, 188–209; and Andrea Broomfield, "Rushing Dinner to the Table: *The Englishwoman's Domestic Magazine* and Industrialization's Effects on Middle-Class Food and Cooking, 1852–1860." *Victorian Periodicals Review* 41, no. 2 (Summer 2008): 102–5, accessed March 27, 2014, *Project Muse*, DOI: 10.1353/vpr.0.0032.

9. See Broomfield, "Rushing Dinner to the Table," 101–23.

10. Andrew Higson, "Fiction and the Film Industry," in *A Concise Companion to Contemporary British Fiction*, ed. James F. English (Malden, MA: Blackwell Publishing, 2006), 66.

11. Andrew Higson, *Film England: Culturally English Filmmaking since the 1990s* (London: I. B. Tauris & Co., Ltd., 2011), 8.

12. Ibid., 31.

13. Ibid., 32.

14. Ibid., 27.

15. Jeremy Musson, *Up and Down Stairs: The History of the Country House Servant* (London: John Murray, 2009), 11.

16. "The Science of Etiquette and Deportment and Dress," *London Journal*, May 2, 1857, 157.

17. Miss Kelman's series ran in four issues of a weekly publication: Kelman, "Popular Papers on Cookery and Domestic Economy," *Bow Bells: A Magazine of General Literature and Art for Family Reading* 34, no. 858 (Jan 05, 1881): 46; 34, no. 862 (February 2, 1881): 142; 34, no. 866 (March 2, 1881): 238; and 34, no. 870 (March 30, 1881): 334.

18. Sarah Stickney Ellis, *The Women of England: Their Social Duties and Domestic Habits* (New York: D. Appleton & Co., 1839), 14, Google Books, accessed April 10, 2014, http://books.google.com/books?id=GwgUAAAAIAAJ&dq=/sarah%20stickney%20ellis&pg=/PR4#v=onepage&q=sarah%20stickney%20ellis&f=false.

19. Ibid., 14.

20. According to Lenore Davidoff and Catherine Hall, "Middle-class men and women were at the heart of the revivals which swept through all denominations. Their most vocal proponents had their sights fixed not only on gentry emulation but on a Heavenly Home. The goal of all the bustle of the market place was to provide a proper moral and religious life for the family." See Leonore Davidoff and Catherine Hall, *Family Fortunes: Men and Women of the English Middle Class, 1780–1850*, ed. Catharine R. Stimpson (Chicago: University of Chicago Press, 1987), 21.

21. Margaret Beetham, "Of Recipe Books and Reading in the Nineteenth Century: Mrs. Beeton and Her Cultural Consequences," in *The Recipe Reader: Narratives–Contexts–Traditions*, ed. Janet Floyd and Laurel Foster (New York: Ashgate, 2003), 20.

22. For a look at the *BOHM*'s complicated print history see Margaret Beetham, "Good Taste and Sweet Ordering: Dining with Mrs. Beeton," *Journal of Victorian Culture and Literature* 36 (2008): 391–406, *Cambridge Journals Online*, accessed March 27, 2014.

23. Ibid., 400.

24. Beetham, "Of Recipe Books and Reading," 20.

25. Beeton, *Mrs. Beeton's Book of Household Management (BOHM)*, 7.

26. Ibid., 27.

27. Ibid., 16.

28. Ibid.

29. Helen Day, "Möbial Consumption: Stability, Flux, and Interpermeability in 'Mrs. Beeton,'" in *Consuming Culture in the Long Nineteenth Century: Narratives*

of *Consumption, 1700–1900*, ed. Tamara S. Wagner and Narin Hassan (London: Lexington Books, 2007), 50.

30. Beeton, *BOHM*, 393.

31. Julian Fellowes, *Downton Abbey: Season 1*, directed by Brian Percival, Ben Bolt, and Brian Kelly, 2011, London, England: PBS Distribution, 2012, DVD, episode 1.1.

32. Ibid.

33. Ibid., episode 1.2

34. Ibid., episode 1.1.

35. Ibid.

36. Ibid.

37. Beeton, *BOHM*, 401.

38. Fellowes, *Downton Abbey*, episode 1.2.

39. Ibid.

40. Ibid., episode 1.1.

41. Musson, *Up and Down Stairs*, 224.

42. Beetham, *BOHM*, 402.

43. Ibid., 403.

44. Beeton, *BOHM*, 33.

45. Ibid., 393.

46. Fellowes, *Downton Abbey*, episode 1.5.

47. Fellowes, quoted in Musson, *Up and Down Stairs*, 11.

48. Julian Fellowes, interview by Dave Davies, *Fresh Air*, NPR, December 11, 2012.

49. Ibid.

50. John Heilpern, "'Downton Abbey': Escapist Kitsch Posing as 'Masterpiece Theatre': Is the Whole World Nostalgic for the Snobbery of the British Class System?" *The Nation*, February 8, 2012, accessed March 27, 2014, http://thenation.com.

51. Martin Pengelly, "Spoiler Alert: *Downton Abbey* Is a Waste of America's Precious TV Binge Time," *The Guardian*, February 23, 2014, accessed March 27, 2014, http://theguardian.com.

52. Pengelly also takes issue with the fact that Julian Fellowes has recently been knighted and elevated to the House of Lords as a Conservative member. Pengelly, "Spoiler Alert."

53. Gail Dines, "*Downton Abbey* and *House of Cards*: Dramas That Live in the World of 1%," *The Guardian*, February 20, 2014, accessed March 27, 2014, http://theguardian.com.

54. Schama, "'Downton Abbey' Returns."

55. See Mollie Hardwick, *The World of Upstairs, Downstairs* (New York: Holt, Rhinehart and Winston, 1976). The book even intersperses historical photographs of the Queen of England and her family with black and white production stills from the series, making it easy for a casual reader to think that both were from the same time period.

56. Schama, "'Downton Abbey' Returns."

57. Ibid.

58. See William Thackeray, "Roundabout Papers—No. 1: On a Lazy Idle Boy,"

The Cornhill (January 1860): 124–28; Geraldine Jewsbury, "Review," The Athenaeum, July 5, 1868, 106.

 59. Thackeray, "Roundabout Papers—No. 1," 27.

 60. Ibid., 127–28.

 61. Jewsbury, "Review," 106.

 62. Jennifer Hayward, Consuming Pleasures: Active Audiences and Serial Fictions from Dickens to Soap Opera (Lexington: University Press of Kentucky, 1997), 2. See also Tania Modleski, Loving with a Vengeance: Mass-Produced Fantasies for Women, 2nd ed. (New York: Routledge, 2008); and Henry Jenkins, Textual Poachers: Television Fans and Participatory Culture, updated Twentieth Anniversary ed. (New York: Routledge, 2013).

 63. Hayward, Consuming Pleasures, 4.

Chapter 9. Pie as Nostalgia: What One Food Symbolizes for Every Generation of Americans

 1. Fredric Jameson, "Nostalgia for the Present," South Atlantic Quarterly 88, no. 2 (1989): 527–37.

 2. This chapter does not attempt to discuss the sexual association with pie found in such films as Revenge of the Nerds or American Pie, as this reference, while certainly worth exploring, does not fit within the scope of this chapter, nor does it in any way alter its interpretation of the nostalgic value of pie.

 3. M.F.K. Fisher, "Apple Pie," in Mom, the Flag, and Apple Pie: Great American Writers on Great American Things, ed. Editors of Esquire (Garden City, NY: Doubleday and Co., 1976), 21.

 4. Jameson, "Nostalgia for the Present," 520.

 5. Fred Davis, Yearning for Yesterday: A Sociology of Nostalgia (New York: Free Press, 1979), 38.

 6. Ibid., 60.

 7. Ibid., 63.

 8. Anita Mannur, "Culinary Nostalgia: Authenticity, Nationalism, and Diaspora," MELUS 34, no. 4 (2007): 13.

 9. Katy Leary, A Lifetime with Mark Twain: the Memories of Katy Leary for Thirty Years His Faithful and Devoted Servant (New York: Haskell House, 1972), 281.

 10. Tracy N. Poe, "The Origins of Soul Food in Black Urban Identity: Chicago, 1915–1947," American Studies International 37 no. 1 (1999): 9–10.

 11. Eugenia Collier, "Sweet Potato Pie," in The Souls of Black Folk: with Related Readings, ed. W.E.B. Du Bois (New York: Glencoe McGraw Hill, 2002), 175.

 12. Ibid., 177.

 13. Ibid., 178.

 14. Ibid., 179.

 15. "Barack Obama: Too Much Pie for One Guy," Fark, accessed October 28, 2008, http://cgi.fark.com/cgi/fark/vidplayer.pl?IDLink=3940291.

 16. Mark Twain, A Tramp Abroad (Hartford: American Publishing Co., 1901), 262.

17. Ibid., 263.

18. *OED Online*, s.v., "pie, *n2.*," accessed October 26, 2008, http://dictionary. oed.com.proxy.lib.siu.edu/cgi/entry/30005204?query_type=word&queryword= pie&first=1&max_to_show=10&sort_type=alpha&search_id=Wgvn-VmAzNX-4616&result_place=3. As a point of distinction it is important to note that this definition falls under the entry for pie as a food, rather than its other usages.

19. Stephen King, "The Body," in *Different Seasons* (New York: New American Library, 1983), Kindle edition.

20. Ibid.

21. Ibid.

22. Ibid.

23. Ibid.

24. Ibid.

25. *Waitress*, directed by Adrienne Shelly (2007; Beverly Hills, CA: 20th Century Fox, 2007), DVD.

26. Ibid.

27. Ibid.

28. Ibid.

29. *Pushing Daisies: The Complete First Season*, performed by Lee Pace, Anna Friel, Chi McBride, Swoozie Kurtz, and Kristin Chenowith (2006–2007; Burbank, CA: Warner Brothers, 2008), DVD.

30. Svetlana Boym, *The Future of Nostalgia* (New York: Basic Books, 2001), 49.

31. Paul Grainge, *Monochrome Memories: Nostalgia and Style in Retro-America* (Westport, CT: Praeger, 2002), 29–30.

32. Jonathan Steinwand, "The Future of Nostalgia in Friedrich Schlegel's German Aesthetics beyond Ancient Greece and Modern Europe," in *Narratives of Nostalgia, Gender, and Nationalism*, ed. Jean Pickering and Suzanne Kehde (New York: New York University Press, 1997), 11.

33. Janice Doane and Devon Hodges, *Nostalgia and Sexual Difference: The Resistance to Contemporary Feminism* (New York: Metheun & Co., 1987), xiii.

34. Ellen G. Friedman, "Where Are the Missing Contents? (Post)Modernism, Gender, and the Canon," in *Narratives of Nostalgia, Gender, and Nationalism*, ed. Pickering and Kehde, 161.

35. Ibid., 162.

36. *Mad Men: Season 1*, performed by Jon Hamm, John Slattery, Vincent Kartheiser, and Peggy Olson (2007; Santa Monica, CA: Lionsgate, 2008), DVD.

37. *Waitress*, directed by Adrienne Shelly (2007; Beverly Hills, CA: 20th Century Fox, 2007), DVD.

38. Ibid.

39. Ibid.

40. *Pushing Daisies: The Complete Second Season*, performed by Lee Pace, Anna Friel, Chi McBride, Swoozie Kurtz, and Kristin Chenowith, 2007–2008 (Burbank, CA: Warner Brothers, 2009), DVD.

Chapter 10. The Last Twinkie in the Universe:
Culinary Hedonism and Nostalgia in Zombie Films

1. Michael Newbury, "Fast Zombie/Slow Zombie: Food Writing, Horror Movies, and Agribusiness Apocalypse," *American Literary History* 24, no. 1 (2012): 90, accessed March 1, 2014, *Project MUSE.*

2. Annalee Newitz, *Pretend We're Dead: Capitalist Monsters in American Pop Culture* (Durham: Duke University Press, 2006), 2.

3. Newbury, "Fast Zombie/Slow Zombie," 97.

4. *Dawn of the Dead*, directed by George A. Romero, 1978 (Hollywood: Anchor Bay Entertainment, 2004), DVD. See also Philip Horne, "I Shopped with a Zombie," *Critical Quarterly* 34, no. 4 (1992): 97, accessed March 1, 2014, *EBSCOhost.*

5. Kyle Bishop, "The Idle Proletariat: *Dawn of the Dead*, Consumer Ideology, and the Loss of Productive Labor," *Journal of Popular Culture* 43, no. 2 (2010): 234–35, accessed February 6, 2014, *EBSCOhost.*

6. Ibid.

7. Gareth Schott, "Dawn of the Digital Dead: The Zombie as Interactive Social Satire in American Popular Culture," *Australasian Journal of American Studies* 29, no. 1 (2010): 63, accessed February 6, 2014, *JSTOR.*

8. Horne, "I Shopped with a Zombie," 108.

9. Bishop, "The Idle Proletariat," 235.

10. Mary Douglas and Baron Isherwood, quoted in Horne, "I Shopped with a Zombie," 104.

11. Warren Belasco, "Food Matters: Perspectives on an Emerging Field," in *Food Nations: Selling Taste in Consumer Societies*, ed. Warren Belasco and Philip Scranton (New York: Routledge, 2002), 2.

12. Newbury, "Fast Zombie/Slow Zombie," 97.

13. Ibid., 103.

14. See, for instance, Sarah Elton's *Consumed*, in which she writes, "How will we feed ourselves in 2050? In the next forty years, the world's population is expected to surpass nine billion. At the same time, climate change is transforming life on the planet. According to the scientists who look at these big-picture issues, in the space of about one generation, a messy combination of climate, population trends, and environmental change will profoundly affect the world as we know it. We need to figure out how to feed the world, dramatically reduce our greenhouse gas emissions, and cope with climate change." Sarah Elton, *Consumed: Food for a Finite Planet* (Chicago: University of Chicago Press, 2013), 3.

15. Newbury, "Fast Zombie/Slow Zombie," 104.

16. Michael Pollan writes, "You're better off eating whole fresh foods rather than processed food products. That's what I mean by the recommendation to 'eat food,' which is not quite as simple as it sounds. For while it used to be that food was all you *could* eat, today there are thousands of other edible foodlike substances in the supermarkets." Michael Pollan, *In Defense of Food* (New York: Penguin, 2008), 11.

17. *28 Days Later*, directed by Danny Boyle (London: DNA Films, 2003), DVD.

18. Newbury, "Fast Zombie/Slow Zombie," 87–89.

19. Ibid. A similar scene occurs in *World War Z*, directed by Marc Forster (Los Angeles: Plan B Entertainment, 2013), DVD.

20. Newbury, "Fast Zombie/Slow Zombie," 89.

21. Elizabeth D. Capaldi, *Why We Eat What We Eat: The Psychology of Food* (Washington, DC: American Psychological Association, 1996), 67.

22. Newbury, "Fast Zombie/Slow Zombie," 90.

23. *Shaun of the Dead*, directed by Edgar Wright (Hollywood: Rogue Pictures [United States Affiliation], 2004), DVD.

24. The other two films in the trilogy are *Hot Fuzz* (2007) and *The World's End* (2013). In each of the films, the characters endure death, destruction, and trauma and experience (and sometimes cause) mindless violence. They also consume ice cream at some point in each of the films, both as palliative against the trauma and because ice cream serves as a dietary staple for most of Pegg and Wright's characters.

25. Newbury, "Fast Zombie/Slow Zombie," 102.

26. *Shaun of the Dead*, directed by Wright.

27. Leon Rappoport, *How We Eat: Appetite, Culture, and the Psychology of Food* (Toronto: ECW Press, 2003), 26.

28. Newbury, "Fast Zombie/Slow Zombie," 102.

29. *Zombieland*, directed by Ruben Fleischer (Hollywood: Columbia Pictures, 2009), DVD.

30. Ibid.

31. Rappoport, *How We Eat*, 34.

32. *28 Days Later*, directed by Boyle.

33. *Zombieland*, directed by Fleischer.

34. Ibid.

35. Ibid.

36. Svetlana Boym, *The Future of Nostalgia* (New York: Basic Books, 2001), xiii.

37. *I Am Legend*, directed by Francis Lawrence (Burbank, CA: Warner Bros, 2007), DVD.

38. Ibid.

39. Ibid.

40. Boym, *The Future of Nostalgia*, 17.

41. Ibid., xv.

42. Ibid., xiv.

43. Ibid.

44. Ibid.

45. *Zombieland*, directed by Fleischer.

46. *28 Days Later*, directed by Boyle.

47. Ibid.

48. Boym, *The Future of Nostalgia*, xvi.

49. *28 Days Later*, directed by Boyle.

50. Boym, *The Future of Nostalgia*, xvii.

BIBLIOGRAPHY

28 Days Later. Directed by Danny Boyle. London: DNA Films, 2003. DVD.

"A Conversation with Bich Minh Nguyen." *Reading Group Guide*. Accessed November 15, 2013, http://www.us.penguingroup.com/static/rguides/us/ stealing_buddhas_dinner.html.

Abdy, Edward. *Journal of a Residence and Tour in the United States*. London: J. Murray, 1835. Accessed September 16, 2014, https://archive.org/stream/cihm_ 28465#page/n7/mode/2up.

"About the Jim Crow Museum." Ferris State University. Accessed March 17, 2014, http://www.ferris.edu/jimcrow/more.htm.

Acton, Sir John. *Acton in America: The American Journal of Sir John Acton*. Edited by Sydney Jackman. Shepherdstown, WV: Patmos Press, 1979.

August, Timothy K. "The Contradictions in Culinary Collaboration: Vietnamese American Bodies in *Top Chef* and *Stealing Buddha's Dinner*." *MELUS* 37, no. 3 (2012): 97–115.

Bakhtin, M. M. "Discourse in the Novel." In *The Dialogic Imagination: Four Essays by M. M. Bakhtin*, edited by Michael Holquist, translated by Carl Emerson and Michael Holquist, 259–422. Austin: University of Texas Press, 1981.

———. *Problems of Dostoevsky's Poetics*. Edited and translated by Caryl Emerson. Minneapolis: University of Minnesota Press, 1984.

———. *Speech Genres and Other Late Essays*. Edited by Caryl Emerson and Michael Holquist. Translated by Vern W. McGee. Austin: University of Texas Press, 1986.

"Barack Obama: Too Much Pie for One Guy." *Fark*. Accessed October 28, 2008, http://cgi.fark.com/cgi/fark/vidplayer.pl?IDLink=3940291.

Barthes, Roland. "Toward a Psychosociology of Contemporary Food Consumption." In *Food and Culture: A Reader,* 2nd ed., edited by Carole Counihan and Penny Van Esterik, 28–35. New York: Routledge, 1997.

Baudrillard, Jean. *For a Critique of the Political Economy of the Sign*. St. Louis, MO: Telos Press, 1981.

Beetham, Margaret. "Good Taste and Sweet Ordering: Dining with Mrs. Beeton." *Journal of Victorian Culture and Literature* 36 (2008): 391–406. *Cambridge Journals Online*. Accessed March 27, 2014, http://www.eifl.net/e-resources/ cambridge-journals-online.

———. "Of Recipe Books and Reading in the Nineteenth Century: Mrs. Beeton and Her Cultural Consequences." In *The Recipe Reader: Narratives–Contexts– Traditions*, edited by Janet Floyd and Laurel Foster, 15–30. New York: Ashgate, 2003.

Beeton, Isabella. *Mrs. Beeton's Book of Household Management*. Edited by Nicola Humble. London: Oxford University Press, 2000.

Belasco, Warren. "Food Matters: Perspectives on an Emerging Field." In *Food Nations: Selling Taste in Consumer Societies*, edited by Warren Belasco and Philip Scranton, 2–23. New York: Routledge, 2002.

Biber, Douglas, and Edward Finegan. *Sociolinguistic Perspectives on Register*. New York: Oxford University Press, 1994.

Bishop, Kyle. "The Idle Proletariat: *Dawn of the Dead*, Consumer Ideology, and the Loss of Productive Labor." *Journal of Popular Culture* 43, no. 2 (2010): 234–48. Accessed February 6, 2014, EBSCOhost.

Bombeck, Erma. "Seize the Moment—June 25, 1991." In *Forever, Erma: Best-Loved Writing from America's Favorite Humorist*, 243–44. Kansas City: Andrews McMeel, 1997.

Bondanella, Peter. "Palookas, Romeos, and Wise Guys: Italian Americans in Hollywood." In *Teaching Italian American Literature, Film, and Popular Culture*, edited by Edvige Giunta and Kathleen Zamboni McCormick, 217–22. New York: *The Modern Language Association of America*, 2010.

Bostad, Finn, Craig Brandist, Lars Sigfred Evensen, and Hege Charlotte Faber, eds. *Bakhtinian Perspectives on Language and Culture: Meaning in Language, Art, and New Media*. Gordonsville, VA: Palgrave Macmillan, 2005.

Bourdieu, Pierre. *Distinction: A Social Critique of the Judgment of Taste*. Cambridge: Cambridge University Press, 1984.

Boym, Svetlana. *The Future of Nostalgia*. New York: Basic Books, 2001.

Broomfield, Andrea. "Rushing Dinner to the Table: *The Englishwoman's Domestic Magazine* and Industrialization's Effects on Middle-Class Food and Cooking, 1852–1860." *Victorian Periodicals Review* 41, no. 2 (Summer 2008): 102–5. Accessed March 27, 2014, *Project Muse*. DOI: 10.1353/vpr.0.0032.

Brown, Linda Keller, and Kay Mussell, eds. *Ethnic and Regional Foodways in the US: The Performance of Group Identity*. Knoxville: University of Tennessee Press, 1984.

Bryant, Dorothy. "Dizzy Spells." In *The Milk of Almonds: Italian American Women Writers on Food and Culture*, edited by Louise DeSalvo and Edvige Giunta, 56–63. New York: Feminist Press at the City University of New York, 2002.

Byrne, Denis R. "Nervous Landscapes: Race and Space in Australia." *Journal of Social Archaeology* 3, no. 2 (2003): 169–93.

Capaldi, Elizabeth D. *Why We Eat What We Eat: The Psychology of Food*. Washington, DC: American Psychological Association, 1996.

Caronia, Nancy. "Go to Hell." In *The Milk of Almonds: Italian American Women Writers on Food and Culture*, edited by Lousie DeSalvo and Edvige Giunta, 95–100. New York: Feminist Press at the City University of New York, 2002.

Carruth, Allison. *Global Appetites: American Power and the Literature of Food*. Cambridge: Cambridge University Press, 2013.

Cheng, Anne Anlin. *The Melancholy of Race: Psychoanalysis, Assimilation, and Hidden Grief.* New York: Oxford University Press: 2001.

Chez, Keridiana. "Popular Ethnic Food Guides as Auto/Ethnographic Project: The Multicultural and Gender Politics of Urban Culinary Tourism." *Journal of American Culture* 34, no. 3 (2011): 234–46. Accessed January 10, 2015, *EBSCOhost.*

Chicago Public Radio. "This American Life TV Show Nominated for Five Emmys." Accessed July 19, 2014, http://www.prnewswire.com/news-releases/this-american-life-tv-show-nominated-for-five-emmys-64933537.html.

"Classic Aunt Jemima Commercial (1967)." Internet Archive. Accessed March 18, 2014, https://archive.org/details/ClassicAuntJemimaCommercial1967.

Colbert, Don. *The Seven Pillars of Health.* Lake Mary, FL: Siloam, 2007.

Collier, Eugenia. "Sweet Potato Pie." In *The Souls of Black Folk: With Related Readings,* edited by W.E.B. Du Bois, 171–79. New York: Glencoe McGraw Hill, 2002.

Collins, Patricia Hill. *Black Sexual Politics: African Americans, Gender, and the New Racism.* New York: Routledge, 2004.

Coontz, Stephanie. *The Way We Never Were: American Families and the Nostalgia Trip.* New York: Basic Books, 1992.

Counihan, Carole M., ed. *Food in the USA: A Reader.* New York: Routledge, 2002.

Curry, Leonard P. *The Free Black in Urban America, 1800–1850: The Shadow of a Dream.* Chicago: University of Chicago Press, 1981.

Daniels, John. *In Freedom's Birthplace: A Study of the Boston Negroes.* Boston: Arno Press, 1914.

Davidoff, Leonore, and Catherine Hall. *Family Fortunes: Men and Women of the English Middle Class, 1780–1850. Women in Culture and Society series.* Chicago: University of Chicago Press, 1987.

Davis, Fred. *Yearning for Yesterday: A Sociology of Nostalgia.* New York: Free Press, 1979.

Dawn of the Dead. Directed by George A. Romero. 1978. Hollywood: Anchor Bay Entertainment, 2004. DVD.

Day, Helen. "Möbial Consumption: Stability, Flux, and Interpermeability in 'Mrs. Beeton.'" In *Consuming Culture in the Long Nineteenth Century: Narratives of Consumption, 1700–1900,* edited by Tamara S. Wagner and Narin Hassan, 49–62. London: Lexington Books, 2007.

De Bruyn, Ben. "Borrowed Time, Borrowed World, and Borrowed Eyes: Care, Ruin, and Vision in Cormac McCarthy's *The Road* and Harrison's *Ecocriticism.*" *English Studies* 91, no. 7 (2010): 776–89. Accessed April 26, 2012, *EBSCOhost.*

de Solier, Isabelle. "Making the Self in a Material World." *Cultural Studies Review* 19, no. 1 (2013): 9–27. Accessed January 19, 2015, *EBSCOhost.*

Deck, Alice A. "'Now Then—Who Said Biscuits?' The Black Woman Cook as Fetish in American Advertising, 1905–1953." In *Kitchen Culture in America,* edited by

Sherrie A. Inness, 69–94. Philadelphia: University of Pennsylvania Press, 2001.

Demaj, Ada. "Touching Race through Play: Sadomasochism, Phenomenology, and the Intertwining of Race." *Annual Review of Critical Psychology* 11 (2014): 97–111.

Dickens, Charles. *American Notes.* 1842. Reprint, Gloucester, MA: P. Smith, 1968.

"Dim Sum Lose Some." *Pushing Daisies.* Perf. Lee Pace, Anna Friel, Chi McBride, Swoozie Kurtz, and Kristin Chenowith. ABC. October 29, 2008. DVD.

Diner, Hasia. *Hungering for America: Italian, Irish, and Jewish Foodways in the Age of Migration.* Cambridge: Harvard University Press, 2003.

Dines, Gail. "*Downton Abbey* and *House of Cards*: Dramas That Live in the World of 1%." *The Guardian,* February 20, 2014. Accessed March 27, 2014, http://theguardian.com.

Dissanayake, Wimal. "Globalization and Experience of Culture: The Resilience of Nationhood." In *Globalization, Cultural Identities, and Media Representation,* edited by Natascha Kramer and Stefan Gentz, 25–45. Albany: State University of New York Press, 2006.

Doane, Janice, and Devon Hodges. *Nostalgia and Sexual Difference: The Resistance to Contemporary Feminism.* New York: Metheun & Co., 1987.

Donnie Brasco. Directed by Mike Newell. 1997. Los Angeles, CA: Mandalay Pictures, 2006. DVD.

Douglas, Mary. "Deciphering a Meal." In *Implicit Meanings: Essays in Anthropology,* 231–51. London: Routledge & Kegan Paul, 1975.

"*Downton Abbey*'s Joanne Froggatt: On Spray Tanning & Saying 'I Love You' to Mr. Bates." The New Potato, February 9, 2015, accessed February 11, 2015, http//:thenewpotato.com.

"*Downton Abbey*'s Laura Carmichael: On Shoes, Wigs, & Why Mary and Edith Will Never Get Along." The New Potato, February 2, 2015, accessed February 11, 2015, http//:thenewpotato.com.

Duis, Perry. *The Saloon: Public Drinking in Chicago and Boston, 1880–1920.* Chicago: University of Illinois Press, 1983.

Durso, Joseph. "Joe DiMaggio, the Yankee Clipper and an American Icon, Dies at 84." *The New York Times on the Web,* March 9, 1999. Accessed August 12, 2014, http://www.nytimes.com/learning/teachers/featured articles/19990309tuesday.html.

Ellis, Sarah Stickney. *The Women of England: Their Social Duties and Domestic Habits.* New York: D. Appleton & Co., 1839. Google Books. Accessed July 1, 2015, https://books.google.com/books?id=5BIEAAAAQAAJ&printsec=frontcover&dq=sarah+stickney+ellis+the+women+of+england&hl=en&sa=X&ei=2ZKVVai_O5TqoASGoqiADA&ved=0CCYQ6AEwAA#v=onepage&q=sarah%20stickney%20ellis%20the%20women%20of%20england&f=false.

Elton, Sarah. *Consumed: Food for a Finite Planet*. Chicago: University of Chicago Press, 2013.

Erby, Kelly. "Worthy of Respect: Black Waiters in Boston before the Civil War." *Food and History* 5 (February 2008): 205–18.

Farrell, Thomas B. *Norms of Rhetorical Culture*. Binghamton: Yale University Press, 1993.

Fellowes, Julian. *Downton Abbey: Season 1*. Directed by Brian Percival, Ben Bolt, and Brian Kelly. 2011. London, England: PBS Distribution, 2012. DVD.

———. Interview by Dave Davies. *Fresh Air*. NPR, December 11, 2012.

Fisher, M.F.K. "Apple Pie." In *Mom, the Flag, and Apple Pie: Great American Writers on Great American Things*, edited by Editors of *Esquire*, 21–26. Garden City, NY: Doubleday and Co., 1976.

———. *The Art of Eating*. Hoboken: Wiley, 2004.

Fisher, Walter. *Human Communication as Narration: Toward a Philosophy of Reason, Value, and Action*. Columbia: University of South Carolina Press, 1989.

Foer, Jonathan Safran. *Eating Animals*. New York: Little, Brown and Company, 2009.

Foucault, Michel. "The Subject and Power." In *Michel Foucault: Beyond Structuralism and Hermeneutics*, 2nd ed., edited by Hubert L. Dreyfus and Paul Rabinow, 208–29. Chicago: University of Chicago Press, 1982.

"Frescorts." *Pushing Daisies*. Perf. Lee Pace, Anna Friel, Chi McBride, Swoozie Kurtz, and Kristin Chenowith. ABC. October 22, 2008.

Friedman, Ellen G. "Where Are the Missing Contents? (Post)Modernism, Gender, and the Canon." In *Narratives of Nostalgia, Gender, and Nationalism*, edited by Jean Pickering and Suzanne Kehde, 159–81. New York: New York University Press, 1997.

Furness, Clifton Joseph. "Whitman Looks at Boston." *New England Quarterly* 1 (July 1928): 356.

Gardaphé, Fred L., and Wenying Xu. "Introduction: Food in Multi-Ethnic Literatures." *MELUS* 32, no. 4 (2007): 5–10. Accessed January 10, 2015, *MLA International Bibliography*.

Gardiner, Michael. *Dialogics of Critique: M. M. Bakhtin and the Theory of Ideology*. London: Routledge, 1992.

Giddings, Paula. "The Body Politic." In *Words of Fire: An Anthology of African-American Feminist Thought*, edited by Beverly Guy-Sheftall, 416. New York: New Press, 1995.

Gillis, John R. *A World of Their Own Making: Myth, Ritual, and the Quest for Family Values*. New York: Basic Books, 1996.

Girardelli, Davide. "Commodified Identities: The Myth of Italian Food in the United States." *Journal of Communication Inquiry* 28, no. 4 (2004): 307–24.

The Godfather. Directed by Francis Ford Coppola. 1972. Hollywood, CA: Paramount Pictures, 2001. DVD.

Goodfellas. Directed by Martin Scorsese. 1990. Los Angeles, CA: Warner Brothers, 2007. DVD.

Grainge, Paul. *Monochrome Memories: Nostalgia and Style in Retro-America*. Westport, CT: Praeger, 2002.

Gritz, Jennie Rothenberg. "New Racism Museum Reveals the Ugly Truth behind Aunt Jemima." *Atlantic*, April 23, 2012. Accessed March 18, 2014, http://www.theatlantic.com.

Guthman, Julie. "Can't Stomach It: How Michael Pollan et al. Made Me Want to Eat Cheetos." *Gastronomica: The Journal of Culture and Food* 7, no. 2 (2007): 75–79.

Haley, Andrew. *Turning the Tables: Restaurants and the Rise of the American Middle Class, 1880–1920*. Chapel Hill: University of North Carolina Press, 2011.

Hall, Basil. *Travels in North America in the Years 1827 and 1828*. New York: Arno Press, 1974.

Handlin, Oscar. *Boston's Immigrants: 1790–1880*. Cambridge: Belknap Press, 1991.

Hardwick, Mollie. *The World of Upstairs, Downstairs*. New York: Holt, Rhinehart and Winston, 1976.

Harris, Trudier. *From Mammies to Militants: Domestics in Black American Literature*. Philadelphia: Temple University Press, 1982.

Hayward, Jennifer. *Consuming Pleasures: Active Audiences and Serial Fictions from Dickens to Soap Opera*. Lexington: University Press of Kentucky, 1997.

Heffernan, Virginia. "This American Life Ira Glass Television Review." *The New York Times—Breaking News, World News & Multimedia*, March 22, 2007. Accessed December 19, 2011, http://www.nytimes.com/2007/03/22/arts/television/22heff.html.

Heilpern, John. "'Downton Abbey': Escapist Kitsch Posing as 'Masterpiece Theatre': Is the Whole World Nostalgic for the Snobbery of the British Class System?" *The Nation*, February 8, 2012. Accessed March 27, 2014, http://thenation.com.

Hernandez, D. "Playing with Race: On the Edge of Edgy Sex: Racial BDSM Excites Some and Reviles Others." *Colorlines* 7, no. 4 (2004): 14–18.

Higson, Andrew. "Fiction and the Film Industry." In *A Concise Companion to Contemporary British Fiction*, edited by James F. English, 58-79. Malden, MA: Blackwell Publishing, 2006.

———. *Film England: Culturally English Filmmaking since the 1990s*. London: I. B. Tauris & Co., Ltd., 2011.

Horne, Philip. "I Shopped with a Zombie." *Critical Quarterly* 34, no. 4 (1992): 97–110. Accessed March 1, 2014, *EBSCOhost*.

Horton, James Oliver. *Black Bostonians: Family Life and Community Struggle in the Antebellum North*. New York: Holmes and Meier, 1979.

Hughes, Kathryn. *The Short Life and Long Times of Mrs. Beeton: The First Domestic Goddess*. New York: Alfred A. Knopf, 2006.

I Am Legend. Directed by Francis Lawrence. Burbank, CA: Warner Bros, 2007. DVD.

Ignatiev, Noel. *How the Irish Became White*. New York: Routledge, 1995.

Ingelow, Jean. "Taste." In *Good Words*, 413. 1888. Accessed July 1, 2015, http://babel. hathitrust.org/cgi/pt/search?q1=jean%20ingelow;id=ien.35556000746594; view=1up;seq=15;start=1;sz=10;page=search;orient=0.

Inness, Sherrie A., ed. *Kitchen Culture in America: Popular Representations of Food, Gender, and Race*. Philadelphia: University of Pennsylvania Press, 2001.

Jacobs, Harriet. *Incidents in the Life of a Slave Girl*. New York: Dover Publications, 2001.

Jacobson, Matthew Frye. *Whiteness of a Different Color: European Immigrants and the Alchemy of Race*. Cambridge, MA: Harvard University Press, 1998.

Jameson, Fredric. "Nostalgia for the Present." *South Atlantic Quarterly* 88, no. 2 (1989): 527–37.

Jenkins, Henry. *Textual Poachers: Television Fans and Participatory Culture*. Updated Twentieth Anniversary ed. New York: Routledge, 2013.

Jewsbury, Geraldine. "Review." *The Athenaeum*, July 25, 1868, 106.

Justin Time. "Marcello's Meatballs/Where's the Oasis?" Episode no. 8, season 1, first broadcast 2011 by PBS. Directed by Harold Harris and written by Andrew Sabiston.

Kalb, Deborah. "Q and A with Writer Bich Minh Nguyen." *Haunting Legacy*. Accessed August 1, 2012, http://www.hauntinglegacy.com/qas-with-experts/ 2012/8/1/qa-with-writer-bich-minh-nguyen.html.

Kelman. "Popular Papers on Cookery and Domestic Economy." *Bow Bells: A Magazine of General Literature and Art for Family Reading* 34, no. 858 (January 5, 1881): 46.

———. "Popular Papers on Cookery and Domestic Economy." *Bow Bells: A Magazine of General Literature and Art for Family Reading* 34, no. 862 (February 2, 1881): 142.

———. "Popular Papers on Cookery and Domestic Economy." *Bow Bells: A Magazine of General Literature and Art for Family Reading* 34, no. 866 (March 2, 1881): 238.

———. "Popular Papers on Cookery and Domestic Economy." *Bow Bells: A Magazine of General Literature and Art for Family Reading* 34, no. 870 (March 30, 1881): 334.

Kessler, Brad. "One Reader's Digest: Toward a Gastronomic Theory of Literature." *Kenyon Review* 27, no. 2 (2005): 148–65. Accessed April 26, 2012, *JSTOR*.

King, Stephen. "The Body." In *Different Seasons*. New York: New American Library, 1983. Kindle edition.

Kraig, Bruce. *Hot Dog: A Global History*. London: Reaktion Books, 2009.

Laurie, Bruce. *Artisans into Workers: Labor in Nineteenth-Century America*. Urbana: University of Illinois Press, 1997.

Laurino, Marino. *Were You Always an Italian? Ancestors and Other Icons of Italian America*. New York: W. W. Norton & Company, 2006.

Leary, Katy. *A Lifetime with Mark Twain: The Memories of Katy Leary for Thirty Years His Faithful and Devoted Servant*. New York: Haskell House, 1972.

Levitt, Theodore. "The Globalization of Markets." *Harvard Business Review* 61, no. 3 (1983): 92–102.

Logan, Rayford, and Michael R. Winston, eds. *Dictionary of American Negro Biography*. New York: W. W. Norton, 1982.

Lott, Eric. *Love and Theft: Blackface Minstrelsy and the American Working Class*. New York: Oxford University Press, 1995.

Luskey, Brian. *On the Make: Clerks and the Quest for Capital*. New York: New York University Press, 2010.

Mad Men: Season 1. Perf. Jon Hamm, John Slattery, Vincent Kartheiser, and Peggy Olson. 2007. Santa Monica, CA: Lionsgate, 2008. DVD.

Mangione, Jerre. "On Being a Sicilian American." In *Studies in Italian American Social History*, edited by Francesco Cordasco, 40–49. Totowa, NJ: Rowman and Littlefield, 1975.

Mannur, Anita. "Culinary Nostalgia: Authenticity, Nationalism, and Diaspora." *MELUS* 34, no. 4 (2007): 11–31.

Manring, M. M. *Slave in a Box: The Strange Career of Aunt Jemima*. Charlottesville: University of Virginia Press, 1998.

Marquette, Arthur F. *Brands, Trademarks, and Good Will: The Story of the Quaker Oats Company*. New York: Basic, 1966.

Mason, Alane Salierno. "The Exegesis of Eating." In *The Milk of Almonds: Italian American Women Writers on Food and Culture*, edited by Louise DeSalvo and Edvige Giunta, 261–69. New York: Feminist Press at the City University of New York, 2002.

McCarthy, Cormac. *The Road*. New York: Vintage International, 2006.

McElya, Micki. *Clinging to Mammy: The Faithful Slave in Twentieth-Century America*. Cambridge, MA: Harvard University Press, 2007.

Mihm, Stephen. *A Nation of Counterfeiters: Capitalists, Con Men, and the Making of the United States*. Cambridge: Harvard University Press, 2007.

Miller, Daniel. *Consumption and Its Consequences*. Cambridge: Polity Press, 2012. Kindle edition.

Miller-Young, M. "Putting Hypersexuality to Work: Black Women and Illicit Eroticism in Pornography." *Sexualities* 13, no. 2 (2010): 219–35.

Modleski, Tania. *Loving with a Vengeance: Mass-Produced Fantasies for Women*. 2nd ed. New York: Routledge, 2008.

Morrison, Toni. *The Bluest Eye*. New York: Vintage International, 1970.

Musson, Jeremy. *Up and Down Stairs: The History of the Country House Servant*. London: John Murray, 2009.

Naranjo-Huebl, Linda. "'Take, Eat': Food Imagery, the Nurturing Ethic, and Christian Identity in *The Wide, Wide World*, *Uncle Tom's Cabin*, and *Incidents* in the Life of a Slave Girl." *Christianity and Literature* 56, no. 4 (2007): 597–633.

Newbury, Michael. "Fast Zombie/Slow Zombie: Food Writing, Horror Movies, and Agribusiness Apocalypse." *American Literary History* 24, no. 1 (2012): 87–114. Accessed March 1, 2014, *Project MUSE.*

Newitz, Annalee. *Pretend We're Dead: Capitalist Monsters in American Pop Culture.* Durham, NC: Duke University Press, 2006.

Nguyen, Bich Minh. "Goodbye to My Twinkie Days." *New York Times,* November 16, 2012, http://www.nytimes.com/2012/11/17/opinion/goodbye-to-my-twinkie-days.html.

———. "How I Found My Mother." In *Requiem for a Paper Bag: Celebrities and Civilians Tell Stories of the Best Lost, Tossed, and Found Items from around the World,* edited by Davy Rothbart, 51–53. New York: Fireside, 2009.

———. *Stealing Buddha's Dinner: A Memoir.* New York: Viking, 2007.

Nick Cave & The Bad Seeds. "Cannibal's Hymn." *Abattoir Blues/The Lyre of Orpheus.* Anti/Epitaph: Mute Records, 2004.

Nissenbaum, Stephen. *Sex, Diet, and Debility in Jacksonian America: Sylvester Graham and Health Reform.* Westport, CN: Greenwood Press, 1980.

OED Online, s.v. "pie, *n2.*" Accessed October 26, 2008, http://dictionary.oed.com. proxy.lib.siu.edu/cgi/entry/30005204?query_type=word&queryword=pie& first=1&max_to_show=10&sort_type=alpha&search_id=Wgvn-VmAz NX-4616&result_place=3.

Padolsky, Enoch. "You Are Where You Eat: Ethnicity, Food, and Cross-Cultural Spaces." *Canadian Ethnic Studies* 37, no. 2 (2005): 19–31. Accessed January 19, 2015, *EBSCOhost.*

Paige, Lucius Robinson. *History of Cambridge, Massachusetts, 1630–1877, with a Genealogical Register.* Boston: H. O. Houghton and Company, 1877.

Paltrow, Gwyneth. "Fed Up with Sugar: The Goop Guide to Alternative Sweeteners." Goop. June 4, 2014. Accessed June 5, 2014, http://goop.com.

Parker, Martin. "Eating with the Mafia: Belonging and Violence." *Human Relations* 61, no. 7 (2008): 989–1006.

Parks, Sheri L. *Fierce Angels: The Strong Black Woman in American Life and Culture.* New York: Ballantine Books, 2010.

Patel, Raj. *Stuffed and Starved: The Hidden Battle for the World Food System.* Brooklyn: Melville House, 2012. Kindle edition.

Pengelly, Martin. "Spoiler Alert: *Downton Abbey* Is a Waste of America's Precious TV Binge Time." *The Guardian,* February 23, 2014. Accessed March 27, 2014, http://theguardian.com.

Peters, Erica J. *Appetites and Aspirations in Vietnam: Food and Drink in the Long Nineteenth Century.* Plymouth, UK: AltaMira Press, 2012.

Pietrykowski, Bruce. "You Are What You Eat: The Social Economy of the Slow Food Movement." *Review of Social Economy* 62, no. 3 (2004): 307–21. Accessed January 11, 2015, *EBSCOhost.*

Pillsbury, Richard. *From Boardinghouse to Bistro: The American Restaurant Then and Now.* Boston: Unwin Hyman, 1990.

Pleck, Elizabeth Hafkin. *Black Migration and Poverty, Boston, 1865–1900.* New York: Academy Press, 1979.

Poe, Tracy N. "The Origins of Soul Food in Black Urban Identity: Chicago, 1915–1947." *American Studies International* 37, no. 1 (1999): 4–33.

Pollan, Michael. *Cooked: A Natural History of Transformation.* New York: Penguin Press, 2013.

———. *In Defense of Food: An Eater's Manifesto.* New York: Penguin Press, 2008.

———. *The Omnivore's Dilemma.* New York: Penguin Books, 2006.

Pushing Daisies: The Complete First Season. Perf. Lee Pace, Anna Friel, Chi McBride, Swoozie Kurtz, and Kristin Chenowith. 2006–2007. Burbank, CA: Warner Brothers, 2008. DVD.

Pushing Daisies: The Complete Second Season. Perf. Lee Pace, Anna Friel, Chi McBride, Swoozie Kurtz, and Kristin Chenowith. 2007–2008. Burbank, CA: Warner Brothers, 2009. DVD.

Ragusa, Kym. "Baked Ziti." In *The Milk of Almonds: Italian American Women Writers on Food and Culture,* edited by Louise DeSalvo and Edvige Giunta, 276–82. New York: Feminist Press at the City University of New York, 2002.

Rappoport, Leon. *How We Eat: Appetite, Culture, and the Psychology of Food.* Toronto: ECW Press, 2003.

Robertson, Roland. "Glocalization: Time-Space and Homogeneity-Heterogeneity." In *Global Modernities,* edited by Mike Featherstone, Scott Lash, and Roland Robertson, 25–34. Thousand Oaks, CA: Sage, 1995.

Roediger, David. *The Wages of Whiteness: Race and the Making of the American Working Class.* London: Verso, 2007.

Rozin, Paul, Maureen Markwith, and Caryn Stoess. "Moralization and Becoming a Vegetarian: The Transformation of Preferences into Values and the Recruitment of Disgust." *Psychological Science* 8, no. 2 (March 1997): 67–73. Accessed January 23, 2015, *JSTOR.*

Said, Edward W. "Orientalism Reconsidered." *Cultural Critique* 1 (1985): 89–107.

Schama, Simon. "'Downton Abbey' Returns." *Daily Beast,* January 16, 2012. Accessed July 23, 2013, http://thedailybeast.com.

Schiffer, Ed. "'Fable Number One': Some Myths about Consumption." In *Eating Culture,* edited by Ron Scapp and Brian Seitz, 288–94. Albany: State University of New York Press, 1998.

Scholes, Lucy. "A Slave to the Stove? The TV Celebrity Chef Abandons the Kitchen: Lifestyle TV, Domesticity, and Gender." *Critical Quarterly* 53, no. 3 (2011): 44–59. Accessed March 27, 2014, *Wiley Blackwell Online.*

Schott, Gareth. "Dawn of the Digital Dead: The Zombie as Interactive Social Satire in American Popular Culture." *Australasian Journal of American Studies* 29, no. 1 (2010): 61–75. Accessed February 6, 2014, *JSTOR.*

"The Science of Etiquette and Deportment and Dress." *London Journal*, May 2, 1857, 157.

Scott, Brandon James. *Justin Time*. Television Episode. Guru Studio. 2011.

Sedikides, Constantine, Tim Wildschut, Jamie Arndt, and Clay Routledge. "Nostalgia: Past, Present, and Future." *Current Directions in Psychological Sciences* 17, no. 5 (2008): 304–7.

Sellers, Charles. *The Market Revolution: Jacksonian America, 1815–1846*. New York: Oxford University Press, 1994.

Sewell, Jessica Ellen. *Women and the Everyday City: Public Space in San Francisco, 1890–1915*. Minneapolis: University of Minnesota Press, 2011.

Shaun of the Dead. Directed by Edgar Wright. Hollywood: Rogue Pictures (United States Affiliate), 2004. DVD.

Sokolov, Raymond. *Fading Feast*. New York: Farrar Straus & Giroux, 1981.

Sontag, Susan. "Notes on 'Camp.'" In *Against Interpretation and Other Essays,* 275–92. 1961. Reprint, New York: Picador, 2001.

Steinwand, Jonathan. "The Future of Nostalgia in Friedrich Schlegel's German Aesthetics beyond Ancient Greece and Modern Europe." In *Narratives of Nostalgia, Gender, and Nationalism*, edited by Jean Pickering and Suzanne Kehde, 9–29. New York: New York University Press, 1997.

"Store Design." Starbucks. January 1, 2014. Accessed September 27, 2014, http://www.starbucks.com/coffeehouse/store-design.

Sullivan, Oriel, and Tally Katz-Gerro. "The Omnivore Thesis Revisited: Voracious Cultural Consumers." *European Sociological Review* 23, no. 2 (2007): 123–37. Accessed January 10, 2015, *EBSCOhost*.

Sutherland, Daniel E. *Americans and Their Servants: Domestic Service in the United States from 1800 to 1920*. Baton Rouge: Louisiana State University Press, 1981.

Taylor, Blair. "2013 Year in Review." "Global Responsibility Report Goals and Progress 2013." January 1, 2014. Accessed September 27, 2014, http://www.starbucks.com/responsibility/global-report.

Thackeray, William. "Roundabout Papers.—No. 1: On a Lazy Idle Boy." *The Cornhill*, January 1860, 124–28. Texas Christian University archives, Fort Worth, TX.

Thompson, Barbara, ed. *Black Womanhood: Images, Icons, and Ideologies of the African Body*. Seattle: University of Washington Press, 2008.

Thompson, Craig J., and Zaynep Arsel. "The Starbucks Brandscape and Consumers' (Anticorporate) Experiences of Glocalization." *Journal of Consumer Research* 31 (2004): 631–42.

Titus, Mary. "The Dining Room Door Swings Both Ways: Food, Race, and Domestic Space in the Nineteenth-Century South." In *Haunted Bodies: Gender and Southern Texts*, edited by Anne Goodwyn Jones and Susan V. Donaldson, 243–56. Charlottesville: University Press of Virginia, 1997.

Toussaint-Samat, Maguelonne. *A History of Food*. Translated by Anthea Bell. Malden: Wiley-Blackwell, 2009.

Turgeon, Laurier, and Madeleine Pastinelli. "'Eat the World': Postcolonial Encounters in Quebec City's Ethnic Restaurants." *Journal of American Folklore* 115 (2002): 247–68. Accessed January 10, 2015, *JSTOR*.

Turner, Patricia A. *Ceramic Uncles & Celluloid Mammies: Black Images & Their Influence on Culture.* Charlottesville: University of Virginia Press, 1994.

Twain, Mark. *The Adventures of Huckleberry Finn.* In *Four Complete Novels,* 141–333. Avenel, NJ: Random House Value Publishing, 1982.

———. *A Tramp Abroad.* 1880. Reprint, Hartford: American Publishing Co., 1901.

Upton, Dell. *Another City: Urban Life and Urban Spaces in the New American Republic.* New Haven, CT: Yale University Press, 2008.

Veblen, Thorstein. *Theory of the Leisure Class.* New York: Dover: 1994.

Waitress. Directed by Adrienne Shelly. Perf. Keri Russell, Nathan Fillion, Cheryl Hines, Adrienne Shelly, Jeremy Sisto, and Andy Griffith. 2007. Beverly Hills, CA: 20th Century Fox, 2007. DVD.

Wallace-Sanders, Kimberly. *Mammy: A Century of Race, Gender, and Southern Memory.* Ann Arbor: University of Michigan Press, 2008.

Wanzo, Rebecca Ann. *The Suffering Will Not Be Televised: African American Women and Sentimental Political Storytelling.* Albany: State University of New York Press, 2009.

Warner, Anne Bradford. "Harriet Jacobs's Modest Proposals: Revising Southern Hospitality." *Southern Quarterly* 30, no. 2–3 (1992): 22–28.

Waters, Alice. *The Art of Simple Food.* New York: Clarkson Potter/Publishers, 2007.

Weiss, John. *Life and Correspondence of Theodore Parker.* Vol. 2. New York: D. Appleton & Co., 1864.

White, Shane. "Freedoms' First Con: Changing Notes: African Americans and Changing Notes in Antebellum New York City." *Journal of the Early Republic* 34, no. 3 (Fall 2014): 385–409.

Whiting, John Eaton. *A Schedule of the Buildings and Their Occupancy, on the Principal Streets and Wharves in the City of Boston.* Boston: Press of W. L. Deland, 1877.

Whitingham, Rayford Logan, and Michael R. Winston. *Dictionary of American Negro Biography.* New York: W. W. Norton and Company, 1982.

Wielenberg, Erik J. "God, Morality, and Meaning in Cormac McCarthy's *The Road.*" *Cormac McCarthy Journal* 8, no.1 (2010): 1–16. Accessed August 20, 2012, https://journals.tdl.org/cormacmccarthy/index.php/cormacmccarthy.

Wilentz, Sean. "Society, Politics, and the Market Revolution, 1815–1848." In *The New American History.* Edited by Eric Foner, 61–84. Philadelphia: Temple University Press, 1997.

Wilhelm, Randal S. "'Golden chalice, good to a house god': Still Life in *The Road.*" *Cormac McCarthy Journal* 6 (2008): 129–49. Accessed August 20, 2012, https://journals.tdl.org/cormacmccarthy/index.php/cormacmccarthy.

Willard, Joseph. *A Half a Century with Judges and Lawyers*. Boston: Houghton Mifflin, 1896.

Williams-Forson, Psyche. *Building Houses out of Chicken Legs: Black Women, Food, and Power*. Chapel Hill: University of North Carolina Press, 2006. Accessed July 19, 2014, http://www.nytimes.com/2007/03/22/arts/television/22heff.html.

Witt, Doris. *Black Hunger*. New York: Oxford University Press, 1999.

Wolfe, Albert Benedict. *The Lodging House Problem in Boston*. Cambridge: Harvard University Press, 1913.

Wong, Sau-Ling Cynthia. *Reading Asian American Literature: From Necessity to Extravagance*. Princeton, NJ: Princeton University Press, 1993.

World War Z. Directed by Marc Forster. Los Angeles: Plan B Entertainment, 2013. DVD.

Zombieland. Directed by Ruben Fleischer. Hollywood: Columbia Pictures, 2009. DVD.

CONTRIBUTORS

JAMES CIANCIOLA is an associate professor of communication at Truman State University, Kirksville, Missouri. His teaching and research focus on the history, theory, and practice of rhetoric. He was named 2010 Educator of the Year (Truman) and received the Governor's Award for Excellence in Education (Missouri). He also wrote for the Italian American magazine *Primo*.

KELLY ERBY is an assistant professor of history at Washburn University, Topeka, Kansas. She received her PhD from Emory University in 2010. Her book *Restaurant Republic: The Rise of Public Dining in Boston* is forthcoming from the University of Minnesota Press.

JOE MARSHALL HARDIN is a professor of English, rhetoric, and writing and dean of the College of Languages and Communication at the University of Arkansas–Fort Smith. His books include *Opening Spaces: Critical Pedagogy and Resistance Theory in Composition* (SUNY Press, 2001) and *Choices: Situations for College Writing* (Fountainhead Press, 2007).

RACHEL S. HAWLEY holds a PhD in twentieth-century American literature from Southern Illinois University, Edwardsville. She teaches literature and composition in the Denver/Boulder area. Her research centers on dark comedy, popular culture, gender issues, southern gothic literature, film, and television.

LINDSY LAWRENCE is an associate professor of English at the University of Arkansas–Fort Smith. She teaches a variety of courses in eighteenth- and nineteenth-century British literature with a focus on publication history and gender roles. She is currently working on a book manuscript looking at Elizabeth Gaskell's use of affect in her serial fiction and how her serials functioned as part of the editorial voice of the nineteenth-century family literary magazine. She is also a co-director of the book *Periodical Poetry Index*.

JENNIFER MARTIN is a University of South Carolina Presidential Teaching Fellow in Social Advocacy and Ethical Life and is working toward her PhD in twentieth-century American literature. Her research interests include southern literature, African American literature, food studies, and women's and gender studies. Her publications include a co-authored article in *Studies in Popular Culture*, an article in the *Journal of Intercultural Disciplines*, and a forthcoming chapter in *Food Cults*, edited by Kima Cargill (Rowman & Littlefield).

KRYSTAL MCMILLEN is a PhD candidate at the University of Colorado, Boulder. Her research interests include dining, culinary output, agriculture and food production, issues of waste, and the consumption of the slave body in the eighteenth century. She is also interested in cultural studies and theories of taste. She has a chapter in *Eighteenth-Century Thing Theory in a Global Context: From Consumerism to Celebrity Culture*, edited by Ileana Baird and Christina Ionescu (Ashgate Press, 2014).

CAMMIE M. SUBLETTE is a professor of English at the University of Arkansas–Fort Smith and specializes in African American literature, race theory, and food studies. Her publications include co-authored articles in *Studies in Popular Culture* and in *Teaching College Literature* and chapters in *Icons of African American Literature: The Black Literary World*, edited by Yolanda Williams Page *(2011)*, *Sacred and Immoral: On the Writings of Chuck Palahniuk*, edited by Jeffrey A. Sartain *(2009)*, and *Movies in the Age of Obama: The Era of Post-Racial and Neo-Racist Cinema*, edited by David Garrett Izzo *(2014)*.

JESSICA KENYATTA WALKER is a doctoral candidate in the Department of American Studies and a certificate holder in women's studies at the University of Maryland, College Park. Jessica's research explores visual cultures that communicate historical, cultural, and social relationships between racial identity and food. She currently teaches in the Women's and Gender Studies and American Studies programs at Kenyon College as a 2015–2016 Marylin Yarbrough Dissertation/Teaching Fellow.

LAURA ANH WILLIAMS is an assistant professor and director of the Women's Studies Program at New Mexico State University. Her research and teaching focus on gender, race, and foodways as well as feminist/queer theory and popular culture. Her current book project explores abjection and foodways in Asian American literature.

INDEX